FOUR

JOE MENZER

CORNERS

How UNC, N.C. State,
Duke, and Wake Forest
Made North Carolina
the Center of
the Basketball Universe

SIMON & SCHUSTER

SIMON & SCHUSTER
Rockefeller Center
1230 Avenue of the Americas
New York, NY 10020

10   9   8   7   6   5   4   3

Library of Congress Cataloging-in-Publication Data
Menzer, Joe.
    Four corners : how UNC, N.C. State, Duke, and
Wake Forest made North Carolina the center of the
basketball universe / Joe Menzer.
        p.   cm.
    Includes bibliographical references and index.
    1. Basketball teams—North Carolina—History.
2. Basketball—North Carolina—History.
3. College sports—North Carolina—History.
I. Title.
GV885.72.N8M46   1999
796.323'63'09756—dc21   98-47550
                                                  CIP

ISBN 0-684-84674-8

Photo Credits:
1, 16, 17, 24: Winston-Salem Journal
2, 4, 19, 20: Durham Herald Co., Inc.
3, 11: U.N.C. Photo Lab
5, 6, 12, 13, 14, 18, 21, 25, 28, 29, 34, 35, 38, 39, 43:
    The Durham Herald-Sun
7, 8, 9: Wake Forest Sports Information Dept.
10: Courtesy of Lennie Rosenbluth
15: N.C. State (Jason Simon)
22: AP/Wide World Photos
23, 26, 27, 33, 37, 40, 41, 45: Howard A. Tillery
30, 31, 32, 36, 42, 44: Dan Sears

For Sarah, Andrew, Elizabeth,
Emma, and, God willing,
yet another basketball player
to be named later.

Acknowledgments

WRITING A BOOK such as this—which was more than two years in the making—is much like joining the army: it's not just a job, it's an adventure. It was also a team effort that could not have been completed without the generous donation of time by countless people and the combined talents of many behind-the-scenes folks who assisted me at every turn. There are so many people to thank that I surely will miss a few. I apologize in advance for that.

First of all, I couldn't have pulled this off without the advance approval and constant encouragement of several people at the *Winston-Salem Journal*, which is a great place to work. My sports editor, Terry Oberle, is the best I have ever worked for or with. The same could be said for working with editors Jeff Neuman and Frank Scatoni at Simon & Schuster, and, as always, with my outstanding literary agent, Shari Wenk.

Others at the *Winston-Salem Journal* who deserve mention are Lenox Rawlings (the best columnist in ACC country in my opinion), John Delong, Dan Collins, Mary Garber, Phil Hrichak, Bill Cole, and Ed Campbell. All offered advice and input, perhaps without even knowing it at times. A very special thanks also must go to Steve Reed of the *Gaston Gazette*. Steve helped interview some sources when my time didn't permit it, and he assisted in painstakingly transcribing countless hours of tape. Without him, I would still be transcribing tape and never would have gotten around to actually writing the book.

Among the many people we interviewed, I would be remiss if I didn't thank at least some of those who were willing to part with ample amounts of their valuable time—especially Michael Jordan and David Thompson, the two best basketball players I have ever seen. Kent McDill of the *Daily Herald* in Illinois assisted with the interview of Jordan, who seemed to enjoy reminiscing about his days at North Carolina. I also appreciate all the time surrendered by busy men such as Mike Krzyzewski, Bill Guthridge, Billy Packer, Charlie Bryant, Brad Daugherty, Danny Ferry, Sidney Lowe, Larry Miller, Les Robinson, Lennie Rosenbluth, Jeff Mullins, Bill Hensley, Skeeter Francis, Phil Ford, Quin Snyder, Dave Odom, Charlie Davis, Gil McGregor, Steve Luguire, and Charlie Dayton.

All the players on the 1998 rosters of North Carolina, Duke, North Carolina State, and Wake Forest were helpful and polite as well. And the sports information directors at those schools, plus their assistants, consistently went above and beyond the call of duty to attempt to fulfill my many requests. Thanks to John Justus at Wake Forest, Mike Cragg at Duke, Rick Brewer and Steve Kirschner at North Carolina, and Jason Simon at North Carolina State.

I also would like to offer sincere thanks for the help I received in all kinds of ways from Leonard Laye, Charles Chandler, and Ron Green, Jr. of the *Charlotte Observer*; Ed Hardin of the *Greensboro News & Record*; Willie T. Smith of the *Greenville* (S.C.) *News*; Joe Macenka and Dave Droschak of the *Associated Press*; Dane Huffman of the *Raleigh News & Observer*; Richard Walker of the *Gaston Gazette*; Denny Seitz of the *Spartanburg Herald*; Al Featherstone of the *Durham Herald-Sun*; Barry Jacobs of the *New York Times*; Mark Packer at WFNZ radio in Charlotte; John Kilgo and Craig Distl of *Carolina Blue*; Darin Gantt of the Rock Hill (S.C.) *Herald*; and former *Winston-Salem Journal* and *Charlotte Observer* ACC beat writer Eddy Landreth. And also to all the countless Big Four basketball fans who offered their encouragement and assistance, such as Walt Doley —who not only is a fine neighbor but quite possibly ranks as the biggest North Carolina fan I came across. He offered countless periodicals, books, and videotapes that spanned decades and aided me greatly in my research.

Most of all I thank my wife, Sarah, for being herself as usual. When she married me, I'm sure she didn't realize that proofreading was part of the deal. And to my wonderful children—Andrew, Elizabeth, and Emma— thanks for staying out of my office most of the times when you were supposed to. And finally, thanks to Kevin McCaughey and Ann McCaughey, two of Sarah's thirteen siblings. Kevin helped with some of the early library research and Ann helped later by watching the kids when Sarah fell ill while I was putting the final touches on the manuscript. The book wouldn't have gotten off the ground without Kevin's help and wouldn't have landed at the publisher's office without Ann's. My two sisters, Diane Menzer and Marti Middlebrook, were also great during a time of need, proving once again that no bond is stronger than family.

What I learned while researching and writing this book is that the schools who comprise the Big Four are like family in their own separate ways. That is a large part of what makes them so special.

Contents

1

THE BIG FOUR

IT WAS JUST after one o'clock in the afternoon and already the temperature was soaring inside Cameron Indoor Stadium. Outside on this last day of February, it was sunny and mild. But inside the stone edifice—one of those rare structures that possesses a soul according to Mike Krzyzewski, coach of the Duke Blue Devils basketball team—the heat was on, literally and figuratively. Coach Krzyzewski saw to that. Legend has it that Coach K always turns up the thermostat when someone special comes to visit. It is a charge he has denied, but there seems to be something to it.

Despite the familiar heat, the legendary Cameron Crazies— student fans who are either clever, rude, creative, or obnoxious depending on one's point of view—jostled for position close to the court and began their pregame ritual. Someone very special was about to walk onto the court.

"Go to Hell, Carolina, Go to Hell!

"Go to Hell, Carolina, Go to Hell!"

These words, familiar to anyone who follows basketball in the Atlantic Coast Conference, would be repeated hundreds of times before the day was done. Sweat began dripping off the Crazies' chins almost as quickly as they settled into the rhythm of their favorite chant, yet that was hardly a concern. Even the bare-chested ones could not possibly stay cool on such an afternoon, nor would they want to. It felt a little like hell must, and that is exactly how they wanted it.

But in reality the heat was on Krzyzewski and the Duke basketball team as much as it was on North Carolina or anyone else. That is usually the case when these two schools get together not so much to play a basketball game but to wage a war with everything they can muster. As the temperature continued to rise inside the arena, the tension level rose to match it.

It was a special day for Duke. It was Senior Day at Cameron, perhaps the most revered day at what is surely the most hallowed court in college basketball. At precisely two o'clock, four senior players on Duke's team would be honored before tipping it off against their most hated rival, the Tar Heels of the University of North Carolina. Aside from everything else, that is what made this game—or any game when Duke and Carolina clashed—different from all others during the basketball season.

It isn't a long trip up Tobacco Road from North Carolina to Duke, or vice versa. But it usually is a difficult and grueling one. Just ask former Carolina forward Mike O'Koren, who after one hard-fought battle at Cameron collapsed from heat exhaustion in front of his locker stall. This was after the Crazies commemorated O'Koren's obvious and sensitive skin problem by brandishing signs that referred to him as the "OXY-1000 Poster Child." Or ask former Duke forward Art Heyman, who once nearly incited a riot by brawling not only with several of Carolina's players but also with one of their cheerleaders. The latter transgression was witnessed by a Durham lawyer who happened to have graduated from North Carolina; he swore out an arrest warrant on Heyman for the alleged assault. Everywhere else in America former North Carolina star Michael Jordan was hailed as daring and stylish for his high-flying moves to the basket with his tongue wagging out in front of him; at Cameron they threw tongue depressors at him in disgust.

There is no place in America like Tobacco Road when it comes to college basketball. And there is no place on Tobacco Road like Cameron Indoor Stadium on a steamy afternoon when Duke is playing host to Carolina.

At twenty minutes to two, the last holdouts from an overflow press corps filtered into Cameron and attempted to wedge themselves into seats on both sides of the court. Mark Crow, a former Duke player, sat next to the media contingent located directly behind the scorer's table near midcourt, shaded just a bit toward the seat occupied by Coach Bill Guthridge on the North Carolina bench. Crow had traveled all the way from Italy, where he now lived, to attend this annual event.

Guthridge had been coming to Cameron for these games for more than thirty years, but this was his first visit as a head coach, having taken over for Dean Smith prior to the 1997–98 season. Smith, college basketball's winningest coach, retired somewhat abruptly the previous October but still talked with Guthridge at least twice a week about strategy and team chemistry. But on this occasion —which also happened to be Smith's sixty-seventh birthday—Dean wasn't in sight. That really didn't seem to matter, though. There wasn't much the Dean could tell Guthridge about the pitfalls of playing Duke in this building that the current North Carolina coach didn't already know, or at least suspect.

Guthridge, a gray-haired, bespectacled gentleman sixty years of age, outwardly wears the image of an easygoing, good-hearted grandfather. He usually displays a calm that seems too serene to be real, even in the heat of the most intense battle. But on this day, he seemed unusually nervous as he paced the sideline in front of his bench.

Shortly before two o'clock, Cameron regular Frances Redding sang the national anthem. This was another Duke tradition that fed the Crazies' insatiable appetite. As she sang the last few bars, they went crazy—there was just no other word for it.

Then, one by one, the Duke seniors were introduced. Todd Singleton—a walk-on who rarely played but was a fan favorite— went first. Roshown McLeod followed. Two years earlier McLeod was an unknown transfer from St. John's who had yet to play a single minute for the Blue Devils. Now, he was an undisputed star. The crowd roared as McLeod made his way to center court, waved, and then motioned toward someone in the stands. He jogged back over to retrieve his two-and-a-half-year-old son, Anthony, and held him high for everyone to see.

Next up was Ricky Price. Two years earlier he had been a star, averaging 14.2 points and earning third team all–Atlantic Coast Conference honors. Now, he was a forgotten backup, his career basically wrecked by his failure to take care of business academically. Krzyzewski had used him only sparingly since his return to the squad in December from an academic suspension.

Finally, it was Wojo's turn. This was the moment the Crazies had been waiting for. As Steve Wojciechowski's name was announced, it seemed as if the old building would burst at the rafters from the noise. The place exploded, or at least it sounded like it had. Wojo, as he was known to teammates and Crazies alike, hugged coaches, players, and managers as he made his way to center court. He would have hugged every Duke fan in the building if he could have. Tears streamed from his eyes as he turned and waved to each crevice and corner that made up this haven called Cameron. It was probably the only college basketball court in the country where Wojo was loved not loathed.

The cheers were deafening. The four Duke seniors embraced at center court.

Guthridge continued to pace.

As Wojo walked from center court, he tried to wipe the tears from his eyes.

"Stop crying, you baby," he thought. "It's time to stop crying and start playing basketball."

But at this moment, he wasn't in control of himself. He was bawling. Mark Crow leaned to a reporter and shouted that this scene was not good for Duke—too much emotion, too many tears.

"It's too close to tip-off for that," Crow warned.

Guthridge sauntered over to the scorer's table.

"When are we gonna start this thing?" he asked.

"Thirty seconds," answered Steve Kirschner, the North Carolina director of media relations who was monitoring the television time-out leading up to the tipoff.

Guthridge turned and walked back to the bench, only to return about sixty seconds later.

"This is some thirty seconds. When are we gonna get going here?" Guthridge asked again, nervously.

Kirschner could only shrug this time. It was out of his control.

Finally, Kirschner gave the signal to the coaches and officials that the TV folks, including bombastic announcer Dick Vitale, were ready.

"What a surprise! Vitale wouldn't shut up," Kirschner announced with a laugh as play at last was set to begin.

It was two o'clock, and no one had yet scored any baskets. But the day's pace already was exhausting.

PRECISELY 10.6 MILES of U.S. Route 15-501 separate the offices of Krzyzewski at Duke and Guthridge at North Carolina. Nowhere else in America are two schools with such rich basketball history and tradition located so close to one another. The proximity of two other ACC rivals—North Carolina State and Wake Forest—makes the situation even more interesting. In a state where college basketball is a serious religion, these four programs are known as the Big Four.

Born layups apart chronologically and geographically, these four schools have endeared themselves to an entire nation through the years. But while legions across the country follow each thundering dunk, every sweet jump shot, and all the gritty defensive stands, it is their local fans and loyal alumni who vicariously experience victory or defeat.

The schools grew up within a 34-mile radius of one another. To this day, North Carolina, N.C. State, and Duke remain situated a half-hour's drive apart. Wake Forest College, which had been located 19 miles west of Durham and 16 miles north of Raleigh in the tiny town of Wake Forest, received a large sum of tobacco money from R.J. Reynolds Company to move to Winston-Salem, a distance of only 110 miles due west, in the summer of 1956. Wake moved (and upgraded its name to Wake Forest University), but its fiercest basketball rivalries had already been set.

"There isn't another place in the country where four schools located so close to each other are the forces in college basketball that these teams are," said Terry Oberle, sports editor at the *Winston-Salem Journal.* "But it isn't just that these teams are close to each other or that they're usually very good every season. It's the way the fans embrace them—and hate the other three schools.

"Either you're for Duke or you're not. If you're not, you hate them. Either you're for North Carolina or you're not. If you're not, you hate them. Same with N.C. State and Wake. The only other place in the United States that I can think of that might be similar is in Philadelphia, where you have Villanova, Temple, LaSalle, St. Joseph's, and Rutgers. But even there, fans aren't as passionate about those teams. They never have been. Part of it might be the pull of professional sports in that area. They've had pro baseball, football, and hockey for years, and even the New York teams aren't far away. Down here, there were only the colleges until Charlotte recently got pro basketball and football. And the only sport anyone gave a damn about for years was basketball."

Those who move to the area feel the force of the Big Four immediately. Krzyzewski, a Chicago native who arrived in Durham to coach Duke in 1980, certainly did.

"There is no other area like this in the United States," Krzyzewski said. "It produces situations and feelings that you really can't accurately express to other people on the outside—because they have no understanding of it. They say they understand it, but they don't. You have to be around here all the time.

"So many times it's like Carolina's got this and Duke's got that.

Or State's got this and Wake's got that. We should have gotten this and they should have gotten that. Those comments come from people all the time—and from all the schools. That creates rivalries that are uncommon in sports and there's no way that people who haven't lived here could realize that."

Those who do live in the area understand that Duke fans wear blue, but not the Carolina blue the Tar Heels wear. State fans wear red. And Wake fans, who recently were awakened from a three-decade slumber to relive past glory, wear gold and black or whatever they can find that pays homage to Coach Dave Odom and Tim Duncan, their program's two saviors.

Jim Valvano, a native New Yorker who coached at North Carolina State from 1980 to 1990, once told Barry Jacobs of *The New York Times*: "When I first got here I thought it was unusual . . . that colors could evoke such unbridled joy or wrath in people. I understand it now. I don't think I'll ever cease to be amazed by it."

Each of the Big Four schools and their basketball programs are unique, yet each one strives for the same ultimate goal. A championship in the highly competitive ACC is always near the top of the list. And so is winning a national championship. North Carolina, N.C. State, and Duke have combined to win seven national championships since 1957. Wake reached the Final Four in 1962 and the Final Eight in 1996, but has yet to capture that final prize.

Woody Durham, longtime radio broadcaster of North Carolina games and a native of the state, once explained it this way to Jacobs: "You live with the rivalries every day. We force you to choose sides. That's just the way we do it, and that's why we've got the tremendous interest we do."

In Chapel Hill, which the *Fiske Guide to Colleges* refers to as "the Southern part of heaven," the University of North Carolina occupies a 730-acre campus dotted with trees, manicured lawns, and thirty miles of brick-paved walkways. The campus was recently ranked among the top twenty in the nation for beauty by Thomas Gaines in his book *The Campus as a Work of Art*. The basketball team plays in the Dean Dome, named after Coach Dean Smith, and there is little doubt about their most feared and hated rivals.

"A game with Duke makes any Carolina fan's heart beat faster," the *Fiske Guide* says. "But N.C. State takes the prize as the most hated rival of all."

Duke fans might take exception to that observation based on their heated games with North Carolina during the 1997–98 season when both teams were for a time ranked number one nationally. While UNC is located on one of the most beautiful campuses in the country, both Duke and State have more of an urban feel about them. Duke's campus is still pretty—buffeted by the 8,300-acre Duke Forest and anchored by the majestic Duke Chapel—but it is located in Durham, where crime is a real-life, day-to-day problem. This could be why only 14 percent of the student population actually hails from North Carolina, with a large portion of the rest migrating from the northeastern states of New York and New Jersey. (At UNC, on the other hand, 82 percent of the student body comes from within the state.) Duke's basketball fans seem to reflect the rougher edge, earning a national reputation as one of the rowdiest, most innovative crowds anywhere in the college game. They enjoy poking fun at Carolina's supposed arrogance and N.C. State's reputation as a party school soft on academics. The feeling at Duke is that students there have the best of both worlds—they know how to study and have a good time, too, and they don't look down their noses at anybody (except, of course, for the students and fans from UNC, State, and Wake Forest).

As for N.C. State, the school continued to fight the renegade image it first earned during shocking scandals in 1957 and again in the early 1960s. The scandal-ridden coaching stints of Norm Sloan and Jim Valvano did nothing to dispel that reputation. It has been a long, uphill fight for the Wolfpack. And as Les Robinson found out, you had better win while you're working on graduating student-athletes, or you'll be gone very quickly. Robinson improved on the academics after Valvano was forced out, but didn't win enough and eventually was asked to step down as coach. Ironically, he now serves as the school's athletics director as it continues to attempt to rediscover the magic that led to national championships in 1974 and 1983.

In recent years, Wake Forest has rekindled memories of the 1950s and 1960s when it was a national basketball power. In the days of Bones McKinney, Len Chappell, and Billy Packer, and before that in the days of Murray Greason, they were as feared and as despised as the other three teams who comprise the Big Four. Their recent return to basketball prominence under Dave Odom and center Tim Duncan, a two-time college Player of the Year who went on to become the first player chosen in the 1997 NBA draft, have served to stoke the fires again.

And while the *Fiske Guide to Colleges* makes a point of inferring that North Carolina State is North Carolina's biggest rival, Wake Forest coach Dave Odom makes it clear that there is absolutely no question about which school is the biggest rival of the other three Big Four schools: North Carolina. And that is why perhaps the only group more prominent in the state of North Carolina than UNC alumni may be the ABC gang—Anybody But Carolina.

"I grew up in North Carolina, and the University of North Carolina is not one of those vanilla schools," Odom said. "Whether you take them or leave them, they're there. And you're either for them or you're against them. There's no in-between on them."

Long before Krzyzewski and Wojo or even Dean Smith, the Big Four scene was inhabited by hoops pioneers like Everett Case, Frank McGuire, Bones McKinney, and Vic Bubas. Magical seasons were forged by players such as Lennie Rosenbluth, Art Heyman, David Thompson, and Michael Jordan.

As coach of Wake Forest and a native of North Carolina who has at various times in his life been touched by all of the Big Four programs, Odom knew how to put this phenomenon into perspective.

"People ask me all the time, 'What's the most difficult thing about your job?' That's typically the question I get, and I always say the same thing. The best and the worst is the same. It's the ACC. It's the best because it's the highest-caliber basketball in the country year in and year out. It *is* a basketball league. It gets the most publicity. It's the most analyzed, the most important, the most intense.

"When you're recruiting, you can knock on any door in the country and at least get in. You may not get the kid, but you can at least get in. I don't think there's another conference in the country where you can say that. We can go anywhere and get in the door. They will listen. So that's part of being the best. Plus the games are the best. The arenas are the best. And the ACC Tournament is absolutely the best.

"But the ACC is also the worst because everything you do, right or wrong, is microscopically analyzed. It's analyzed and rehashed and retalked about. It's the most unforgiving league in the country. When you make a mistake, everyone knows about it and everyone talks about it the next day at the water cooler. There's nowhere to hide. So it's the best and the worst all at one time."

But would Odom consider coaching anywhere else?

He smiled at the question.

"There's nothing like it in this country," he said. "I'm always amused when I'm out recruiting and I hear some of the things coaches outside our league say to paint the picture that going to their school would be better than coming to one of ours. But in the back of my mind, I know that nine times out of ten, those coaches would switch places with us right away."

ON THIS FINE DAY in February, at Cameron Indoor Stadium, the Big Four stage solely belonged to the Big Two and their very different basketball teams. This February meeting was the two hundredth in the history of the Carolina-Duke rivalry. And it was shaping up to be one of the best.

When the teams had met three weeks earlier in Chapel Hill, some mischievous Duke students stoked the rivalry's home fires by swiping a retired North Carolina Michael Jordan jersey from the rafters at the Smith Center. The Jordan jersey was later discovered hanging outside Cameron Indoor Stadium on the day of the two hundredth showdown in the storied series.

Not to be outdone, North Carolina students responded by stealing not only a Grant Hill jersey from the rafters at Cameron, but also a signed poster of the 1992 Olympic "Dream Team," valued at twenty thousand dollars, from Coach Krzyzewski's office. Krzyzewski had been one of head coach Chuck Daly's assistants on that team and he was more than a little steamed about it getting stolen. Three weeks later, it was recovered after an anonymous tip led police to a garbage bag outside the Smith Center in Chapel Hill.

This wasn't the first time such high jinks had preceded a Duke-Carolina showdown. In fact, this kind of behavior occurred between the Big Four schools every day. Once, before a Carolina–N.C. State game, a national championship banner was taken from Carolina's building and draped in disrespect over a nearby highway overpass. Ed Hardin, a columnist for the *Greensboro News and Record*, laughed as he assessed the latest antics just prior to the Duke-Carolina tip-off.

After all, the two buildings where these teams played their home games were about as different as the fans who followed them. The Dean Dome was a modern, antiseptic, imposing structure where fans usually sat in relative calm while they watched the action unfold in front of them on the court. Cameron was old, dusty, small, and cramped, and looked to the naked eye from the outside nothing like a basketball arena at all.

"What's great about all this is that you know the Duke students probably had to come up with some elaborate scheme just to get into the Smith Center and take the Jordan jersey. I can just imagine them scaling walls and all sorts of stuff," Hardin said. "Then here at Cameron, all the Carolina folks had to do was break a window. Then they probably walked right in and took whatever they wanted."

Duke entered this game ranked number one in the nation, a distinction it also held earlier in the year when North Carolina, then ranked number two, had run roughshod over the Blue Devils in meeting number 199 in Chapel Hill. As a result, Carolina took the number-one ranking until they suffered an upset loss at home to another Big Four rival, North Carolina State, just sixteen days later. When Duke hammered UCLA the very next afternoon at Cameron, they laid claim to the top spot in the nation's polls.

Carolina's loss to State had dropped them to number three in the polls, but Guthridge's squad did not look like the number three team in the nation at the start of this game. And Duke certainly didn't look like they were number one. Indeed, it seemed as if the two teams had swapped positions once again. Carolina jumped to a quick 25–9 lead before Duke even called their first time out. Carolina was dominating, and it appeared the Cameron Crazies were heading for a long, painful afternoon.

With 12:49 left in the first half, Krzyzewski sent in Wojcie-chowski, McLeod, and freshman Shane Battier, to check in for Chris Burgess, Elton Brand, and Trajan Langdon.

Carolina assistant Pat Sullivan, who was in charge of keeping track of the opposing team's substitutions, made his way to the scorer's table and sought out Kirschner.

"Who's coming in for them?" Sullivan asked.

Kirschner wasn't sure.

"There's so many of them, it doesn't make any difference," Sullivan joked.

Indeed, Duke had supposedly gained an advantage in depth and endurance on Carolina earlier in the year by developing a bench while Guthridge ignored his. The Blue Devils ran ten-deep some games, sometimes substituting five-for-five at a time. Guthridge usually stuck to six or seven players. His "starting six," as he called them, consisted of leading scorer and rebounder Antawn Jamison, Shammond Williams, Vince Carter, point guard Ed Cota, and his interchangeable big men Makhtar Ndiaye and Ademola Okulaja. Guthridge's starting lineup changed each game; he had one of his six starters come off the bench in an unusual alphabetical rotation.

Jamison, who had burnt the Blue Devils for 35 points and 11

rebounds in the first game between the two teams, was on his way to another big afternoon. But with roughly nine minutes, thirty seconds left in the first half, Jamison was called for his first personal foul. He complained about it, and the Crazies finally had some spontaneous ammunition.

They began to chant: "Whine-y bitch! Whine-y bitch!"

Jamison just smiled.

But he wasn't smiling a moment later, when Cota dribbled away half the thirty-five-second shot clock and then missed a field-goal attempt without even thinking about getting the ball down low on the block to Jamison. As they ran back down to the other end of the court, Jamison gestured to Cota and angrily yelled, "Give me the damn ball, man!"

Cota nodded. He knew Jamison was right.

When the halftime buzzer rang, Carolina had a comfortable 42–30 lead.

Krzyzewski stormed off the court and into the locker room, where he immediately ripped off his sport coat, his shirt, and his tie. Everything was drenched with sweat. He angrily discarded his shirt and tie. In the other locker room, Guthridge stayed dressed and calmly told his team that all they had to do was maintain their composure and victory, along with the number-one ranking in college basketball, would be theirs some time shortly after four o'clock.

Krzyzewski addressed his team with his upper body covered only by a simple white T-shirt. It fit his approach. He wanted his guys to get back to the basics, the pure fundamentals of basketball, that helped them win 26 of their first 28 games.

"We're too tentative. We're getting beat to rebounds and loose balls. We're not playing like ourselves," Coach K fumed. "We play differently against these guys and it doesn't make sense. Just be yourselves out there. Do all the things we've been doing for the last month and a half and we'll be fine.

"We've played sixty minutes of basketball against this team this year—three halves. And we haven't played with the kind of passion or energy we need."

To his assistant coaches, Krzyzewski wondered aloud as he donned a white golf shirt and grabbed his blazer before heading back out: "Why is it that we always seem to play a different game against North Carolina?"

No one could answer him.

After intermission, Mark Crow returned to his seat in the

stands and mentioned again that the Duke seniors had much on their shoulders. Perhaps too much.

"It's Senior Day and you're defending the number-one ranking —and it's Carolina," Crow said. "One of those alone, especially just playing Carolina, would be enough. You have to be an awful mature man to carry all that weight. There is such a thing as having too much adrenaline.

"I remember my Senior Day. I shot about three for fifteen. I got a lot of rebounds, but I couldn't hit a shot. I was too wound up —and I didn't have all this going on."

Crow looked at Guthridge, who had just returned to the court from the locker room. He shook his head.

"There's the real story in college basketball this season, if you ask me," said the Duke man. "The job he's done following Dean is remarkable. Following a legend in anything is never easy. Sometimes it's impossible. And look at him. Everybody else in here is sweating their asses off, and he looks like he just got a cup of tea and he's getting ready to read the morning newspaper."

Guthridge wouldn't look like that in an hour.

As GUTHRIDGE sat down with not a bead of perspiration in sight, Krzyzewski marched past to his spot on the Duke bench. With his fresh white golf shirt, Krzyzewski looked like a new man. He hoped his team would look rejuvenated, too.

It didn't happen right away, but it did happen. After falling behind 64–47 with 11:39 left, Duke rallied furiously.

Freshman Elton Brand hit a jump hook, drawing a foul from Ndiaye in the process. Though ten minutes were still left to be played, the 6-11 Ndiaye had just collected his fifth foul. As Ndiaye walked slowly to the bench, the Crazies tried to time their chant with the precise moment he would sit down, humming slowly until they reached a certain decibel level then shouting in unison: "See ya!"

Ndiaye faked them out. He feigned like he was going to sit down, but remained standing, smiling at the student section across from the Carolina bench.

The chants grew louder.

"Sit! Sit! Sit!"

Ndiaye wouldn't play along. He kept standing and smiling.

Finally, Guthridge tugged at Ndiaye's jersey and told him to sit. For the first time all day, it looked as if there might be some sweat glistening on the forehead of the now-agitated coach.

Ndiaye was done, but Brand was just getting started.

The freshman hit a layup, then another jump hook after grabbing his own rebound off a missed free throw.

Trajan Langdon, the classy junior who had been struggling with his shooting, drilled an outside shot.

The crowd erupted, and the Carolina lead was under 10.

Brand took a feed from Wojciechowski and hit another jump hook. With Ndiaye out of the middle, no one could stop him. He had scored a remarkable 11 points in just over three minutes.

Guthridge began to sweat profusely. He called a twenty-second time-out.

Crow leaned over to shout to the reporters standing next to him, but he could barely be heard above the din.

"Is there any place louder?" he asked to heads that quickly shook no.

The last 6:55 of the contest was a blur.

Wojo hit one of two foul shots to cut it to 72–69 with 4:42 left. McLeod hit two jumpers, and suddenly it was 75–73 with 2:35 to go. The seniors had come alive.

"I think I'm going to have a heart attack," Crow joked.

A few plays later, Okulaja made a bad pass that was stolen by McLeod. Chris Carrawell made a driving basket that tied the game at 75.

The place was rocking.

"Go to Hell, Carolina, Go to Hell!"

Some Crazies held up a sign, heretofore tucked away in embarrassment, that read: "Welcome to Hell, Carolina."

For Carolina it really must have felt like Hell.

After Carolina committed their 18th turnover, McLeod hit a layup to give Duke its first lead of the day at 77–75.

Crow shouted that it wasn't over yet. He pointed to a spot on the floor where more than two decades earlier Carolina's Bobby Jones had stolen an in-bounds pass in the final seconds, and then dribbled the length of the floor to stun Duke with a game-winning layup at the final buzzer. He gestured to another area on the court, some thirty feet from the basket, and mentioned that former Tar Heel Walter Davis once banked in a shot from about that distance to complete a remarkable Carolina comeback from 8 points down in the final seventeen seconds of regulation to force overtime. Although that game was played at old Carmichael Auditorium in Chapel Hill, Crow and his Duke teammates were beaten that time by Carolina as well.

"We must have played Carolina ten times during my career, and it seemed like they were always doing that stuff to us. I think we beat them once when I played," Crow said.

These were exactly the kinds of games Carolina somehow pulled out. The Heels were usually the team that came from 17 down to win. Not Duke.

But this day was different.

Neither team scored again.

Cota, usually one of Carolina's most reliable free-throw shooters, missed two foul shots with 3.8 seconds left—missing the second on purpose. Carolina's Brendan Haywood grabbed the rebound and was fouled by Brand with 1.2 ticks remaining. Haywood had no chance. A below-average foul shooter, he was a freshman playing in Cameron for the first time. He missed the first, then had to attempt the same intentional misfire that Cota had on his second attempt. This time Carolina didn't get the rebound.

Final score: Duke 77, North Carolina 75.

Seasoned veterans of Cameron are conditioned to ask the students sitting behind them, "Are you coming over?" If the answer is yes, then those in front had better get the hell out of the way. It means the students are going to do whatever they can to climb over the crowd, the press tables, and the scorer's table to get onto the court at the final buzzer.

For a game like this one, the question didn't even need to be asked. Everyone was coming over.

As the fans stormed the court and began a wild and lengthy celebration, the North Carolina players tried to make their way off to the locker room through the crowd. A Duke student inadvertently smacked Okulaja in the head. Okulaja retaliated by clearing some space with a forearm that happened to find the student's face.

Blood streamed from the student's nose, running onto his T-shirt that read: "Go to Hell, Carolina."

The noise in Cameron Indoor Stadium didn't die at the final buzzer. If anything, it only got louder. Students remained in the building for another twenty minutes before they finally started filing out. They didn't want to leave; they wanted this moment to last forever.

"Yessssss!" yelled Mark Crow. "This is why I came all the way from Italy!"

Kenny Dennard, whose playing career at Duke began one year after Crow's ended, stopped by to say hello. He pounded his chest.

"I thought I was going to have a heart attack!" Dennard shouted to Crow above the din.

As the the two former Blue Devils turned to walk out of the building, their hearts pounded fiercely. They were not alone.

AFTERWARD, KRZYZEWSKI COULDN'T STOP smiling or heaping praise on his team. He was especially pleased with the play of Wojciechowski. Despite Wojo's slow start and a box score stat line that revealed little to the naked eye, in Krzyzewski's mind, Wojo was the key to this game.

"I'll take my point guard through any alley, any dark street." Krzyzewski said. "I'm not saying he's the most talented or whatever, but he was remarkable today. Not good. Steve Wojciechowski was remarkable. He wouldn't let us lose.

"Wojo's played pretty well here. It was Senior Day today. Everything was on the table, everything was at stake. For him to get eleven assists and one turnover and play great D, it was one of the great performances here."

Then Krzyzewski paused before asking, "Did he have any points?"

"One," came the answer from the press corps.

"One," repeated Krzyzewski, eyeing Wojo's line again. "It's one of the great one-point performances in the history of the game. You know what? My daughter, Jamie, is a sophomore point guard for Durham Academy. I always tell her she's too concerned with her shot. I'm going to take this box score, get it printed up, and highlight what you can do scoring one point."

Then he folded the box score and put it in his pocket.

Someone asked about Krzyzewski's change of clothes at halftime.

"[My shirt] was all wet, and I was so mad because we were playing so poorly. Not that I tore anything up. I didn't . . . I was just all wet, so I decided to go with my cool look—as cool as you can look at fifty-one," said Krzyzewski, smiling.

And he had every reason to smile. Not only did Coach K beat a very talented North Carolina team, but he also collected his 500th career coaching victory in the process.

For every coaching victory, there must be a loss. Bill Guthridge took loss number three of his career with dignity and aplomb.

"It's hot in here," Guthridge joked as he arrived in the press interview room. "After being in that air-conditioned gym, it seems hot in here.

"It was a tough one to lose, obviously."

Obviously? He could already hear the critics gathering 10.6 miles away down U.S. 15-501: *Dean never would have lost this game. See, if you had developed a bench earlier in the year, maybe your boys could have survived in this heat without falling apart.* The criticism would be endless.

But Guthridge took the high road. He credited Duke and faulted himself.

In the winning locker room, Wojciechowski admitted this was a perfect way to go out in his final appearance at Cameron Indoor Stadium.

"This is a special place to play and we play for a special coach. There isn't a better way to end my career at Cameron than this. There was a lot of emotion going into this one."

The real beauty of this classic confrontation was that if all went as it was supposed to, they would get together to do it again in seven days in the championship game of the ACC Tournament in Greensboro. And they would keep doing it over and over long after Guthridge and Krzyzewski were gone, just as they had been doing it for years, long before these two coaches had even arrived.

Twenty-four hours after Duke pulled off its remarkable comeback against Carolina, the other two Big Four schools, Wake and N.C. State, met in Winston-Salem, a short drive down Interstate 40. Wake Forest and North Carolina State weren't playing for the same high stakes Duke and North Carolina were playing for, but there was plenty on the line. Both teams had hopes of making the sixty-four-team NCAA tournament field. Both needed a victory to move one step closer to securing that, and both were jockeying for favorable seeding in the ACC Tournament.

In a game that matched Duke–North Carolina in intensity and emotion, Wake won. Bones McKinney, the legendary old Wake coach, would have been proud. Everett Case, the old N.C. State coach who probably did more than anyone else to make basketball what it is today in North Carolina, probably turned over in his grave. No one doubted that wherever these two deceased gentlemen were resting, they definitely tuned in.

That's the way college basketball is in the Big Four arena. It's larger than life.

2

THE OLD GRAY FOX

I T WAS AFTER NINE O'CLOCK in the evening, and young Dave Odom knew he was supposed to be sleeping. But he just couldn't. He was too excited. His ears strained to hear every sound—not only from the radio beside his bed, but also from outside his room where his mother was just down the hall. His pulse quickened. If his mother came into his room, he knew he would be in big trouble.

But that didn't matter. The Wolfpack game was on and that made the risk well worth it in his mind. Odom was just a kid, but he already had a passion for basketball that was unmatched by anything else in his life. Growing up in Goldsboro, North Carolina, fifty-two miles east of the state capital in Raleigh, it hadn't taken him long to latch onto the Wolfpack of North Carolina State. He even had a backup team that was only sixteen miles or so north of Raleigh, but Wake Forest was a little harder to follow because their games weren't regularly broadcast by the voice of basketball authority, Ray Reeve.

Sitting on the edge of his bed, Odom leaned forward to hear Reeve call the game.

If he heard his mother coming down the hall toward his room, he knew what to do. He had done it countless times. "I was just a kid and I was supposed to be asleep at nine o'clock," Odom recalled. "But it would just be halftime then, so I would turn the radio down real low and I'd listen for my mother. The door would be closed, but she would come by. I could hear her coming down the hall, so I'd cut the volume all the way down so she couldn't hear it. She would open

27

the door to see if I was asleep, but then she would close the door and I would immediately tweak it back up in the cover of darkness."

Like everyone else from North Carolina, Odom was hooked on hoops.

If you weren't a North Carolina State fan, there were three other teams within a thirty-four-mile radius of one another to root for. In Raleigh, the Wolfpack reigned under the watchful eyes of Everett Case, their enigmatic coach. Sixteen miles to the north in tiny Wake Forest, Coach Murray Greason and his wild-eyed assistant, Bones McKinney, were turning the Demon Deacons into a national power. Nineteen miles to the east of Wake Forest was the city of Durham, home of the Duke Blue Devils. And sitting almost within shouting distance of that campus was the University of North Carolina in Chapel Hill, where Frank McGuire, a brash coach from New York was about to make history twice—first by guiding the Tar Heels to a national championship and next by hiring a young assistant coach named Dean Smith.

If you're from North Carolina, chances are your life has been touched by more than one of these institutions. Odom was lucky enough to be touched by all four. He started out an N.C. State fan, became friendly with Duke coaches when he coached at Durham High, did some television work for UNC, and ultimately became the head coach of the Demon Deacons.

Charlie Bryant, who served as an assistant coach at Wake Forest and N.C. State, and later became head of the Wolfpack Club in Raleigh, puts it this way: "We've got a unique situation here in the Big Four. It has a dramatic impact on the way people live their lives in this state. It dominates conversations. It's at everyone's breakfast table and every dinner table in the state during the basketball season. You can't get away from it. You can't escape it. You couldn't get away from it if you wanted to."

Charlie Dayton, another local who grew up a State fan and later became sports information director at Wake Forest before getting into public relations for several National Football League teams, used to walk to State games from his house as a kid.

"Growing up was great because there was no pro influence. I'm not saying the pro influence is bad—but for us, it just didn't exist," said Dayton, who is now director of communications for the NFL's Carolina Panthers. "Only the local teams were really on television at the time [during the late 1950s and early 1960s]. The southernmost baseball team was the Washington Senators, and the next closest team would have been Cincinnati or St. Louis. Professional basketball hadn't even broken the egg yet. And in football, there were a lot of [Washington] Redskins fans, but that was about it.

"So really, as you grew up, your whole world was college sports."

Dayton, Bryant, and Odom are not alone. Growing up in North Carolina then and now, people usually talk about college sports in cities big and small across the state. And basketball is the college sport that draws the most talk. Everett Case, the coach of those early Wolfpack teams that Odom just had to listen to on the radio, is the man responsible for making college basketball the state's personal pastime.

THE OLD GRAY FOX, Everett Case made his mark coaching high-school basketball in Indiana, a state that was already certifiably crazy over the sport as early as the 1940s. In twenty-three seasons as a high-school coach, Case's teams posted an astounding 726-75 record and won four Indiana state championships. He spent two years as an assistant coach at the University of Southern California, but didn't really attract national attention until he coached service teams as a lieutenant in the U.S. Navy during World War II. During the war, a team he coached at DePauw Naval Training Station in Indiana posted a 29-3 record, and in 1946 just before his discharge, he coached a team at Ottumwa Air Station in Iowa to a record of 27-2.

One week before the Southern Conference basketball tournament in 1946, Dick Herbert, the sports editor of the *Raleigh News and Observer*, went to the N.C. State campus to attend a spring football practice. Sitting in the stands were Dr. H. A. Fisher, the faculty chairman of athletics, and John Von Glahn, the business manager of athletics.

Herbert asked the two gentlemen if they had picked their new basketball coach yet.

They answered no.

"Are you open to suggestions?" Herbert asked.

"Yes," Fisher replied.

"Who is it that you have in mind?" Von Glahn added.

"Everett Case. He was a heck of a high-school coach, spent two years as an assistant under Sam Barry at Southern Cal, and then coached during his stint in the navy. He's just getting out now," Herbert said.

"But don't listen to me. Let me get you in touch with Chuck Taylor from Converse. He'll tell you all about Ev."

Taylor, who put on basketball clinics throughout the country and later gained immortality when he stamped a certain Converse basketball shoe with his name, did not mince words when Fisher and Von Glahn contacted him. He told them that in his opinion Case was the best coach in the United States.

The previous coach, Bob Warren, had been forced to operate within the confines of a limited annual budget of about two thousand dollars, gleaned from concession profits at the Southern Conference tournament. When Fisher and Von Glahn approached Case about the job, they assured him that as the new coach he would be appropriated an adequate number of scholarships worth far more than the amount of money they had committed to Warren. Within a few days, Case accepted the job without ever having seen the North Carolina State campus.

It was a job Case would love for the rest of his life.

Case recruited heavily from his home state, earning his early teams the nickname "the Hoosier Hotshots." His first team in 1946–47 included Norm Sloan, who later would follow in the Old Gray Fox's footsteps to coach State himself. The official team nickname that season was the "Red Terrors" but the following season it was changed to the "Wolfpack."

Case was one of the first true innovators of the game. Although he wasn't the first coach to use the full-court press or other pressing-type defenses, he was the first to use them for long periods of play. One longtime referee, Lou Bello, later credited Case with bringing in "not only the fast break, the one-hand shot, and speed, speed, speed, but also the pressing defense." He fiddled with the matchup zone years before anyone else in the state tried it. Case even brought the traditions of pregame introductions and the clipping of nets after a big victory to North Carolina, having established the now time-honored rituals first with his high-school teams in Indiana. He was also one of the first coaches anywhere to film games and then spend hours dissecting them. In 1927, he infuriated the opponents of his Frankfort High team by holding on to the ball after every basket their opponent scored. The ten-second violation was adopted as a result.

But perhaps more than anything, Case understood that he had to sell himself, his program, and the game of basketball to the general public. He made it a point to talk with reporters on a regular basis and he always returned their calls.

When Case heard of a coaching gimmick from up North that he thought had merit, he quickly adopted it. He also thought up some of his own.

One time when the Wolfpack were preparing to face a Rhode Island team that moved the ball up the court especially fast, Case added a sixth man to the second team and a second ball to the practice scrimmage against the first team. The first team spent the entire scrimmage scrambling on defense. It seemed outlandish, but when tip-off came against a Rhode Island squad operating with only five players and one ball, Case's players found Rhode Island's vaunted fast break amazingly easy to defend.

Another time, Case placed his second-team center on a chair in front of the basket before facing South Carolina and their 7-foot center, Jim Slaughter. Case's point was that Slaughter was big, but not much more mobile than a chunk of wood.

"Learn to avoid having your shot blocked in practice by the second-team center standing on the chair," Case told his players, "and you should be able to avoid having Slaughter block it in the game."

The strategy worked. Case's team slaughtered South Carolina by 20 points.

Of course, it always helped that State had extra time to put this stuff in during practices before big games. This was no accident. Case spent many hours in the off-season figuring out when and where it would be best for his team to face its better nonconference opponents. He would create a master sheet so he knew when an opponent had a tough game immediately before playing his squad, and he would make certain that he scheduled notoriously strong teams only after State had a week off to prepare.

It helped that he usually penciled State in as the home team no matter who the opponent was. From 1954 through 1960, the Wolfpack never played more than ten away games and posted a 108-22 record at home. During the same time span, their road record was a mere 36-29. In 1956, when State posted a 24-4 record en route to winning the ACC regular-season and tournament titles, Case scheduled only five away games.

State fans were very appreciative and came out in droves to support their team. Sometimes, they even got a little carried away. One February night in Raleigh in 1948, students broke down the doors at old Frank Thompson Gym, so the fire marshal cancelled the game. Two days prior to that contest, tragedy had struck when the bleachers at Purdue collapsed and two students were killed during a game there. An hour before tip-off against North Carolina in Raleigh, Frank Thompson's 3,500-seat bleachers were already filled when one of the front entrance doors was broken down by a group of onrushing students and fans who had been deprived of tickets. Eight policemen and ten firemen rushed to the scene and, mindful of what had happened at Purdue, promptly called off the game. The rowdy crowd chanted repeatedly, "We want a ball game! We want a ball game!" State's team remained in the dressing room; Carolina's never even made it into the building.

Skeeter Francis, who later would go on to serve for years as Wake Forest's sports information director and later as an official with the Atlantic Coast Conference, was a sportswriter at the time for the *Durham Herald*. He remembered games at cramped Frank Thompson Gym.

"On occasion, I covered a game there and had to crawl through a window in the basement to get in the building," Francis said. "Then I would go into the actual gym through the men's room because the fire marshal had already closed the doors and wouldn't let any more people in."

Case loved it. Not only did he forge a natural rivalry with the nearby school from Chapel Hill, but he also had an obvious reason to lobby for a quicker completion to a new arena that already was under construction. This was no small task. The design of William Neil Reynolds Coliseum originally was trotted out in late 1939 and was identical to that of Indoor Stadium on Duke's campus right down Tobacco Road. It was supposed to cost $300,000 and serve the dual purpose of basketball arena and ROTC armory. When Governor J. Melville Broughton announced plans to build the facility at State's commencement ceremonies in 1941, the United States Secretary of War declared the project one vital to the nation's military defense.

He must have been exaggerating, since the project stalled and then reached a complete dead end during World War II. It would be ten years, three governors, four General Assemblies, four State Budget Commissions, and $3 million later before the arena was finally completed.

When he had first viewed the outer shell of Reynolds Coliseum upon his hiring in 1946, Case moaned, "It's too small. It needs to be bigger."

Proving that the coach had clout, the school huddled with architects and the construction crews and agreed to make it bigger. The steel girders that had been in place for years remained, but both end zones were extended to increase seating capacity from 9,000 to 12,400. Hence, the unusual shoe-box shape of the facility. Three and a half years later Case had what was at the time one of the finest facilities in all of America.

When Reynolds Coliseum was completed in 1949, sports editor Smith Barrier of the *Greensboro News and Record,* wrote that Raleigh had just become "the basketball capital of the world. Immediately, at once." Case paid visiting teams what were at the time outstanding fees to play there because he knew he would pack the place to the rafters. Reynolds regularly outdrew other basketball meccas in the nation, even Madison Square Garden.

Nineteen forty-nine was also the year Case established the Dixie Classic—pitting State, North Carolina, Duke, and Wake Forest against four of the best teams in the nation. It became an instant success.

Young Dave Odom was among those who attended some of the first Dixie Classics. His father, Bill, was a Pontiac-Cadillac dealer in Goldsboro and knew the owner of a construction and lumber company in Raleigh who saw that he received tickets to the Dixie Classic each year. Bill Odom would take his son and two others and always sit in Section 12, Row 4, Seats 1–4, right behind what was then the Governor's Box.

"They were the best seats in the house," Odom said. "That was the highlight of the year for me. We watched four games a day against some of the best teams in the country. You were watching the very best players in the nation."

As he watched, Odom would make it a point to watch the gray-haired coach roaming the sideline in front of the North Carolina State bench.

"Everett Case wasn't a man who was given to a lot of histrionics," Odom said. "He looked like he was in total command of his team and himself. He was a man that, if looks could kill, then he was guilty a lot during a game because he could stare down an official or one of his players or even an opponent or an opponent's player.

"You know the old thing about a picture being worth a thousand words or that kind of thing? Well, he had a way of really letting you know what he thought without saying it. Word has it that he could put a tongue-lashing on you pretty good. But he did it in a private way. He wasn't loud at the games. He was more in control."

Charlie Dayton remembered attending an early Dixie Classic game between State and the University of Dayton.

"It was the first time I can ever remember being exposed to Big Four basketball. I guess I was nine years old. Maybe ten or eleven at

the most," Dayton said. "It was North Carolina State versus Dayton
—and in retrospect, it might have been the worst Dixie Classic game
ever played. I think the final score was something like thirty-eight
to thirty-two. It must have been a horrible game to watch for the
sophisticated fan, if there was such a thing at the time. But I thought
it was the greatest thing in the world, to go there to the Coliseum
and have this happening right in front of you.

"So after that, my family got me season tickets to all the State
basketball games. I think it was eight dollars for a season ticket at
that time. I still have one that I saved back home in Raleigh."

Case loved the Dixie Classic because he loved tournament basketball. Whether it was the Dixie Classic, the ACC Tournament, or
the NCAAs, Case thrived in the festive atmosphere. He loved the
attention his team received and he enjoyed entertaining the media,
with whom he had a good relationship.

"A tournament is like a banquet and every game is a feast,"
Case would tell his players.

CASE KNEW MORE than a little about banquets and feasts, but he
kept most of his focus on basketball. He was a hard-driving, hard-
drinking man who cursed before it was fashionable for coaches
to do so. He had never been married and had no intentions of
wedding himself to anything or anyone but his chosen profession.
He was driven to succeed. One N.C. State player, Lou Pucillo, described him this way: "He won too much; he had a real fear of
losing."

Case earned the nickname The Old Gray Fox because he was
crazy like a fox. But he always had his reasons for everything
he did.

During a slump by his team in 1958, Case received word from
some of his sources around town that his players had been drinking
regularly and excessively. He was peeved and called assistant coaches
Vic Bubas and Lee Terrill into his office immediately.

"This has to stop! Let the players know that I know about it
and that this has to stop!" Case shouted. "Any player caught drinking from here on out will be kicked off the team and out of school. I
want you guys to keep an eye out."

Case ranted and raved for more than thirty minutes. Finally, he
was finished. Bubas and Terrill turned to leave.

"Wait. You'd better not go into the Players Retreat lounge or
any other bar because you might find Richter," Case added.

John Richter was Case's star center at the time and his only true big man. Richter also loved his beer. Case did not want to risk losing his best player.

Truth be told, Case was also a man who enjoyed a good, stiff drink. Friends would tell him when they thought he was drinking too much, but Case would shrug it off. He liked nothing more than having a few drinks or coffee and dessert with his assistant coaches and friends, and he often invited them over to his house after games.

Bill Hensley was the sports information director at State during Case's final years as coach. In those years, he was often among those who visited the coach after hours. He knew of Case's legendary temper—which could surface in tense moments during practices or games—but said he was usually a perfect gentleman around him and his wife Carol.

"In five years of working with Case, we never had a cross word between us," Hensley said. "He was the easiest person to get along with I've ever seen. People think he was fiery and had a horrible temper. But he was the most kind, gentle, laid-back individual I ever saw. Now he could get mad. But it was not often. Usually, his demeanor was wonderful."

Hensley knew there were times when Case drank too much.

"He could get bombed. He loved his booze," Hensley said.

Hensley also knew Case was prone to use a certain swear word. Shortly after Hensley had been hired away from Wake Forest to work at State, he and his wife went over to Case's house after a home game that the heavily favored Wolfpack had lost. Case answered the door and invited the Hensleys inside.

"Coach, this is my wife Carol," Bill Hensley said.

"Carol, nice to meet you. C'mon in. Have a drink," Case replied.

"We didn't look so good tonight, did we Coach?" Hensley said as he stepped through the door.

"We looked like shit . . . S-H-I-T!" Case shot back.

Years later, Hensley laughed when he thought of the moment.

"I looked at my wife and her eyes must have been as big as saucers because you just didn't say that back then," he said. "Four-letter words just weren't used like that then. It's so funny when I look back on it because of the way people swear now. But that was the first time my wife had ever met Everett, and she sure didn't know what to think after that."

Bryant, who was an assistant coach on Case's last team at State, remembers how Case did not like a whole lot of dribbling during his practices. When point guard Eddie Biedenbach first arrived at the school, he didn't know this.

"Biedenbach was a new recruit and a terrific ball-handler," Bryant said. "So he starts dribbling all over the place in his first practice and Everett just goes nuts. He starts stomping all over the place, yelling SHIIIIITTT! He could say shit and you could actually smell it. He could chew ass as well as anyone."

Case was also as frugal as anyone.

When Pucillo received his first paycheck as one of Case's assistant coaches, he asked Case out to dinner. One of the basketball program's biggest boosters visited their table while they were eating and offered to pay the bill. Pucillo politely declined, saying it was his night to treat. The booster tried to insist, and Pucillo again resisted.

Then Pucillo felt Case kick him underneath the table.

"Let him pick up this tab and then you can take me out again later," Case whispered.

Long-time State assistant coaches Lee Terrill and Vic Bubas often joked with each other that they needed to take extra money out of the bank before going on the road with Case.

"If they stopped to eat somewhere, they knew they would have to pay," said Charlie Bryant, who later felt the same pinch as one of Case's last assistants.

Another time when the team was in New York to play at Madison Square Garden, Case gave a cab driver such a small tip that the cabbie looked at the coin in the palm of his hand and returned it to the coach.

"I think you might need this more than I do," the cabbie said in jest.

Case accepted the coin without embarrassment, replying: "You know, I believe I do."

In reality, he didn't. Case had made lots of money in Indiana before ever coming to North Carolina. He had made extra cash for years by setting up and running basketball clinics. He even owned a popular drive-in restaurant.

Les Robinson, who would later go on to coach State himself, was a player under Case. He remembers visiting the coach at his home on numerous occasions. One of Case's hobbies was dabbling in the stock market. He often would dispatch Robinson or another player down to the local Merrill Lynch broker to deliver a transaction.

"Back then you didn't just pick up the phone and call your broker," Robinson said. "I didn't know what it was all about. I didn't even know what a stock was. I swear to God I didn't. So several of us would run errands for him down to Merrill Lynch. They would wrap something back up that we would then take back to him. It was like making a deposit at a bank. I would come back and hand him his receipts or whatever and he would give me a quarter.

"Frugal is a kind way of putting it in describing him. He would give me a quarter for driving down there and back. The NCAA could never have gotten him on that [giving money to recruits]. He was tight."

Case didn't like parting with his money, but there were things he would spend it on. Usually they had something to do with basketball. He believed, for instance, that every kid in North Carolina should have a basketball hoop in his backyard. He realized that for basketball to flourish at the college level, it had to develop grass roots—and he helped plant them in North Carolina.

He was passionate about having the state go to an open high-school tournament without regard to the size of the school. It was like that in Indiana when he coached high-school ball there. It never happened in North Carolina, but he never stopped lobbying for it or telling friends why he felt it was needed. Decades before the movie *Hoosiers* documented the triumph of a tiny high school over a big school from Indianapolis in the Indiana state championship game, Case sat around regaling anyone who would listen with the same tale.

"That kind of thing makes basketball," he told Hensley more than once. "That's what makes basketball so great. For a little two-hundred-student school to come in and whip some huge school from Indianapolis for the state title, that's the greatest thing in the world for them. It makes their program. It's great for the game."

Hensley recalled that Case would often tell that story and encourage parents of young children to get their kids to play the sport.

"He encouraged people to put goals in their backyard," Hensley said. "That was something he would help pay for occasionally if a kid needed a goal in their backyard."

If Case wasn't working the general public or the media as an ambassador of the sport, he was talking the game with fellow coaches or checking out young prospects.

When Press Maravich was coach at Clemson, Maravich would invite Case and Hensley to the Maravich home after games. They would sit around, talk basketball, and watch young Pete Maravich, Press's ten-year-old son, put on a dribbling exhibition.

"Press and his staff and Case and his staff would have dessert and coffee. Could you see something like that happening today?" Hensley said. "We would go to Press's house and watch Pete put on a show. He would put on gloves and a blindfold and dribble the ball behind him, between his legs, off the wall. Press would make him wear gloves and dribble with either hand. He made him wear the gloves so Pete couldn't feel the ball, so Pete would have a better touch handling it once he took the gloves off."

Case was so impressed with young Pete that he later made plans to hire Press Maravich as his top assistant, so Maravich could eventually replace him as coach when Case retired. He made these plans mainly because he admired Press Maravich's coaching abilities, but also because he figured Pete Maravich would follow his dad to Raleigh.

Through the years, Case's teams usually feasted on opposing teams no matter what the circumstances. He won more than his share of Dixie Classics and guided the Wolfpack to national prominence. He helped elevate everyone's appreciation of basketball not only in the state of North Carolina, but also across the country. He won nearly 74 percent of the games he coached over nineteen seasons, finishing with a record of 377-134.

But when Case failed to maintain control of his players and his team, he felt like a miserable failure. He twice ran into trouble with the NCAA over recruiting violations, getting State placed on a one-year probation for the recruitment of Ronnie Shavlik in 1953 and for four years of probation for the alleged illegal recruitment of Jackie Moreland in 1956. State was charged with conducting illegal tryouts for Shavlik; school boosters and even assistant coaches were charged with the more serious NCAA crime of luring Moreland to Raleigh with illegal offers of gifts and cash. Case proclaimed his innocence each time, but to no avail.

The probations bothered Case, but not nearly as much as the time some of his players became involved in a point-shaving scandal.

In the early 1950s, though, times were good and were about to get better. Case had established State as a program of national recognition, and the birth of a new conference was on the horizon. With the formation of the Atlantic Coast Conference in 1953, new rivalries were forged and old ones were intensified in a way even Case could not have imagined.

For years after his arrival in Raleigh, Case had his way with North Carolina, beating the Tar Heels in fifteen consecutive games from 1947 through 1952. Administrators at the University of North Carolina were fed up, so they decided to do something about it. They hired Frank McGuire, a brash but savvy coach out of New York City.

The Old Gray Fox was about to be challenged as he had never been challenged before.

3

McGUIRE'S MIRACLE

LIKE EVERETT CASE, Frank McGuire arrived in North Carolina with an impressive basketball resume in tow and some innovative ideas in mind. In 1952, while North Carolina was struggling to a 12-15 record overall and an embarrassing eleventh-place finish in the packed Southern Conference, McGuire was coaching St. John's in New York to the NCAA Tournament. To outsiders it looked like McGuire, a New York native through and through, had found a place to call home.

Lennie Rosenbluth knew otherwise. In March 1952, Rosenbluth was a New York kid from the Bronx who was just finishing his senior year of high school. He knew McGuire through Harry Gotkin, a New York talent scout who often took him to college and professional basketball games at Madison Square Garden.

At not more than 170 pounds on a 6-5 frame, Rosenbluth was a lanky young man. But his physical appearance was deceiving. He was a fine basketball player, an explosive scorer who unfortunately lacked the academic qualifications to get admitted into college. His high-school playing career had consisted of all of five games because of circumstances largely out of his control. High schools in the Bronx were crowded at the time with older, more mature athletes who were back in school to finish their eligibility and earn their diplomas after serving their country in the difficult years following World War II. As a result, Rosenbluth was cut from his high-school team as both a sophomore and junior. The next year, he took only a minimum number of courses so he could keep his status as a junior.

That year, he made the team, but was thwarted yet again when New York City's coaches went on strike to demand more pay and better conditions for their teams. The strike lasted two years, leaving the city without any high-school athletics during that time and forcing Rosenbluth to find other places to play.

That was okay with the determined Rosenbluth. He still wanted to play. His own affinity for demonstrating his skills on playgrounds and in church halls led to his discovery by Hy Gotkin, Harry's cousin, who coached the team at the 92nd Street YMCA. Hy Gotkin asked Rosenbluth, a Jewish white kid, to come and play on a squad otherwise made up of all black players. Rosenbluth accepted and went on to help the team—led by future Duquesne and NBA player Sihugo Green—win 65 straight games.

This was a different era for New York basketball. High school players were forced to showcase their skills wherever they could. Playing for the local YMCA or even on a nondescript playground in front of the right people was the best way to make a name for yourself. Rosenbluth's exposure with the YMCA club earned him an invitation to play for Laurel Country Club in the Catskills Hotel League, where a big guy by the name of Wilt Chamberlain was also busy making himself known.

At first, Rosenbluth's playing time in the summer league was limited. He was, after all, playing with and against the area's best high school players and its best pro and college stars as well. When a tragic automobile accident killed one of his teammates and injured two others Rosenbluth cracked the starting lineup and quickly began averaging more than 20 points per game. He played well enough to catch the eye of Red Auerbach, coach of the Boston Celtics.

Auerbach approached Rosenbluth one afternoon.

"We're holding a rookie camp in September. Would you be interested in coming and working out with us?" Auerbach said.

"You bet I would," Rosenbluth replied enthusiastically.

Rosenbluth thus spent two weeks in September 1951 working out with the Boston Celtics, who employed the likes of Bob Cousy and Bill Sharman and the eccentric center (and future Wake Forest coach) Bones McKinney. Auerbach was impressed enough to offer Rosenbluth a contract, but when the NBA reviewed a list of the Celtics' prospective players and found Rosenbluth's name on it, the league ruled that its teams could not sign high-school players. Rosenbluth later admitted he had intended on accepting Auerbach's offer, even though he had not yet earned his high-school diploma.

Rosenbluth had no choice but to turn elsewhere. Despite his apparent physical limitations and lack of academic qualifications, Rosenbluth still hoped to play in college for Everett Case at North Carolina State. For a time Case wanted him, too.

After point-shaving scandals rocked the New York–area schools in 1951 and led to several colleges deemphasizing the sport, many star players fled the area for out-of-state schools. Rosenbluth was no different. And even though Rosenbluth knew McGuire at St. John's, he initially had no plans to play for him.

"If he had stayed at St. John's, I probably wouldn't have gone there because of all the scandals that were hitting New York in 1951," Rosenbluth said. "Those were the first point-shaving scandals in the country, and because of them, New York basketball kind of died.

"Long Island had great teams and they deemphasized the program. St. John's wasn't touched, but Manhattan deemphasized and so did City College. Players were leaving New York City then. If there hadn't been a scandal, then New York would have kept all of the best ballplayers. To play in the Garden was every kid's dream."

It was while sitting with Harry Gotkin at a game in the Garden that Rosenbluth first learned of McGuire's intentions to flee South.

At this point, Rosenbluth was steamed at State and he wasn't sure what he was going to do. His heart had been set on playing for Case and the Wolfpack. Case had even invited him down for a visit his junior year, but it was not the type of visit that Rosenbluth had envisioned.

"I got invited down by Everett Case to look at the campus. Everything was supposed to be all set," Rosenbluth said. "But I got down there, and before I knew it there was a tryout. I had known nothing about it and done nothing to prepare for it. In New York that year there was no basketball because the coaches were all on strike. I was in terrible shape. I couldn't run up and down the court, let alone have a good showing.

"After all those practices, Everett told Harry and my father that he wasn't interested in me anymore."

Harry Gotkin was perhaps more upset over the matter than even Rosenbluth. So that night at the Garden, he leaned over to Rosenbluth and told him a secret.

"Forget about State. I have something to tell you," Gotkin said.

"What?" Rosenbluth said.

"Frank isn't coming back to St. John's next year. He's going to coach either at Alabama or North Carolina, and he told me that he wants to take you with him wherever he goes," Gotkin said.

At first Rosenbluth was confused.

"McGuire had taken St. John's to the NCAA Tournament, where they had lost to Kansas," Rosenbluth said. "And St. John's was giving Frank a testimonial dinner. But here Harry was telling me Frank wasn't going to be at St. John's the next year.

"I had known Frank McGuire for quite a while. I knew him because I would go with Harry to the Garden and we would sit up there with Frank, [long-time McGuire associate] Buck Freeman, and everyone else. So I had known him. And when Case said to forget about it, and Harry told me that McGuire wanted me, that's where I wanted to go. I was one of the few people at the time who knew he wasn't going to be back at St. John's.

"But the thing was I didn't have language or math [courses required to get into college], so I had to go to prep school. Frank went to Carolina for the 1952–53 season and I went to prep school. Then I went to Carolina the next year."

It would prove to be a wonderful relationship between McGuire and Rosenbluth.

The same could not be said of McGuire and Case, who in the 1953–54 season took their teams out of the Southern Conference and into the new Atlantic Coast Conference. The ACC, in actuality, was formed with football in mind much more than basketball. Maryland and Duke were national football powers at the time. The formation of the nine-team ACC meant that a more desirable round-robin schedule format could be adopted. This enabled the new league to secure an automatic berth to the Orange Bowl on an annual basis. The Southern Conference, of which the Big Four schools were members prior to formation of the ACC, had become bloated with 17 schools—many of whom could not hope to compete with the likes of Duke and Maryland on the football field.

The four schools from the state of North Carolina had been doing battle on the basketball court ever since Wake Forest played Trinity College (which would go on to become Duke University) on March 2, 1906. N.C. State and Wake had played each other since 1910, with Duke added to State's schedule in 1911, and North Carolina added in 1912. State and Carolina then joined the Southern Conference together in 1921, joined later by Duke in 1928 and Wake in 1937. But the idea in 1953 was to have the top football schools from the Southern Conference—North Carolina, North Carolina

State, Wake Forest, Virginia, Clemson, and South Carolina in addition to Duke and Maryland—form the ACC. That this new league might quickly develop into one of the best college basketball conferences in the country was an afterthought to almost everyone but the likes of Case, McGuire, and Duke's Hal Bradley.

"There's no doubt that this area is a hotbed of college basketball," Bradley said at the time. "And in another few years, we will rank with any such area in the nation. Basketball in the high schools of our state is improving steadily and this, too, will hasten the growth and popularity of the sport in North Carolina."

Bradley was right. Along with Case and McGuire, and Bones McKinney and Murray Greason at Wake Forest, Bradley helped shape a new image of big-time college basketball in the state.

Case was the first coach to consistently go out of state to recruit players, establishing the pipeline to his home state in Indiana and bringing in the likes of Dick Dickey, Norm Sloan, and Vic Bubas. Once the pipeline was established, it became a perpetual link to the best players in the state. All Case had to do to snare a top recruit was tell one of his former players from Indiana how much fun it was to whip up on everyone in North Carolina and just about anyone else the Wolfpack cared to play.

McGuire, in a way, had the same sort of recruiting philosophy, only he believed the best college basketball recruits were located in New York City. He had lived there and coached there and he had all sorts of guys like Harry Gotkin to keep him informed and in touch with the up-and-coming players. It didn't take long for him to establish the same type of pipeline as Case, only to a different city. It became known as the Underground Railroad.

Once this happened, people took notice of Frank McGuire and North Carolina basketball. And he loved the attention. He once told *Sports Illustrated* magazine: "New York is my personal territory. Duke can scout in Philadelphia and North Carolina State can have the whole country. But if anybody wants to move into New York, they need a passport from me.

"All the people in New York are my friends. No one gets paid for helping, but everybody looks out for me. The whole police department looks for players for me. So do the high-school coaches, and so do the brothers at the Catholic schools. Even the waterfront looks out for me."

New York was McGuire's bread-and-butter territory, but there was some dispute about whether he was telling the complete truth about no one getting paid to help him. If they didn't get paid in cold cash, they usually were paid in favors of some form or another. These were the days before the NCAA crackdowns on recruiting, and both Case and McGuire did pretty much as they pleased at first to get the players they wanted.

Regardless, when McGuire first arrived at Carolina in 1952, it didn't take long for him to realize that Case had better players than he did. It also didn't take long for the two men to begin agitating one another.

In his first confrontation with Case on the court, McGuire coached his Tar Heels to a 60–59 upset victory. Case never forgot it. The next two times the teams met, Case laid on the full-court pressure early and never let up. State won by 21 and 32 points, respectively. McGuire was furious with Case for what he believed was unnecessary pressing and for running up the score when those games were already out of hand. He bit his tongue. He knew he didn't yet have the same caliber of players to work with as Case, but he was working on it.

When State beat North Carolina again in January 1954, McGuire could hold back no longer. He lashed out at Case when talking with reporters following the game.

"[Case] ruined the game by using the press," McGuire insisted. "It was ridiculous. He could beat us by 25 points without doing it, but he comes over here and tries to lick us by 40. If that's the way he wants to play, I'll fight him right back when we get the boys to compete with him."

Case, in turn, was furious with McGuire for making such claims. For one thing, on this particular occasion, State had won by a mere 7 points, 84–77. That hardly constituted running up the score.

"Why, that's the most childish thing I've ever heard of," Case told reporters when informed of McGuire's postgame comments. "Since when did he get to the place where he could coach my ball club? I'll do anything I please as long as it's within the rules. Didn't he press us over here [in Chapel Hill] last year?"

McGuire added: "I am declaring open war against Everett Case. And some day, perhaps in a year or two, the shoe will be on the other foot."

THE CHAMPIONSHIP SHOE was firmly on Case's foot the first three years in the ACC, which from the first year of its existence relied on a postseason tournament to determine its true champion. The winner would then represent the conference in the NCAA Tournament. It would be decades before more than one school from the conference was permitted entrance into the tournament that determined the national champion. The ACC tournament, then, was the most important series of games in North Carolina.

The first ACC Tournament in March 1954 gave an early indication of how competitive the Big Four schools were going to be in the new league. State beat Carolina 52–51 in the first round, eased past Duke 79–75 in the semis, and then held off Wake Forest 82–80 in overtime to win the first ACC championship.

It helped that the tournament was held at Reynolds Coliseum, giving Case and his Wolfpack a decided home-court advantage. His teams won the ACC Tournament each of its first three years, winning the regular-season title as well in 1955 and 1956. The Big Four schools combined would go on to win 17 of the first 18 ACC Tournament titles, 23 of the first 25 and 31 of the first 35. It wasn't until the league's seventeenth season in 1970 that a school outside of the Big Four would capture a regular-season title—when South Carolina, coached by Frank McGuire, made it through 14 league games unbeaten.

McGUIRE BLEW onto the scene in Carolina like a hurricane from the North. He was brash and cocky and not afraid to share his views on any subject. He dressed like a model out of a men's fashion magazine, wearing tailored suits and starched white shirts with neckties pulled up tight around the collar. He usually wore diamond cuff links and had a fancy handkerchief of some type stuffed carefully into the breast pocket of his suit coat. He almost looked like a New York mafioso. And in later years, when he coached at South Carolina, he often would drop hints that he had certain friends with connections in New York City. He even told reporters once that he knew where the body of former Teamster Jimmy Hoffa was buried.

But McGuire was most outspoken when it came to discussing his rival, Case. McGuire even accused Case of using music to establish an unfair advantage at Reynolds Coliseum. In other subtle innovations that would catch on in a big way, Case was the first coach to authorize a pep band to play at home games and the first to have an applause meter for fans installed. State also employed an organist. McGuire used to argue that when the organist cranked up "Dixie," the old Southern anthem, it was worth at least a ten-point swing in State's favor.

At the same time, McGuire was openly critical of Case's habit of playing a schedule top-heavy with home games. He noted State's repeated failures at Madison Square Garden, offering Case a clear backhanded compliment by saying: "Every time I go to New York, I rave and rave about State. Then when they go north to play, they never live up to expectations."

Another time McGuire told reporters: "Good teams win on the road. Fair ones do not. Basketball is a game where the home court has its advantages. But a good team, in order to stay on top, has to win on the road."

Case's teams were good, no doubt, but after reaching the Final Four in the NCAA Tournament in 1950, they never did much again to make noise on a national level. Recruiting violations hurt. Despite winning the 1955 ACC regular-season and tournament titles, State was banned from participation in the 1955 NCAA Tournament for paying the travel expenses of recruiting prospects to Raleigh for open tryouts two years earlier. The key figure in the violations was Ronnie Shavlik, an outstanding player from Denver who went on to have a fine All-America career at State. But perhaps one of Case's biggest disappointments was letting Lennie Rosenbluth get away. McGuire, who had lured Rosenbluth from New York City, would capitalize on this failure in a big way.

Many insiders, among them Case himself, would say in later years that the 1955 State team, which went 28-4, may have been his best. It irritated him to no end, then, when Carolina and McGuire, led by none other than high-scoring newcomer Lennie Rosenbluth, roared into Reynolds Coliseum and laid an 84–80 defeat on the Wolfpack that season. McGuire ordered his players to clip the nets, further infuriating Case, the man who had brought the net-clipping tradition to the South in the first place.

Earlier, Case took a shot at McGuire for playing a game that was too slow-paced.

"It's not basketball. It's not good for the game," Case argued.

This came from a coach who in 1954 had held the ball for the final six minutes of a 57–48 State victory over McGuire and Carolina at Reynolds Coliseum. Then he refused to shake McGuire's hand once the contest was over. Or was it McGuire who refused to shake hands? The answer depended on which coach reporters talked to.

"The losing coach should be the first to offer congratulations, not the other way around," Case fumed.

"He shouldn't be holding the ball like that. That's not basketball," McGuire shot back.

Later, McGuire added an interesting twist to his ongoing feud with Case by claiming that Everett himself wanted the public to think the men hated each other. That, in Case's mind, *was* good for the game. It was especially good for creating a healthy rivalry between the two schools.

"He'd always say, 'Don't shake hands with me on the court. Let the people think we're mad at each other,' " McGuire said.

But others close to Case knew that the State coach disliked McGuire, and vice versa.

"They didn't like each other," Bill Hensley said. "They would get mad at each other for everything. Back in those days, they would really get mad if you held the ball. One of Everett's favorite tricks was holding the ball.

"If he felt a team was better than his, he would hold the ball. He would slow it down. They would shoot about every five minutes. So sometimes he would admit that a team had more firepower or manpower and was favored to win. Then he would hold the ball and slow the game down. But if he felt his team was better, he would play racehorse basketball."

So when holding the ball was good for State, Case considered it good for the game. When it wasn't good for State, the Old Gray Fox sniffed in disgust at the tactic.

Basically, when Case wanted to bend the rules a little bit, he didn't care what anyone thought. Since his team was banned from participating in the NCAAs in 1955 and the ACC had adopted a policy that prohibited its teams from playing in the National Invitation Tournament, Case opted to enter the twenty-five-team AAU national tournament in Denver instead. State beat Wuthnow Furniture of Hope, Kansas, in the first round before losing to the San Francisco Olympic Club. The following year, league officials voted not to allow participating schools to play in the AAU tournament again.

In 1956, though, Case didn't care about the AAU tournament. His team was finally going to be eligible for the NCAAs, and this time he wanted to atone for past failures.

His team rolled through the early part of the season, beating fifth-ranked Brigham Young and capturing yet another Dixie Classic championship over a field that included two other unbeaten top-ten teams. After winning their first 11 games to run their two-year unbeaten streak to 22 games, State stood ranked number two in the nation behind only San Francisco and its great center Bill Russell.

The streak ended when Duke upset State 68–58 after State's starting guard Vic Molodet missed the January 7 game due to an illness.

More bad luck followed. Cliff Hafer, a reserve forward, was booted off the team in mid-February for violating the school's honor code. And Shavlik, the 6-9 scoring wonder, broke his left wrist in the regular-season finale.

With his wrist in a cast, Shavlik still managed to play in the ACC Tournament, concentrating on rebounding instead of scoring. He grabbed 16 rebounds in a revenge victory over Duke in the semifinals and 17 boards in the championship final against Wake Forest. He became an instant celebrity in and out of North Carolina. He even got invited onto the Perry Como Show prior to State's first-round NCAA game against heavy underdog Canisius.

The game against Canisius wasn't to be played at Reynolds Coliseum. It was to be played at Madison Square Garden, where Case's teams always seemed to have trouble.

True to form, even 25 points and 17 rebounds from Shavlik could not prevent another disappointing NCAA tournament defeat. State fell in a four-overtime thriller. Case was crushed.

"This is the greatest disappointment I've suffered in my thirty-six years in basketball," he told reporters afterward. "If I hadn't recognized the players on the floor, I wouldn't have believed this is the same State team I coached all year. The boys were so high. They wanted to do the right thing so badly that they did everything wrong."

It was about to get worse for Case. As he pondered the pending departure of the fabulous Shavlik from his own team, he scanned a sheet listing the final league statistics and noticed a familiar name at the top of the scoring charts. The ACC's leading scorer that season: Lennie Rosenbluth, who had scored 26.7 a game for Frank McGuire at North Carolina.

ROSENBLUTH FELT something special might happen to North Carolina during the 1956–57 season. He was one of several players returning for the Tar Heels, who had proven the previous year that they were one of the top teams in the ACC. They had beaten State at Reynolds Coliseum in Raleigh and they had actually reigned with State as cochampions of the regular season. But then Wake Forest upset the Heels 77–56 in the semifinals of the ACC Tournament, and a possible dream season had ended brutally and suddenly.

That defeat may have made North Carolina a better team the following season. McGuire certainly never forgot it, and he reminded his players of it so often that they would have had to have been brain-dead to forget it. Nonetheless, McGuire was less certain than Rosenbluth, his team captain, of the team's potential entering the '56–57 campaign. He told friends and reporters that another 18-win season would be acceptable; more than 20 wins was perhaps possible.

McGuire had several reasons for these reservations. For one thing, several of his boys were having trouble hitting the books. Harvey Salz, a sharp-shooting sophomore guard, had dropped out of school. Senior Tony Radovich, another guard who might have provided important depth, was only eligible the first semester of the season. And later in the season, 6-11 Bill Hathaway, a starter when the season began, and sophomore Stan Groll, a reserve guard, were declared academically ineligible. Plus this team had a difficult schedule.

Unlike Everett Case, McGuire believed a good team could only become a great team by the character and experience it built playing under adverse conditions on the road. One year after Case scheduled only five away games for State, McGuire and his Tar Heels played only eight home games at tiny Woollen Gym on the Carolina campus.

They played anybody and everybody, usually in hostile environments. McGuire particularly enjoyed the time they beat New York University in Madison Square Garden early in the season. Even though Rosenbluth was triple-teamed most of the game, managing only 9 points, others picked up the scoring. Whenever too much attention was paid to Rosenbluth, others like Tommy Kearns, Joe Quigg, and Pete Brennan picked up the slack. Ultimately, it made North Carolina a better, more balanced offensive team.

They avenged the previous season's loss to Wake Forest by beating the Demon Deacons—after first beating Utah and then demolishing Duke—to win the Dixie Classic. They handily dispatched State at Reynolds Coliseum again, building a huge early lead before cruising to an 83–57 victory.

Someone asked McGuire if his players ever got rattled.

"Rattled? These boys are too young to get rattled. They haven't got enough sense to get rattled," he replied. "Nothing bothers them. They just go out and play ball. They don't worry about nothing."

The questioner should have asked McGuire if he was getting rattled as the win streak grew.

"We knew the pressure was getting to McGuire in 1957," Rosenbluth said years later. "The first time we beat State, we must have had an eighteen-point lead at halftime. That was unheard of. And he was getting on us because he said we weren't playing well. He was raking us over the coals in the locker room at halftime.

"The players, well, we couldn't even look at each other because we would burst out laughing. We all had our heads down while he was screaming at us because we were afraid to look at each other."

It had by then become obvious that Rosenbluth's feeling was right from the start. This team *was* something special. As team captain, Rosenbluth organized weekly team meetings where players could air their gripes openly and honestly without fear of retribution from teammates or the coaching staff. Things were going so well for the Tar Heels that the players usually talked only about how many games they had to go to complete a perfect season. As the wins piled up, McGuire scratched his head and wondered if someone was going to wake him up from this wonderful dream season.

"I don't know how we keep winning," he told reporters at one point. "Every opponent is playing harder against us and our kids are feeling the pressure building up from our winning streak. I think we'd be a better ball club if we got knocked off a couple of games. There's no such thing as an undefeated season in basketball."

With that thought in mind, McGuire actually conceded defeat in the huddle during a time-out in the final seconds of a game at Maryland. Eighteen seconds remained. Maryland led 53–49 and had their best foul shooter at the line with a chance to ice the upset victory.

"Okay fellas, we lost this ball game. But go out with class. Act like true champions. Shake their hands when it's over because they played a great ball game," McGuire told his players in the huddle.

Rosenbluth was stunned. He knew McGuire was probably right, yet it seemed strange to hear the coach say it. But the impossible happened. The sharpshooter from Maryland missed his free throw, and Carolina grabbed the rebound. The Heels got quick baskets from Bob Cunningham and Tommy Kearns in the final eighteen seconds to force overtime.

"It looked like there was no way we could win that game," Rosenbluth said. "Remember, there was no three-point shot back then. So even if you were down three with less than ten seconds to play, you could forget about it.

"But once we tied that game up and went to overtime, we knew we would win it. That was the kind of season it was. It was after that game that some of us starting sitting around thinking, 'Hey, we're not going to lose.' "

By then, the Tar Heels were riding an 18-game unbeaten streak and ranked number one in the country. They took over the top spot in mid-January when Kansas and their remarkable center, Wilt Chamberlain, were upset by Iowa State.

This team was McGuire's handiwork, and it had New York City imprints all over it. The entire starting five at the beginning of the season—Rosenbluth, Kearns, Quigg, Brennan, and Hathaway—was from the New York area. Later Bob Cunningham, another New York native from West Harlem, was added to the lineup when Hathaway was declared academically ineligible. They played a style of offense popular in New York, but unseen until that time in the South. They always made the extra pass and played unselfishly. They rarely turned the ball over, and they played gritty team defense.

"We had a freelance offense, basically," Rosenbluth said. "We didn't have set plays where Player One would pass to Player Two, and then he does this or he does that. McGuire set up a pattern and we ran off the pattern. It was like a New York–style offense. It played to everyone's strengths."

Rosenbluth's strengths were the most obvious. Because of his long arms and his ability to score inside as well as outside, he played forward and center at a mere 6 feet, 5 inches. He could score on hook shots over big men in the paint, and on twenty-foot jump shots over smaller forwards and guards.

When games got heated, McGuire knew to go to Rosenbluth.

"Feed the animal," he often said. It was McGuire's way of saying the other guys had to get the ball to Rosenbluth more.

But the beauty of Carolina's team that season was that it wasn't a one-man show. Shut down Rosenbluth at all costs, and others like Quigg or Kearns or Brennan could hurt you. Quigg was a banger who had a nose for the ball. Kearns was the point guard who could penetrate to break down opposing defenses. Brennan was automatic on the jump shot from the corner.

Like most coaches present and past, McGuire absolutely disdained turnovers that cost his team a chance to put points on the board.

"The ball is gold, boys. You don't throw away gold," he would tell his players.

Practices were mental tests more than physical ones. McGuire would set certain scenarios for his players and ask them what they would do in them.

"Everything was the clock. The clock, the clock, the clock," Rosenbluth said. "We would practice situations like being down two points with thirty seconds to go. Or he'd say we're ahead by one point with fifteen seconds to go. Then he'd ask us, 'Okay, what are you guys going to do now?'"

The constant drilling paid off more than once.

Besides the miraculous Maryland game, there was also a time where Duke's Bobby Joe Harris handed the Tar Heels a critical ACC victory by misreading the scoreboard at Woollen Gym. Or maybe the score was posted too slowly, leading to Harris's gaffe. Whatever the case, Harris had just made two key steals that led to Duke baskets and a score tied at 73 all. But before the second Duke field goal could be posted on the scoreboard, Harris looked up and saw UNC 73, Duke 71. Harris assumed he needed to foul Tommy Kearns intentionally to even have a shot at winning. With sixteen seconds left, Kearns made the free throws and Carolina won, 75–73.

Harris and Duke coach Hal Bradley went ballistic, claiming the slow-handed scorekeeper had cost them a legitimate shot at victory, but to no avail. The Heels then beat Duke again in the final tuneup for the ACC Tournament, completing a 24-0 regular season that included a remarkable 14-0 mark in conference play.

"Congratulations, boys. I didn't think you could do it, but you fooled me. This is the happiest night of my life," McGuire told his players.

State's Case and Duke's Bradley both offered only faint praise, each predicting that Carolina's run would end soon enough.

"They've got a fine ball club. But I believe someone will knock 'em off before the end of the season," Case said.

Bradley added: "Carolina has a fine team and I'm glad to see them ranked number one in the nation. It looks good for our conference. But I don't think they have a great team."

McGUIRE HAD BY THEN grown pretty fond of this group. Knowing they listened to him and played intelligently and hard, he allowed his players certain liberties.

Rosenbluth, for instance, did not like to participate in the traditional team meal before games. McGuire believed in feeding his players a hearty meal precisely four hours before tip-off. It usually consisted of steak, baked potato, dry toast and hot tea—except for Rosenbluth. Usually, he was too nervous to eat. But if he did eat, the only thing he would eat before games were shrimp cocktails.

McGuire told waitresses at The Pines, where the team ate before home games and games against the Big Four schools, to give his players whatever they wanted.

"Keep the shrimp cocktails coming," Rosenbluth said.

"If that's what he wants, keep 'em coming," McGuire would tell the servers.

Rosenbluth once devoured eleven shrimp cocktails before a game, but insists today that he usually saved his insatiable appetite for shrimp cocktails for after the game.

"Most of the time I wouldn't eat at four p.m. with the rest of the guys," Rosenbluth said. "I would eat lunch around one and then wait for the game to be over. Then after the game I would go out and eat something. But it's true that shrimp cocktails were big with me.

"Shrimp was always on the entree for home games. McGuire would arrange that. Everybody liked it, not just me. In fact, when we went to the first round of the NCAA Tournament—I think it was one of the few pregame meals I ever ate—we went to a seafood place and they just kept bringing on the shrimp. We kept eating."

They kept winning, too. And as long as they were winning, McGuire wanted to make no trouble with his players.

Times were different then. The school was located on Tobacco Road, and tobacco was king. Most of the players smoked despite the objections of their coaches. Joe Quigg was even the campus representative for Marlboro cigarettes. Rosenbluth was one of Quigg's favorite customers and he knew that Quigg handed out free samples to students.

"Joe, you've got to take care of us on the team first," Rosenbluth would say.

Quigg would. He often would deliver cigarettes to teammates by the case, which didn't exactly figure in the training regimen preferred by McGuire.

Then Rosenbluth, Quigg, and Ken Rosemond would conspire to drive to away games in the Ford station wagon driven by team manager Joel Fleishman. They knew as long as they stayed in the rear of the three-car caravan, McGuire, riding shotgun up front in the lead car, would never realize they were chainsmoking all the way to the next visiting locker room.

"I always found that it killed the nerves," Rosenbluth said.

Then again, maybe McGuire knew more than he was letting on. Rosenbluth remembered a card party the players held in one of their hotel rooms before an away game at Louisiana State his sophomore year. It was getting late and the party was getting loud.

Suddenly, McGuire opened the door to the room and walked in.

The players, who were all puffing on cigarettes, were stunned and at a loss as to what to do in the smoke-filled room.

Then McGuire blurted out, "Whoops, wrong door."

And he left, closing the door quietly behind him without another word.

"We never heard anything more about it," Rosenbluth said years later.

McGuire's trusted assistant coach was Buck Freeman, who had come with him to Chapel Hill from New York and handled much of the game strategy and pregame discussion of player matchups. McGuire would often dispatch Freeman to the Varsity Theater on Franklin Street to make sure Rosenbluth wasn't cutting class again. One time Freeman found Rosenbluth, a movie buff, but ended up getting so caught up in the action on the big screen that he sat down next to the star player until the credits rolled. Rosenbluth never made it to class that day.

Freeman also had another position as McGuire's assistant. He figured it was his job to keep the players away from attractive coeds of the opposite sex, lest it affect their focus on the basketball court.

"He thought basketball and girls did not mix," Rosenbluth said. "Whenever we saw Buck, the girls in the car had to hide."

Freeman would walk around the campus virtually every night around 11:00 P.M. when he figured the players would be taking their dates back to their dormitories. If he saw them, he would let them know exactly what he thought right then and there.

"You need to keep your mind on basketball, not girls," Freeman often said.

Rosenbluth added: "If he saw you with a girl and you had a bad practice the next day, he would get all over you."

But the players actually enjoyed when Freeman ran practice in McGuire's place. They figured they could mess with him just enough to have practice cut short, leaving more of the evening for doing things like chasing young coeds or going to the movies or hanging out and puffing on a few Marlboros.

"With McGuire, you never fooled around in practice. You just didn't," Rosenbluth said. "But when McGuire would be off somewhere and would say, 'Okay, fellas, Buck is taking practice today,' we would be thrilled. We used to say, 'Okay, Buck's running practice and it starts at seven. Make a date for eight o'clock.'

"The guys on the team knew we would be thrown out of the gym. Practice would last a half-hour to forty-five minutes before Buck would go berserk and throw us out of the gym. You could count on it. We knew it was coming. He would start yelling and cursing you and telling you, 'You're doing this wrong or that wrong! Just get out of the gym!' He had no patience."

By March 1957, Rosenbluth and his teammates were through fooling around and seemed entirely focused on what they could accomplish on the basketball court. Even McGuire believed by then that anything was possible, and he privately stewed over the backhanded compliments handed out by Case and Bradley as his team completed its perfect regular season.

Again, the pressure to win the ACC Tournament was enormous. Stumble once there and the season was over.

"There was tremendous pressure," Rosenbluth said years later. "There was only one winner and only one team went on. We all knew that. Today, of course, you can get five or six teams from a conference into the NCAA Tournament. Back then, you win the tournament and you go to the NCAAs; if you don't, that's it. Pack your bags and go home."

"It was like Russian Roulette," McGuire once said.

It made every shot, every pass, every defensive stand of each game important. One mistake could lead to another and make even the undefeated Tar Heels susceptible to an upset. Clemson was up first in the ACC Tournament and was disposed of easily, 81–61. This was no surprise and hardly a test. Clemson had finished the regular season 3-11 in the ACC and 7-17 overall.

But next up was Wake Forest in what would be Murray Greason's last year as coach of the Demon Deacons. In fact, assistant Bones McKinney already was pretty much running the show. The Deacons were 19-9 overall, even though they had finished just 7-7 in the ACC. Regardless of their record, they always seemed to play the Tar Heels tough. They had played Carolina three times already in 1957—twice in the ACC regular season and once in the Dixie Classic—and every game had gone down to the wire. North Carolina had won one game by 3 points, the other two by 5 apiece.

Furthermore, the Deacons had embarrassed the Tar Heels and McGuire in the ACC Tournament one year earlier, eliminating the regular-season cochampions in the semifinals in blowout fashion,

77–56. That was on McGuire's mind as he spoke to his team before the 1957 tournament rematch.

"I have not forgotten how those boys celebrated right in this building last year after they humiliated us," McGuire told his players. "We've had such a great year. Don't let them spoil it for you.

"Just remember that they'll do anything to try and win. We've never had an easy game against Wake, those sons-of-bitches. Just remember last year, fellas."

Finally, McGuire clenched his fists and shook them at his players before sending them onto the court.

"Get out there and beat the hell out of 'em! I want to beat the hell out of 'em!" he roared.

They didn't beat the hell out of them, and they almost didn't beat them at all. It came down to a controversial play involving Rosenbluth, who made a hook shot just after Wake's Wendell Carr collided with him in the lane with forty-six seconds left. McKinney howled for a charging foul on Rosenbluth. McGuire implored the referees to call a blocking foul and let the basket stand, plus award his star an additional free throw.

McGuire won the argument with the referees. As his Catholic teammates made the sign of the cross, Rosenbluth made the subsequent free throw. Carolina won the game, 61–59.

In an interview with Ron Morris for the book *ACC Basketball: An Illustrated History*, McKinney argued thirty years after the fact that Rosenbluth should have been called for charging. McKinney added that the Wake locker room after the game was "like a tomb."

"Of all my days in the pros, all my playing, and all my coaching days, this was the saddest moment of my entire basketball career," McKinney told Morris. "The whole damn place was broken up. I've never seen anything like it in my life. There wasn't one dry eye in the place, mine included."

The Baptist minister still retained his sense of humor. He was even able to manage a weak smile when a friend who worked for UNC, Billy Carmichael, approached and said: "Bones, I know you feel bad and that's understandable. But I thought it was funny as hell that you Baptists and Catholics were out there fighting like hell and a Jew stepped in and settled the whole thing."

Earlier in the season, McGuire had called Rosenbluth "my Jewish Joe Dimaggio."

Jewish Joe Rosenbluth wasn't finished. He scored 38 points in the ACC Tournament final against South Carolina, leading the Tar

Heels to an easy 95–75 victory. Four players accounted for 94 of North Carolina's points—as Brennan added 22, Quigg 18, and Kearns 16. Bob Cunningham was the only other UNC player to score, and he registered only one free throw.

Cunningham was another example of McGuire's unfailing loyalty to players. Cunningham had been a hot prospect in high school in 1954, recruited by about thirty schools who were telling him they were prepared to offer a full scholarship. But when he stumbled in his family's West Harlem apartment and his shooting hand went through a window, severing nerves, all but one of the coaches who had been pursuing him scattered and were never heard from again.

The injury was bad enough that doctors suggested amputating his thumb. Cunningham's father, an immigrant from Ireland, refused to let them. Several operations later, a dejected Bob Cunningham went home to find McGuire waiting for him on the steps to the family's apartment.

"Don't worry, Bobby," McGuire told Cunningham. "No matter what happens, you've still got your scholarship to the University of North Carolina."

As Rosenbluth celebrated in the winning locker room after the twenty-point victory over South Carolina that clinched the ACC Tournament title, he shouted: "This is a team that honestly feels it can lick the world!"

Three straight wins in the ensuing NCAA Tournament backed up Rosenbluth's claim and landed Carolina in the Final Four in Kansas City, where it faced Michigan State and its star forward, Jumpin' Johnny Green. Again Carolina seemed blessed. First a shot by Michigan State's Jack Quiggle was disallowed at the end of regulation, sending the game into overtime. Then Green missed a free throw at the end of the first overtime, allowing Brennan to grab the rebound and dribble the length of the floor for a layup that tied the game 64–64 with four seconds left. It wasn't until the third OT that Carolina finally took control for a thrilling 74–70 victory.

Now only one team and one huge man stood between Carolina and a perfect 32-0 season and the national championship. The team was Kansas, and the huge man, a young Wilt Chamberlain.

The 7-2 Chamberlain was everybody's All-American, the nation's tallest and finest player. He had poured in 32 as Kansas romped past defending national champion San Francisco 80–56 in the other semifinal.

"He was a big guy—and I mean a big, big guy," Rosenbluth

said. "He is a big man. But everybody was saying we didn't have a chance. It was 'Kansas this and Kansas that. And Wilt Chamberlain this and Wilt Chamberlain that.'

"But we weren't in awe of Chamberlain. A lot of us played in the mountains in Chamberlain's senior year in high school. It was the summer and we played against him. It wasn't the Carolina team, but it was Joe Quigg and myself and we played against him. He would dunk it every which way—but we weren't awed by the dunk shot. To us, it was the same thing as a little jump shot from the foul line. It counted the same. It's basically the same shot as long as you don't get intimidated by it."

McGuire knew he could not devise a defense that would stop Chamberlain completely. So he decided to do it by committee. Rosenbluth and Quigg would double-team him whenever possible. The guards could drop back to try to take away the entry pass, creating in effect a triple-team and gambling that Kansas could not consistently knock down the outside shot.

"Listen," McGuire told his players, "we're going to hold Chamberlain if we have to. We're going to keep him surrounded. If he shoots, box him out and make sure we get the rebound. And if he does score, just don't give him the dunk shot."

Unlike Rosenbluth, McGuire didn't look at a dunk by Chamberlain as just another shot. He looked at it as a way for Chamberlain to ignite the pro-Kansas crowd of 10,500 in Kansas City. He didn't want it happening.

As the players warmed up before the game, North Carolina Governor Luther Hodges walked up and sat down next to McGuire on the Tar Heels' bench. He sat there, chatting and simply soaking up the electric atmosphere, until Buck Freeman politely ran him off.

"Governor, with all due respect, we've got a ball game to play here," Freeman finally said.

As the players strode to center court for tip-off, Rosenbluth walked up to Chamberlain and sized up the Kansas star.

"I came up to his shoulders," Rosenbluth said.

Then McGuire pulled a surprise. He didn't have Rosenbluth or Quigg jump center against the 7-2 Chamberlain. Instead, he had Tommy Kearns, the smallest player on the team at 5 feet, 11 inches, line up opposite Wilt for the opening tap.

"I wanted him to think, 'Is this coach crazy? What other tricks does he have up his sleeve?' " McGuire said of Chamberlain.

The only other trick was playing solid team defense on the

imposing center. At times it seemed like there was a human fence surrounding Chamberlain, who scored 23 points anyway. That was still nearly seven points below his season's average.

Rosenbluth scored 20 before fouling out with 1:45 remaining in regulation of what would become a wild three-overtime game. Neither team scored in the second overtime, which was marked by a scuffle in which McGuire cursed at several Kansas players and a Kansas assistant shoved McGuire. Carolina trailed 53–52 in the third overtime when Quigg drew a foul with six seconds left. Kansas called time-out to make him ponder the free throws, but McGuire quickly calmed Quigg down and confidently told his team the opposite of what he told them two months earlier in a similar situation at Maryland. He told them they would win the game, and he told them precisely how they were going to do it.

First McGuire paused and took a deep breath. The largely pro-Kansas crowd around him was going crazy. The noise seemed deafening. Then McGuire leaned forward and looked into the eyes of the young men surrounding him. He stared at Quigg.

"Joe, after you make these two foul shots, get back on defense as quick as you can," McGuire said.

Not *if* you make the foul shots, but *after* you make these foul shots.

The air of confidence sunk in. There was no doubt in any of the players' minds that Quigg was going to make both foul shots.

Then McGuire turned to the rest of those in the huddle.

"All of you get back on defense as fast as you can after Joe makes the foul shots. The ball is going into Chamberlain, so get ready for it," he said.

The final seconds unfolded exactly as McGuire anticipated. Years later, Bob Cunningham told the *Charlotte Observer:* "It was like Frank had seen film of the last six seconds."

Quigg made both foul shots, then Kansas tried to force the ball into Chamberlain. Quigg made another big play, slapping the pass away to Kearns, who caught it with two seconds remaining. He immediately tossed it as high as he could over his head to let the clock run out and prevent Kansas from fouling him. Carolina won the game 54–53 and the national championship.

It was another miracle finish in the season that would come to be known by Carolina fans as "McGuire's Miracle." The perfect 32-0 season was preserved forever.

Rosenbluth, the kid who wasn't good enough to play for Everett

Case at North Carolina State, was named to the All-Tournament team along with Pete Brennan. Rosenbluth finished his three-year North Carolina career with 2,045 points in 76 games for a 26.9 average that still ranks best in school history. His point total was the most in school history at the time, a record that stood for twenty-one years until Phil Ford came along and broke it in 1978.

"I think we were a team of destiny," Rosenbluth said. "Coach McGuire had a lot of faith in me. And I never wanted to let him down. It was one of those things where I felt it was a privilege to get a basketball scholarship and play for him. I don't think he owed me anything. I felt I always owed him for giving me a chance."

Most of McGuire's players felt the same way.

4

ACC: MADE FOR TV

O<small>N THE MORNING</small> of the championship game against Kansas, March 23, 1957, North Carolina coach Frank McGuire hosted a breakfast in his hotel suite where a number of coaches were invited. Two of the coaches present were Bob Spear, the head coach at Air Force, and a young Spear assistant named Dean Smith. McGuire was interested in hiring a new freshman coach and asked Smith if he would be interested. Smith, who ironically was all set to root against the Tar Heels that very night, did not say no. But he didn't say yes right away, either.

"You'll have to talk to Bob first," said Smith, a 1953 graduate of Kansas and a member of their 1952 national championship team.

It would be another year before McGuire lured Smith away from Air Force to Chapel Hill, but it wouldn't be as a freshman coach. Buck Freeman, a recovering alcoholic, had by 1958 become a casualty of the '57 title season. Expectations were high for the Tar Heels the next season, even without their star Lennie Rosenbluth, but the team struggled, finishing with a 19-7 record and losing to Maryland in the ACC Tournament final. Somewhere along the way, Freeman began drinking again. McGuire tried to ignore the problem for a while because Freeman had been his top assistant since their days together at St. John's. They were close friends. But McGuire soon came to realize he needed a new assistant coach. Smith turned out to be the perfect man for the job. He began duties as McGuire's assistant prior to the 1958–59 season.

"Buck was on the wagon a long time," Lennie Rosenbluth said.

"But I think the pressure of the 1957 season just got too much for him. There wasn't much pressure on us, the players. We were just playing ball and having fun. But to those who were sitting and watching the games, or coaching the games, they were under tremendous pressure. We didn't worry about it. But I think the pressure finally got to Buck and he started drinking again."

Indeed, Freeman's fall from grace wasn't the only fallout from the 1957 season. The culmination of McGuire's Miracle was witnessed not only by those in attendance at the championship game in Kansas City, but also by the thousands of folks watching it on television back home. The national championship earned by North Carolina changed everything for Big Four basketball. Until then, the games were great for the few locals who showed up for them or cared enough to at least casually follow them in the newspapers. But the masses had not yet caught the fever.

Until, that is, C. D. Chesley saw to it that Carolina's two Final Four games in '57 were televised back to the region. Television was at the time just beginning to catch on as a viable news and entertainment medium. Some homes had them in North Carolina, but many still did not. Right about the time Carolina put on its championship run, folks were beginning to learn of the power of the little black-and-white box. Soon television sets would be in every living room across America. Chesley couldn't have had two better games to broadcast on TV—a pair of triple-overtime thrillers won by North Carolina over powerful teams from Michigan State and Kansas.

Leonard Laye, sports editor of the *Charlotte Observer*, remembers the impact that the televised Final Four games had on his community, particularly among the younger fans.

"The first memory I really had of ACC basketball, which was really Big Four basketball back then because the Big Four was so dominant, was the '57 national championship," Laye said. "I was twelve or thirteen years old at the time. I grew up in Belmont, an area just outside of Charlotte, and we had just gotten our first television set. An old black-and-white. I can remember sitting up both nights, watching those two triple-overtime games and just going nuts in the process. I think my parents got hooked on basketball because of the TV. I know I did."

Laye was not unlike most other young teenage boys at the time.

"I was a baseball fan. As a kid, I read all the major-league box scores and all that," Laye said. "I paid no attention at all to college basketball until that national championship happened right there in front of me on the television. And from that point on, I grew up with it. I think all my buddies were the same way. That's what we talked about at school—I mean, other than girls and the normal things. When we talked about sports, we talked about what was happening with Belmont High's teams or what was happening in college basketball, mostly at the Big Four schools.

"The championship introduced us all to it. And soon after that, they started televising the Saturday afternoon ACC Game of the Week. I can remember planning my Saturday around whatever game was on."

Dave Odom, who had grown up listening to the radio broadcasts of North Carolina State games by Ray Reeve, was growing older and was about to become a three-sport star at Goldsboro High School in eastern North Carolina. But he did not turn on the radio the night North Carolina won the national championship. He didn't have to. His mother let him stay up late to *watch* the Tar Heels beat Kansas on television.

"I was still a North Carolina State fan. But my greatest memory of that is that I was proud of North Carolina that night," Odom said. "I guess my greatest memory was twofold: number one, I was amazed at Wilt Chamberlain's influence on the game. And number two, I remember the last play [of the third overtime] when Tommy Kearns ended up with the basketball with about two seconds left on the clock, and he throws the ball as high as he can in the arena, letting the final two seconds tick off. I remember thinking to myself, 'In most games, that's a great move. In this one, that's probably the only place Wilt Chamberlain can go and get it.' I was in eighth or ninth grade at the time. I remember watching Kearns and saying, 'I'm going to do that one day.'

"And I did. Probably more than once. With two seconds on the clock, you end up with the ball and here's a guy coming at you, and you know he's going to try to foul you. So you just throw the ball up in the air and the clock runs out. That's probably one of the great moves. But in that game, that's not so smart because Chamberlain can get it up there."

Odom, then only a teenager, was already beginning to think like a coach.

TELEVISING THE FINAL FOUR GAMES in 1957 had been a stroke of genius, or incredible luck, by one Castleman DeTolley Chesley. More likely, it was a combination of the two.

Chesley always had believed in the power of television and had worked within the sports divisions of the ABC, NBC, and Dumont networks from almost the advent of the new medium. He produced the national telecasts of Notre Dame football highlights every Sunday morning. Fighting Irish fans quickly grew accustomed to hearing the voice of announcer Lindsey Nelson describing the previous day's action.

Chesley had a powerful ally at the time in Frank McGuire. McGuire was among a group of school officials who granted permission in 1955 to a Chapel Hill public TV station to telecast a Carolina game against Wake Forest on a one-game experimental basis. Like all coaches, however, McGuire worried about televised games keeping fans from attending them in person.

"There is no doubt that the sport is in for a change," McGuire said at the time. "Whether this change will be good or bad from the standpoint of attendance, I don't know. I do know, however, that the game will become more popular as a result. More youngsters will be permitted to stay up at night to see the telecasts. And even the younger girls seem to like it. We already have started receiving letters from the girls asking for pictures of our players."

That experimental broadast in 1955 was only an appetizer. The two Final Four games in 1957 proved to be the entrée the fans would keep coming back for time and time again. But it almost didn't happen. Chesley, who actually operated out of Philadelphia, had produced a few televised ACC football games with only mixed results. But in 1957, he watched as college basketball fans grew increasingly passionate with each North Carolina victory. Chesley figured televising the Final Four games would generate a little revenue and a little more excitement for the sport.

So he hastily assembled a small "regional" network that included WBTV in Charlotte, WFMY in Greensboro, and WTVD in Durham. He lined up a couple of sponsors, rented broadcasting equipment in Kansas City, and bought time on phone lines to transmit the signal from the noisy, packed arena straight into the comfort of living rooms across North Carolina.

Chesley, who went on to form a network that televised ACC games every week, was stunned by the enormous interest the two games generated. He heard reports from all over the state about folks with TVs inviting over those without, just so they could watch the game; about furniture stores that had placed sets in display windows, where crowds quickly had gathered to watch.

"They were renting TV sets for hospitals [all over North Caro-

lina]," Chesley told the *Greensboro Daily News.* "It was the damnd-
est thing you ever heard of. I knew right then and there that ACC
basketball could be as popular as any TV show in North Carolina.
We were in Kansas City at the game. We didn't know how it had
gone over back in North Carolina. The game started so late in the
East, we wondered if anyone had stayed up to watch it.

"The next day we found out that almost everybody had stayed
up. We got letters from fans two years later thanking us for televising that one game against Kansas."

The impact was evident at once. More than fifteen thousand
fans showed up at Raleigh-Durham Airport to greet the championship team upon its return to North Carolina. McGuire and Lennie
Rosenbluth were invited to appear on the *Ed Sullivan Show.* And
Chesley already was thinking about the future of television as it
related to ACC basketball.

The next morning in Greensboro, Dick Andrews, the public
relations director at Pilot Life Insurance, rushed into the office of
company President O. F. Stafford.

"Did you see that game Saturday night?" Andrews asked
Stafford.

"Dick, my gosh, who didn't?" Stafford answered.

The next season, Pilot Life footed most of the bill for a slate of
ten televised ACC regular-season games on Saturday afternoons.
Chesley later expanded his coverage of the conference to include the
ACC Tournament.

Lindsey Nelson, the famed Notre Dame announcer, once told
Chesley, "There are four sports events you ought to see before you
kick the bucket: the Masters, the Kentucky Derby, a Notre Dame
home game, and the World Series."

Chesley shook his head, and responded.

"Those are all great events. But the atmosphere and the enthusiasm at an ACC Tournament are better than the World Series ever
thought about being."

WHILE MCGUIRE WAS CELEBRATING North Carolina's national championship and pondering a change to his coaching staff, a subtle coaching change was taking place a hundred miles due west in
Winston-Salem, where Wake Forest had relocated less than two
years earlier. There was nothing subtle about the school's move to
Winston-Salem. That was done because the R. J. Reynolds Company
offered lots of money in perpetuity if the school would relocate to a

plot of 320 acres on Reynolda, the estate of a Reynolds heiress and her husband. Founded in 1834 by Southern Baptists, the conservative school was originally a men's college that didn't permit women until it was deemed necessary to do so to keep the school's enrollment up during World War II.

But by 1956, all that tobacco money and land (even if it was being offered by a woman) was far too enticing to be ignored by school leaders, most of whom didn't smoke, drink, or have a great deal of respect for women. So the school moved from the tiny town of Wake Forest, and changed its name to Wake Forest University.

Horace Albert McKinney—better known to friends and foes as Bones—had been around Big Four basketball for years and was considered one of college basketball's most colorful characters even before succeeding Murray Greason, his friend and mentor, as coach of the Demon Deacons in 1958. McKinney played basketball at both North Carolina State and North Carolina, switching schools after his collegiate playing career was interrupted by a stint in the army during World War II. He was good enough to play professionally with the Boston Celtics and Washington Capitols when both teams were coached and managed by the legendary Red Auerbach. At 6 feet, 6 inches, and with a weight that would fluctuate between 175 pounds and 210 pounds depending on how much he "was sweatin'," it was easy to see how McKinney earned the nickname Bones.

Bill Hensley, who later would become McKinney's roommate on the road when Hensley was sports information director at Wake Forest, recalled attending a Celtics exhibition game in Raleigh when McKinney played for the team.

"He was dribbling the ball down the court and some fan in the front row was eating popcorn," Hensley said. "Bones stopped and kept dribbling. Then he reached over to help himself to the fan's popcorn. He got a handful and started eating it right there.

"The crowd went absolutely berserk. He never missed a beat. He ate the handful of popcorn and kept right on playing."

In 1988, McKinney wrote a book with Garland Atkins, *Honk Your Horn If You Love Basketball*, that detailed his storied career. In it, he declared, "I don't remember exactly when everyone started calling me Bones. But with a name like Horace Albert, the sooner the better, right?"

He also wrote at the time: "I plead guilty to driving through life at about 80 miles an hour, drinking 60,000 Pepsi-Colas, smoking some 2 million cigarettes, and threatening the lives of several hundred referees . . . I still drink Pepsis, but now I prefer the Diet ones. And I don't have to drink 25 a day now since I'm not coaching and sweatin' like I used to."

Hensley confirmed McKinney's love for Pepsi.

"He would drink twenty or thirty a day. I'm not exaggerating," Hensley said. "He would drink more than a case of Pepsi a day. That's not good for you."

Neither was the way in which McKinney operated an automobile. Hensley was well aware that Bones was a maniac when it came to driving. He would often find himself far behind McKinney when the Wake Forest team commuted by cars to games.

"Bones would fly," Hensley said. "He knew one speed—wide open. He should have been a stock-car driver."

Adding to his legend was the fact that McKinney was an honest-to-God ordained Baptist minister—never mind the language he used around referees or the fact that he often preferred to soothe his soul after wins or losses with something a little stronger than Pepsi-Cola. He once joked that March 1982 was a big month for him. Within a two-week span that month, he quit smoking and received a letter from his insurance company that he claimed began: "Dear Bones, If you get one more speeding ticket, you'll be walking."

McKinney swore that convinced him to slow down at age sixty-five. But earlier in life, no one moved faster than Bones McKinney. He toiled for years as Greason's trusted assistant, ace recruiter, and Wake Forest's jack-of-all-trades. One year McKinney was even asked to coach the Wake golf team. A year earlier, the star of that golf team was Arnold Palmer.

"I'm sorry I missed Arnie," McKinney said. "I probably could have helped his game."

That is highly doubtful. McKinney loved his golf and was pretty good at it, but he didn't know much about teaching it. So he kept his strategy simple.

"Coaching golf ain't hard," McKinney claimed. "You just pair up the players, tell them to play good, and get back to the clubhouse as fast as you can. Then as soon as they get out of sight, you tee it up yourself.

"What else was there for me to do? The boys practiced on their own and all I had to do was drive them to the matches. The only way I could lose the job was to lose my license. So I slowed down to seventy-five miles an hour."

In later years, McKinney occasionally played golf with Palmer.

By accounts from both men, the preacher once stole a putter from Palmer's bag when Arnie wasn't looking. He promised to give it back for years thereafter, but never did.

"I always wondered what it would have been like to have Bones McKinney as my golf coach," Palmer said in McKinney's 1988 book. "I'm sure he would have helped me with my game. Either that, or he would have destroyed it altogether.

"I have always remembered one thing Bones taught me: always grip the club with both hands."

In truth, McKinney was a fairly accomplished golfer.

"He was a hell of a golfer," Hensley said. "He was like John Daly. He could hit a golf ball a mile. He didn't know where it was going, but when he connected, he could put it into orbit."

He just didn't know much about coaching the sport. Hensley once pressed McKinney on his approach to teaching golf.

"What exactly is it that you do as coach of the golf team?" Hensley asked.

"I told you. I drive the van," McKinney answered. "Then I give the guys two golf balls each before a match and tell them, 'Y'all play good.' That's it."

McKinney knew a whole lot more about the sport of basketball than he did golf, but he basically stumbled upon his coaching opportunity at Wake Forest while attending religious courses at the seminary.

The highest salary McKinney ever earned playing in the pros was eleven thousand dollars. With a family that was growing (four children, with two more to come), McKinney wasn't sure what he was going to do when he retired as a player in 1952. At first he took on a paper route, but later joked that he couldn't stay awake long enough to deliver all the papers he was supposed to. That was when Greason stepped in with an offer and asked Bones to be his assistant.

McKinney was ecstatic. He thought to himself, "I wonder how much they'll offer me—three thousand, four thousand, maybe even five thousand dollars a year?"

He already had figured that the least he and his wife, Edna, and their four children could live on was $750, which would be $50 a week for the remainder of Wake's basketball season. But surely he would be offered more than that to become Greason's right-hand man.

McKinney told Greason he wanted the job even before the official salary offer came through. The next morning, Jim Weaver, who was then Wake's athletics director and later would go on to become commissioner of the Atlantic Coast Conference, called McKinney into his office.

"Come right on in, Bones," said Weaver, smiling and throwing an arm around McKinney. "I'm happy you've decided to help Murray. Of course we don't have any money in the budget for this, but I think I could scrape up seven hundred and fifty dollars. That would be fifty dollars a week for the rest of the season."

McKinney, then thirty-three, accepted, but decided to keep the paper route as an additional source of income.

"I was probably the oldest paper boy in the United States. When I was playing in the pros, I never thought I would be using my hook shot to deliver papers," he said.

To supplement his income from coaching and the paper route, Bones began renting out rooms at his home to athletes. Luckily for them and the boarders, they had a fairly large home—and Bones often joked that he wanted it filled to the brim with paying customers, if at all possible.

"We stopped when we got to seventeen [boarders]," he said.

Finally, at the end of the 1952–53 season, Wake increased his salary to $5,300 and McKinney felt he could devote himself more to serving God and Greason while leaving delivery of the daily newspaper to younger folk.

"I was now getting paid for doing what I loved and I was as happy as a mule eating green briars," he said.

But he was still Greason's assistant, with much to learn about the intensity of Wake's rivalries with the other Big Four schools. Playing Carolina in the semifinals of the ACC Tournament in 1956, Wake was winning by a large margin. North Carolina State already had wrapped up the other spot in the finals, and McKinney knew a tough game for the championship lay ahead. He turned to Greason on the bench.

"What do you think about putting some subs in and resting the first team?" McKinney asked.

Greason didn't even look at McKinney. He stared straight ahead. He was thinking only of whipping McGuire, his hated opponent on the North Carolina bench.

"I've got that SOB where I want him and I'm going to beat the hell out of him!" Greason growled.

The Demon Deacons won 77–56. But they lost to State the next night, 85–70.

Greason knew he should have listened to McKinney. Most of

the time, he usually did. By 1956, it was highly unusual for Greason to ignore McKinney's advice. As the years passed with McKinney sitting by Greason's side, the older coach had grown to trust his assistant and good friend more and more. In fact, by the end of Greason's twenty-three-year tenure as coach (he had been at it since 1934), McKinney had more to do with running the team than Greason. During timeouts, Greason usually let McKinney do most of the talking to the players. The game was passing Greason by, and even before the end of the 1957 season, he knew it was time to pass on the reins to McKinney.

McKinney knew the cupboard was bare when he took over for Greason in 1958. The Demon Deacons were coming off a successful 19-9 campaign but were looking at having to rebuild. Talking about his first season at the helm with Garland Atkins years later, McKinney said: "I tried to let my players off as much as I could 'cause I didn't think practice that first year was going to help us that much . . . I could tell this team had a lot to learn. We took the backboards down one week to paint them, and the players never knew they were gone.

"When we did practice that first year, we worked on the little things that are really important in basketball. Every player knows how to shoot, rebound, dribble, and pass. We worked on important things like moanin'. We worked thirty minutes a day on How to Impress a Referee By Moanin'."

Like other Wake Forest coaches, McKinney found recruiting against the other members of the Big Four difficult. Before Wake relocated to Winston-Salem, the campus of North Carolina State—with all its tradition, impressive Reynolds Coliseum, and all the attractions of the big city of Raleigh—was just a few miles away. Down the road from there were Duke and North Carolina with their sprawling, beautiful campuses.

McKinney used to joke that Wake football coach Peahead Walker was the first to discover the key to successful recruiting when it was still located in Wake Forest.

"Peahead brought in recruits on the train and picked them up at the Raleigh train station at dusk, when they couldn't see good," McKinney said.

Then Walker would put them up in a motel close to the Duke campus. The next day he would drive them around Duke, showing them the sights and "all the pretty girls on the East Campus."

"The recruits were so busy picking themselves out a girl, they never knew they were at Duke and not Wake Forest," McKinney said. "Then Peahead put them back on the train and sent them home. If they signed, when they arrived back for school, the train stopped this time at Wake Forest."

Some newcomers would protest that this wasn't the same place they saw on their recruiting visit. One was Bill George, who went on to have an outstanding NFL career as a linebacker with the Chicago Bears.

"They had shown him the Duke stadium and the Duke campus during his visit," Hensley said.

When George stepped off the train in Wake Forest, he looked around and frowned.

"This isn't the campus that I saw," George said.

"Yeah, well, that was our South campus. You'll be on this one," Walker replied.

Legend has it that McKinney did more than chuckle and tell this story about Peahead Walker. He learned from it and used to drive Greason's basketball recruits past Reynolds Coliseum in Raleigh after they got off the train, telling them that that was the building where they would play some of their college basketball if they signed with Wake Forest. It wouldn't have been an outright lie. They would play there—every time they played an away game against N.C. State or played in the Dixie Classic or ACC Tournament. They just wouldn't play their home games there.

In truth, prior to moving to Winston-Salem for the 1956–57 season, the Deacons played in a place McKinney had grown to love —cramped Gore Gymnasium. Capacity there was a mere 2,200— 1,300 less than the old Frank Thompson Gym that North Carolina State had abandoned years earlier. But it was always packed with pro-Wake crowds. Only 600 tickets were set aside for sale to the general public each game, assuring the Demon Deacons a decided home court advantage. When State, North Carolina, or Duke visited, the place would be packed even more than usual. Children would often climb trees outside to sneak into the upstairs bathroom windows. Then they would sit in the rafters to watch the games that unfolded below. On a court that measured only ninety feet long (instead of the NCAA regulation ninety-four), and with seating extremely close to the sidelines, opposing players found it difficult to play against Wake on their home court.

Lennie Rosenbluth, the great North Carolina player, eventually refused to take the ball out of bounds there because the fans were so close to the court they would pull his leg hairs and pinch him as he got set to throw it in. Visiting teams learned to run their fast breaks closer to the center of the court because the fans on the sidelines could—and would—stick out a foot to trip opposing players who got too close to them.

"They were nasty," Rosenbluth said. "The three feet you were supposed to have to throw it in? Well, the fans' knees were there. It was a tough place to play."

That's why McKinney loved it.

PRIOR TO PLAYING North Carolina in the semifinals of the 1957 ACC Tournament at Reynolds Coliseum, McKinney had the Wake players check out of the Plantation Inn north of Raleigh early on the morning of the game. He ran the players through a special practice at old Gore Gymnasium, trying to revive old memories and give his players an edge before they took the court to face undefeated North Carolina, which was then ranked number one in the nation.

McKinney had another reason for the workout at Gore that morning. He later told reporters he suspected the janitor in the Winston-Salem Coliseum where his team usually worked out was "a Carolina man." He said he was convinced that the janitor had been spying on his practices and sending information back to Frank McGuire, Carolina's coach.

McGuire laughed off the absurd charge. But he did acknowledge that McKinney was an up-and-coming coach who knew what he was doing. What McGuire and the others feared most was that McKinney was actually starting to get better players. They knew that if that happened, Wake Forest would be even more difficult to deal with than they had been in the past.

Anytime McKinney ran across another ACC coach who was pursuing the same player he was, the minister was ready with a standard line: "Oh, you're recruiting him, too? I preached at the boy's church last Sunday."

Years later, McKinney laughed at the memory.

"I liked to see those other coaches sweat," he said.

They didn't sweat often that first season when they played McKinney's team. Wake won only 6 games, lost 17, and quickly had ol' Bones thinking about getting another paper route. He killed the pain of losing with humor most of the time.

There was the time Wake Forest was playing in a four-team invitational tournament at Kentucky in those early years. The Dea-

cons were playing Princeton—coached by Bill Van Breda Kolff and
led by Bill Bradley, a superb player who would go on to gain fame
first as a player in the NBA and later as a U.S. senator—in the first
round for the right to face Kentucky in the championship.

In his book, McKinney related his version of what happened:
"Van Breda Kolff hated the box-and-one defense, so naturally I used
it all night on Bradley. In the second half, I called a time-out to set
up a play. The team usually didn't run the plays I gave them anyway,
but I had to say something in the huddle. We usually scored on
busted plays.

"This time, though, the play I called worked like a charm. Butch
Hassell scored and we went ahead in the game. I was so happy I
kicked my leg up in the air and my cheap loafer, that didn't fit, flies
out to center court. Well, somebody's got to get it. I knew the referee
wasn't going to get it. He couldn't see it.

"So I charged out on the court and when I bent over to pick it
up, out fell pencils, a notepad, some chalk, my glasses, and a Pepsi
bottle."

That wasn't all. When McKinney looked up, Princeton was
coming "on a fast break, heading toward me like a frieght train."

Knowing he was in trouble no matter what he did, McKinney
decided to have a little fun and play some defense. He later complained that "the referee called me for a technical just because I was
playing out of uniform."

True to form, McKinney cussed the official.

"I thought you were a preacher," the man in stripes said.

"Yeah, well, I thought you were a referee," McKinney shot
back.

There were times, though, when McKinney exploited a referee's
blind spot to his own advantage. During one game against Manhattan, he was standing two feet out of bounds when one of his players'
errant bounce passes ended up in his hands. McKinney didn't hold
onto the ball long. He spotted Billy Packer, one of his best players,
breaking for the basket, and hit him in stride with a perfect pass for
a layup. It all happened so quickly that the referees never saw him
do it and didn't realize what had happened.

"Manhattan's coach absolutely went wild," recalled Hensley,
who was sitting near McKinney at the time and saw the whole
thing. "The crowd went wild. Nobody could believe that the basket
counted. Bones just smiled and never said a word."

Another time, the Deacons were playing North Carolina State

in Winston-Salem. McKinney knew that Case, State's coach, had false teeth and needed to drink water during a game or his mouth would get unbearably dry. So McKinney made certain there was no water at Case's bench.

Early in the second half, referee Red Mahalic backed up to McKinney's bench and said, "Bonesy, ol' Ev ain't got any water."

"Gosh, Red," replied McKinney, "I didn't know ol' Ev didn't have any water."

"Yeah, his mouth's so dry he hasn't been able to talk to his boys the last three time-outs."

"Well, ol' Ev can have my water then," said McKinney, trying to sound sincere.

"Have your manager take it over," the ref said.

"He's busy right now. Why don't you take it over, Red?"

Mahalic looked at the water bucket, then at Case before turning back to McKinney.

"I don't guess ol' Ev is gonna get any water tonight," Mahalic finally said before striding away.

McKINNEY KNEW what he had to do to make Wake Forest competitive again, like they had been most years under Greason. But he wanted to do more than that. Even in the best years under Greason —and there had been several good ones, including a 22-7 record in 1953, the first year of the ACC—Wake Forest always had played in the shadows of North Carolina and North Carolina State. McKinney wanted Wake to outshine his dual alma maters.

It burned McKinney that North Carolina and State had so many more resources. He had even seen State and Case steal away his good friend and road roommate, Bill Hensley.

Hensley loved Wake and wanted to stay there, but both Greason and McKinney told him he owed it to his family to explore his options when State requested he come over to Raleigh for an interview in 1956. Hensley loved sports so much that he had left his job as a special agent with the FBI to become Wake's sports information director several years earlier, taking a big pay cut to do so. Case knew Hensley was good at what he did and Case wanted him when the SID position became available at his school.

"I was making forty-eight hundred a year at Wake Forest," Hensley said. "State offered me six thousand dollars, plus I got five hundred for handling the ACC Tournament and five hundred for handling the Dixie Classic. So their total offer came to seven thousand dollars, which was a big increase for me back then—even though my kids break up today every time I tell this story."

When Hensley arrived back at the Wake campus after his State interview, McKinney and Greason were anxiously waiting for him on the steps of the old gym.

"How did it go?" Greason wanted to know.

"Coach, it went good," Hensley replied.

"Well, did they offer you the job?"

"Yes, they did."

"What are you going to make?"

"It amounts to seven thousand," Hensley replied.

"God, take it! That's more than I make as head basketball coach here," Greason shouted.

To improve the team after Greason left and at least get back to the point where Wake was competitive with Carolina and State, McKinney knew he had to recruit better players. And to help him do that, he turned to new assistant coach Charlie Bryant. They would prove to be a good team for a while.

"Even that first year, when we were six and seventeen, everybody was real upbeat because Bones was such a colorful character and everybody knew he could coach," Bryant said. "Then we just went out and hit the bushes."

Mostly, Bryant hit the bushes. McKinney did not care much for the recruiting process, despite his outgoing manner.

"He was one of the best Xs and Os coaches I had ever seen," Hensley said. "But he was not a good recruiter. In fact, he was terrible. Bones and I were about as close as you could get, and he told me he did not like it.

"He and Press Maravich were two of the worst recruiters I've ever known. They knew it was necessary, but they didn't put their hearts into it. It was kind of degrading to them to lower themselves to go kiss a sixteen-year-old's tail. Other people were great at recruiting; those two were two of the worst I've ever met. But yet, they were two of the best coaches I'd ever seen.

"Bones loved coaching, planning for games, the game activity itself. But he didn't like that recruiting part. I'm not even so sure the story about him driving recruits past Reynolds Coliseum and telling them they would be playing there is true. That wouldn't be him. He wouldn't do something like that. He was more the type of recruiter who would get a Pepsi, pat a kid on the back, and just say something like, 'I hope you come here.' And then he would be done with it."

He needed to do more, or have a little luck. He was about to get it when Billy Packer, the son of a coach who wanted to play baseball more than basketball, and big man Len Chappell, who had appeared headed for Duke until the very last minute, suddenly were persuaded to join forces on the basketball court at Wake instead.

"We had a great recruiting year. It was considered the best freshman class they ever had at Wake Forest," Bryant said. "Suddenly, things really seemed to be looking up for us. We were excited about our future."

The Big Four schools were entering a new age that would include a higher regional and national profile because of the advent of television. Bones McKinney and Wake Forest were poised to take center stage.

5

SCANDALS STRIKE

ALONG WITH THE INCREASED EXPOSURE that television brought to the Big Four came increased scrutiny from the NCAA governing body in terms of how Case, McGuire, McKinney, and the other coaches were conducting their recruiting business in the ACC. The days of open tryouts, favored by Case, were over by 1956. Case had landed North Carolina State on probation in 1955 for allegedly paying the way of Ronnie Shavlik and others to tryouts in 1953. McGuire often bragged about his New York network and how everyone in the Big Apple was looking for players who might help him, but no one really believed him when he said he didn't pay any of those talent scouts. Ultimately this brash comment would come back to haunt him.

The Shavlik incident bothered Case, but not as much as what came later. A much bigger blow to his program was the alleged illegal recruitment of Jackie Moreland. Until going after Shavlik in Denver, Colorado, Case had almost always stuck to his habit of targeting out-of-state recruits from Indiana. Moreland though, was a gifted 6-7 center from Minden, Louisiana, and by 1956, colleges across the nation were beginning to step up their recruiting efforts. Moreland apparently was impressed by all the attention. He signed a letter-of-intent to attend not only North Carolina State, but also Kentucky, Texas A&M, and Centenary College.

Eventually it was State that Moreland came to choose. Case had beaten all the others out again for a terrific player, and he was excited about the future impact Moreland would have on his program. What he did not envision was what actually happened. Moreland scored 30 points in his first freshman game before the NCAA came down hard on the player, the coach, and the entire school for what they believed were blatant and reckless violations of the recruiting guidelines they had laid down years earlier.

Moreland never put on a State uniform again although he did go on to play five seasons in the NBA and ABA. Case was stunned when terms of the school's punishment were handed down by the NCAA: four years probation for the entire athletic program. Until the NCAA handed down the "death penalty" to Southern Methodist University's football program in 1987, this stood as the stiffest penalty ever assessed by the NCAA for recruiting violations.

Here is what the NCAA claimed it found, even though Case disputed the facts:

• Moreland had been offered a five-year scholarship instead of a four-year scholarship.

• Moreland was promised two hundred dollars a year for clothing over the five-year period.

• Moreland was promised an annual cash "gift" from alumni of one thousand dollars.

• State paid Moreland eighty dollars to cover his transportation fees to Raleigh to enroll in classes.

• Betty Clara Rhea of Minden, Louisiana—Moreland's girl-friend—had been promised an all-expenses-paid trip to Raleigh to visit Moreland during Thanksgiving break.

Walter Byers, executive director of the NCAA, dismissed Case's rebuttal arguments.

"We have enough concrete evidence to convince a board of eighteen men from all parts of the country that these are the facts," Byers told reporters. "In other words, our decisions aren't based on hearsay."

Case stood fast. He denied all charges except for the one involving the eighty dollars, which he said was paid not by State officials, but by a friend of Moreland's in Louisiana.

But the ACC conducted its own investigation into the matters and announced that it agreed with the NCAA's findings. In addition to ruling Moreland ineligible to play again for State, the conference denied contact with prospective recruits by the State basketball staff for one year and fined the school $5,000, although Case later had the fine reduced to $2,500.

"If you're going to convict schools on charges like these, I can tell you that there wouldn't be very many left to play basketball or anything else," Case fumed. "They are getting mighty thin, splitting hairs, grasping at technicalities."

State's probation would require the school's football team, coached by Earle Edwards, to sit out the 1958 Orange Bowl even though the Wolfpack won the ACC that season.

When it was suggested years later that this must have made Case feel sick, Bill Hensley, State's sports information director at the time, laughed and said of his old friend: "Um, how can I put this? Everett didn't really care about the football team. He didn't like football. Occasionally he would make a sarcastic remark when the football team would do something. He would say, 'I hope they know who's paying for their pleasure.' He would say something to let it be known that, hey, if it wasn't for a good basketball team there wouldn't be as good a football team there. He believed the basketball program, as good as it was, helped the football program get better recruits. He was not enemies with Earle Edwards when I was there, but he was not the best of friends with him, either."

In other words, State was a basketball school. Period. And as the man in charge of the basketball program, Case was dumbfounded by the NCAA's heavy-handedness in dealing with his alleged recruiting violations. There was, however, little he could do about it besides have the school serve its time and try to keep the program clean as a whistle thereafter.

Just a few miles to the northwest McGuire had his own problems at North Carolina. *Sports Illustrated* magazine did a story in 1956 entitled "Basketball's Underground Railroad" that claimed both State and Carolina were paying talent scouts in New York. One of the names dropped in the article was Harry Gotkin, the New York City garment manufacturer who had guided the great Lennie Rosenbluth into McGuire's outstretched arms at Carolina. Howard Garfinkel was named as the chief scout for Case and State. Although Garfinkel admitted that in the story, he denied getting paid by anyone. He then added to the controversy by saying, "As far as I know, Gotkin is the only scout who gets paid. And I don't know why anyone would pay him."

The story went on to tab Mike Tynberg, a North Carolina graduate, as another talent scout on the McGuire payroll. A nephew of Harry Gotkin's, Tynberg even foolishly admitted as much in the article. "I'm on the North Carolina payroll. So is Uncle Harry," Tynberg said. "We're listed as assistant coaches."

They weren't listed as assistant coaches, of course. And what they were doing was illegal. But McGuire denied it, and for a while basketball life at North Carolina went on, business as usual. The exposure from a national magazine like *Sports Illustrated*, however, increased public scrutiny of the programs being run both by Case and McGuire. And by the early 1960s, that kind of scrutiny would begin taking its toll on two coaches who were used to doing things their way without being questioned.

Vic Bubas *was* officially listed as an assistant coach at North Carolina State, but he was no ordinary assistant coach. He had a nice history with the program. He was on the 1950–51 State team that advanced to the Final Four, and he had the distinction of being the first player to score a basket in Reynolds Coliseum. That was by design. He used to go over to Reynolds while the finishing construction touches were being laid on the building. Once there, he would envision himself scoring that first basket.

When the Wolfpack tipped it off against Washington & Lee on December 2, 1949, the opening tap went to Bubas. He dribbled straight to the basket to attempt a layup.

He missed.

He grabbed his own rebound and shot again.

He missed again.

Finally, he grabbed the second rebound and put the ball through the hoop. In doing so, he went down in the record books forever as the player who made the first basket in the new building. State went on to beat Washington & Lee by 20 points, 67–47.

That was the kind of guy Bubas was—organized and stubbornly determined to succeed at whatever he put his mind to. Bubas came to State in part because Case had promised him a chance to get into coaching once his playing days were over. Bubas had always wanted to coach and thought he would make a good one. After watching him play, Case agreed.

"Vic was always a keener student of the game than most," Case told *The Raleigh Times* once. "He studied basketball with the idea in mind that someday he would coach it."

When Bubas completed his playing career at State, Case gave Bubas that opportunity by hiring him as the school's freshman coach. Over the next four seasons, Bubas's freshmen teams posted a record of 64–10. And after Case promoted Bubas to his top assistant's position in 1955, the Old Gray Fox had so much confidence in him that he often allowed Bubas to run practices and even sometimes call the plays and make the substitutions in games.

One night in 1959 against Kansas, Bubas was running the team and State was having a tough time of it. Each time he called a play that didn't work or made a substitution that proved faulty, Case reminded Bubas of it.

"Nothing's working here tonight. We're going to lose this game if we don't come up with something to wake us up. What should we try next?" an exasperated Case said.

"I don't know. It seems like I've tried everything," Bubas replied.

"I don't pay you not to know," Case snapped.

Bubas was upset. If Case didn't want him running the team, why did he put him in charge for the night in the first place?

"What do you want me to do, pull a rabbit out of a hat?" Bubas asked.

"If that's what it takes to win this game, you're damn right I do," Case said.

They didn't win that game, but the two of them experienced plenty of success during their eight years together on the State staff. Yet it was during that 1959 season that Bubas decided he was going to leave the school. If a head-coaching opportunity didn't surface, he planned to attend graduate school at the University of Florida. He applied for the head-coaching position at the University of New Mexico but did not get it.

Then Hal Bradley left Duke to become head coach at the University of Texas. That opened up a head-coaching position just down Tobacco Road. Bubas was interested, but uncertain at first about jumping to a rival Big Four school. He did not formally apply, but eventually let the school know that he was interested in talking. Word quickly spread through the grapevine, even though Duke athletic director Eddie Cameron was in the process of screening what would amount to more than 135 prospective candidates over a six-week period.

Cameron was well aware of Bubas's ample qualifications, but he was worried about one thing. Bubas had been one of the State assistant coaches reprimanded for involvement in the illegal recruitment of Jackie Moreland. That black stain on Bubas's otherwise spotless record almost kept the Duke AD from giving Bubas serious consideration.

The sports editor of the Durham newspaper called Bill Hensley at North Carolina State.

"What do you know about Vic Bubas? Cameron has been told Bubas is interested in the job, but he's worried about Bubas's involvement in the Moreland incident," the newspaperman asked.

Hensley gave Bubas, a close friend, a glowing endorsement. Then Hensley called Cameron directly.

"Please take my word for it," Hensley told Cameron. "If you hire him, he'll be the best coach you ever hired. He'll never embarrass you."

"But what about the Moreland thing? That was an embarrassment to State. What did he have to do with that?" Cameron replied.

"Listen, the Moreland issue looks bad for him. He was one of the coaches who helped recruit him. But none of that stuff was his doing. I'm telling you he's going to be a great coach. He will not embarrass you or the university. He's a class act," Hensley added.

Cameron thought about it some more and on Thursday, May 1, 1959, he sent word to Bubas that he would ask the Duke Athletic Council the following Monday to hire him as the school's next head coach. If the council approved the recommendation, the hiring would be made official at a news conference the next day. Cameron called Bubas on the phone Monday morning and arranged a meeting at a restaurant near the Raleigh-Durham Airport. When Bubas walked in, Cameron stood up and shook his hand.

"Don't you think it's time you go recruiting?" asked Cameron, grinning.

Bubas had the job. He was thrilled, even though he took a pay cut in actual salary—from $9,500 as Case's top assistant to $9,000 as Duke's head man. Bubas didn't care. He was a head coach and he knew he would make up the difference, plus much more, on the side by holding basketball clinics.

He told Cameron: "Pay me what you want, but what I make on the side is mine as long as it is honorably earned."

The next day, when Cameron introduced the thirty-one-year-old Bubas to the media and a crowd of students who had gathered in front of Indoor Stadium, the AD beamed.

"Gentlemen, this is our new basketball coach. We hope he will be here forever."

Thus, Bubas packed up his family and moved barely fifteen miles down Tobacco Road from State and the city of Raleigh to Duke and the city of Durham, two communities so close they share an airport that bears each of their names. Yet to the naked eye, the two schools seem worlds apart. Both campuses are considered more urban than Carolina or Wake Forest, but Duke's is unquestionably more beautiful and occupied largely by a different clientele than State. State's students actually hang out at places in the heart of Raleigh; Duke's students mostly stay away from Durham's tough inner city and inhabit their own little world in and around campus.

Duke was founded in 1838 as the Union Institute. It later became Trinity College and remained named as such until 1924 when, according to the *Fiske Guide to Colleges,* "it became the beneficiary of a stack of tobacco-stained dollars called the Duke Endowment." The athletic nickname also was changed at the time from the Methodists to the Blue Devils. Located in the lush North Carolina piedmont, the campus has the look and feel of a northern Ivy League–type school. This could explain why most of its students come from the Northeast, with as few as 10 percent actually hailing from the state of North Carolina most years. Derisive UNC fans often refer to Duke as "the University of New Jersey."

The first collegiate basketball game played in the state of North Carolina was between Wake and Duke on March 2, 1906, when Duke was still named Trinity College. But it wasn't until Eddie Cameron became coach in 1928 that the basketball program really took off. Cameron coached until 1942, a season marked by his finest record of 22–2 and his third Southern Conference championship. He quit to become Duke's head football coach, leading that team to a Sugar Bowl victory in 1945. Then Cameron became athletics director, serving in that capacity until 1972. He eventually had the hallowed building where Duke plays their basketball named after him.

Cameron had made Duke a lifelong commitment and expected Bubas to do the same. But first Bubas had to endear himself to a community that was skeptical of a man who had for years made his living just down the road by trying to beat Duke's brains in. No coach, assistant or otherwise, had ever made the jump from one Big Four school to another.

BY THE 1959–60 SEASON, Bones McKinney was busy making progress with his plan to upgrade the Wake Forest program. Bubas, a tireless recruiter who would elevate the art McKinney did not care for to a new level in the coming decade, was ready with a plan of his own at Duke. Changes were brewing at the top in the other two Big Four programs as well.

Case was getting older and losing steam at State. McGuire was feeling underappreciated and was beginning to lose patience at Carolina. Both men had experienced much success. Perhaps so much success that they stopped paying attention to the little things that make a successful basketball team.

It was difficult to tell what bothered Case the most—being placed on four years probation, or having to watch McGuire and North Carolina rake in all the glory after their perfect 32-0 national championship season in 1957. But after finishing 18-6 and 22-4 in the 1957–58 and 1958–59 seasons, the State program started slipping in a big way.

The team's record was 2-5 heading into the Dixie Classic in December 1959. Case looked at the tournament as a way of turning the season around. He had never experienced a losing season at State and did not intend this to be his first.

Unbeknownst to Case, some of his players were looking at the 1959 Dixie Classic in drastically different terms. They were looking at it as a way to make some extra cash. Don Gallagher, a starting forward, had cut a deal with gamblers to help throw State's game against Wake Forest only a week earlier. Gallagher, a young father who had been struggling to make ends meet, had accepted a thousand dollars to make certain State lost to Wake by at least 12 points. He did it by allowing Wake forward Dave Budd to power his way to 17 points and 19 rebounds in a 73–59 victory for the Demon Deacons.

Gallagher was part of the acclaimed 1956 recruiting class that had included Moreland. But Moreland was long gone and so were several others from the group, and State, for perhaps the first time under Case's command, was seemingly undermanned.

Realizing this, Case decided to play a slowdown game against Dayton in the opening round of the 1959 Dixie Classic. Gallagher was approached before the contest by a man named Joe Greene, his gambling contact. Greene told Gallagher he could earn another thousand dollars if State won by fewer than four points or lost.

Gallagher was nervous. Case's decision to slow the game down made it difficult for Gallagher to attempt to control the outcome without looking painfully obvious. As a result, he did little or nothing to that end. Dayton won the game anyway, 36–32, and Greene slipped Gallagher a thousand dollars inside a comic book in a Reynolds Coliseum rest room after the game. A year earlier Gallagher had celebrated winning the 1958 Dixie Classic with his jubilant teammates. Now he was turning on them and throwing games.

It would get worse. Encouraged by Greene, Gallagher eventually involved teammate Stan Niewierowski, who helped make certain

Greene's bet in a game against Maryland was safe. The next season, the point-shaving cancer spread. Niewierowski, Alton Muehlbauer, and Terry Litchfield all accepted bribes with the intent of controlling the outcomes of certain games. The only code of honor they seemed to agree on was that they refused to take any money to fix games against their bitter rivals at North Carolina. They refused gamblers more than once on lucrative offers to fix those games, saying they wanted to play their best and try to beat Carolina every time.

As noble as that small gesture may have been of them, State's record suffered overall, dipping to 11-15 in 1959–60 for Case's first losing season and to 16-9 in '60–61. The school's reputation would suffer even more.

Case was distraught when he learned of his players' involvement in the point-shaving schemes. These were players who often visited Case's home at 611 Daniels Street near Cameron Village in Raleigh—located barely one mile from Reynolds Coliseum—where they would sit and talk basketball for hours at a time. Case didn't even care if his players drank alcohol in front of him on occasion— the legendary story being that one player, George Stepanovich, once showed up on Case's doorstep with three six-packs of beer after previously announcing to the coach that he had given up scotch and popcorn for Lent.

"Come right on in," a smiling Case told Stepanovich.

Case, a lifelong bachelor, treated his players like the sons he never had. For years, he had figured he knew what they were doing or what they were going to do even before they did it. He knew, for instance, that they often used to pile into a twenty-four-foot-long hearse station wagon owned by State guard Davey Gotkin, another of Harry's nephews, and drive to the beach for parties that could last an entire weekend.

"Just remember not to get into any trouble. And remember, old Joe Hayes is watching you," Case often told his players.

One of the players finally asked Case just who in the hell old Joe Hayes was. Case smiled and replied: "He's about six feet, nine inches tall and weighs about two hundred and ninety pounds. And he's black. If any of you get out of line, old Joe Hayes knows what to do about it."

There was no old Joe Hayes watching his players, of course. And by 1959, the notion that Case had his finger on the pulse of his program and his beloved players was little more than a myth as well. It was all beginning to slip from his tight-fisted control.

Gallagher had fooled Case and everyone else. He graduated with honors from State in August of 1960, and was named winner of the Alumni Trophy, handed out annually to the school's outstanding senior athlete. He earned another award for being in the best platoon in State's ROTC program, and immediately made plans to join the army after graduation.

"Don Gallagher used to come by my office every day," Hensley said. "He was the nicest kid you ever met. I was crazy about him, and so was Everett."

Bucky Waters, who played with Gallagher at State and later served as an assistant there and as an assistant and head coach at Duke, remembered that Gallagher was in school at the same time as Jim Hunt, who later would go on to serve as the governor of North Carolina. Waters told Ron Morris in *ACC Basketball: An Illustrated History* that if anyone had ventured a guess back then, they would have said Gallagher would have gone on to become governor before Hunt.

"He was the kind of guy everyone respected," Waters told Morris.

Finally, in 1961, while Gallagher was off serving in the army, Case began to grow suspicious that something might be awry with some of his players. It was Muehlbauer's obviously poor defensive play during a game against Georgia Tech, which Muehlbauer had tried to fix and failed, that ultimately tipped Case off. By then, the scam was being suspected by others as well.

"I remember being at that Georgia Tech game," said Charlie Dayton, the loyal State fan who would go on to serve as sports information director at Wake Forest. "State was up by thirty points or something, and Georgia Tech ended up cutting it to a half-dozen or so. I was just a kid, but I remember State taking shots in that game that even at a young age I wondered, 'Why are they taking those crazy shots? What are they doing?' And I guess that was the game Everett Case ended up reporting to the authorities that something seemed to be wrong."

That was the kicker. Case turned his own guys in.

Then he watched in horror as a federal investigation of the scandal around him grew to include others, including the trusted Gallagher.

The Old Gray Fox was crushed. He felt personally betrayed.

It was something he never completely recovered from, according to close acquaintances.

"He wasn't married and had no family except these kids and his job," Hensley said. "That job and those kids were his family. He couldn't believe any of them would do what they had done."

McGuire was busy encountering his own problems just down the road from the disillusioned Case. Winning the 1957 national championship had not quite brought about the financial windfall that McGuire had envisioned. The blue-and-white, air-conditioned Cadillac that school boosters had presented him with following the '57 season was beginning to show some mileage, and so was the guy driving it.

McGuire had been awarded a five-year contract extension worth $11,600 annually following the championship—good money, but not a great salary for a coach of his caliber, in his opinion. Others agreed with him.

On the very night the Tar Heels won the national championship in Kansas City, McGuire arranged to have a lavish party thrown for his boys. When the party became too expensive for school officials, McGuire reluctantly paid for some of it out of his own pocket. For later road games, McGuire wanted the school to pay the way of some of his New York cronies. The school refused.

Nine years after his arrival in Chapel Hill, McGuire still worked out of cramped quarters in antiquated Woollen Gym.

"When I played, his office was like a ticket booth," said Lennie Rosenbluth, the star on the '57 championship team. "McGuire didn't even have a desk in the office. There wasn't room for one. He and [assistant coach] Buck Freeman had a shelf in there. That was it. When you walked in and anyone else was with you, you had to walk in single file. And that was his office."

The small office bothered McGuire, but not as much as Woollen Gym itself. He repeatedly stated that it was too small for a big-time college program like his, and he often looked with envy to the southeast, where Everett Case operated out of a spacious office in sparkling Reynolds Coliseum. It galled him that he had to go to Case's place every year to play in the Dixie Classic and even the ACC Tournament—and not just because of the large pro-State crowds that would pull for Case's teams, sending the noise meter Case had installed for the fans soaring to its peak. The Wolfpack had a home lair of which they could be proud; McGuire, on the other hand, scheduled more away games than home ones, mostly because he believed difficult road games strengthened his team for the long haul but also because he really didn't like playing in Woollen Gym that much.

"The damn roof still leaks," McGuire moaned in 1961.

On top of all the slights, however real or perceived they may have been by McGuire, was the fact that Carolina was the subject of a growing point-shaving scandal—and McGuire's recruiting practices, like Case's at State, were coming under greater scrutiny as the 1950s gave way to a new decade.

Lou Brown, who played for McGuire in 1959 and 1960, was charged with and admitted to helping arrange the fixing of seven games in New York in exchange for a total of $4,500. None of the games in question involved North Carolina, but it was a stain on the program nonetheless.

During his testimony in the Durham County courthouse, Brown indicated under oath that North Carolina teammate Doug Moe accepted seventy-five dollars from a gambler and spent the money, but never did anything to help fix a game. Brown also said that gamblers had approached teammate Ray Staley and offered him a thousand dollars for fixing a game, but that Staley refused. Moe and Staley were later suspended from school by the university for failing to report these contacts with gamblers.

This proved to be just the tip of the iceberg that would sink the coach.

McGuire fielded another great team in 1961, going 19-4 and winning the ACC regular-season title. The Heels were ranked fifth in the nation—but that was as far as that squad would go. After being placed on NCAA probation for one year for violating dozens of recruiting rules, including payments to one Harry Gotkin and Gotkin's alleged illegal payments of entertainment and other expenses to prospective recruits and their families, the faculty board at North Carolina decided not to let McGuire's boys participate in the 1961 ACC Tournament. In a telegram to Commissioner Jim Weaver, school officials stated simply that they did not think it would be fair for the Tar Heels, who were not eligible for the NCAA Tournament anyway, to possibly eliminate one or more teams that would be eligible by defeating them in the ACC event.

It was the final straw for McGuire, who now wanted out. With one year remaining on the five-year extension he signed after crafting "McGuire's Miracle" in 1957, the brash coach from the Big Apple resigned to become coach of the Philadelphia Warriors in the National Basketball Association. The Warriors' star player was center Wilt Chamberlain, the same guy who almost denied McGuire the national championship four years earlier. The Warriors agreed to pay McGuire an annual salary of $22,500—plus $2,500 in travel expenses so he could continue living in Chapel Hill whenever the Warriors' schedule would permit it. McGuire loved the area too much to vacate it completely after nearly a decade.

Alumni were not upset about McGuire's departure. He had pretty much worn out his welcome in the folksy town, not to mention the surrounding communities who had good reason to despise him.

McGuire had infuriated fans and faculty at Duke in 1958 when he refused to leave the court following a loss to the Blue Devils, whose fans had rushed the floor in celebration. McGuire said he would not leave until police protection was provided, prompting Duke's football coach, Bill Murray, who was in charge of arena operations for the game, to say: "It was an uncalled-for demonstration. . . . It was the most revolting act by a college coach that I have ever witnessed. The very idea of McGuire requiring police protection to go to his dressing room is absurd."

McGuire's slick New York City style had long annoyed the folks at Wake Forest and North Carolina State as well. When Weaver made a ruling that was unfavorable toward Carolina following a wild fight between the schools—during which both Bones McKinney and McGuire were decked—McGuire accused Weaver of making a prejudiced ruling because he had been Wake's athletic director prior to taking the ACC job.

But what made matters worse for him was his decision in 1959 to basically throw the ACC Tournament championship game.

Both Carolina and State had spent portions of the regular season ranked number one in the nation. At Reynolds Coliseum on January 14, 1959, Carolina, then ranked number three, beat the top-ranked Wolfpack 72–68 in overtime. In one of his favorite showmanship tricks, McGuire called a timeout with one second left to let the loss sink in on State. When they met about a month later in Chapel Hill, the Heels were ranked number one and State was number five. Carolina won again, 74–67. This set the stage for a dramatic showdown in the ACC Tournament final, but McGuire stunned fans and school officials everywhere when he pulled his best players early in the game and basically let State win. The catch: he knew State, which was on probation for the recruitment of Jackie Moreland, could not go anywhere. His team had clinched the ACC's automatic NCAA Tournament berth just by getting to the championship game.

One insulted ACC fan sneaked off into the basement during the contest and cut the lights in Reynolds Coliseum as a sign of protest, causing an eight-minute delay in the action. McGuire defended his decision, saying he was resting his starters for the NCAA Tournament.

State won easily, 80–56, but it was a tainted victory and a championship almost by default. The extra rest for McGuire's starters didn't help much in the NCAAs, either. Carolina lost in the first round to a Navy squad that hadn't been given much chance of pulling off the upset.

McGuire would last two more seasons, but some Carolina fans never forgave him for letting State win the '59 ACC Tournament title. They also resented his attempts at times over the years to quiet them at home games, as he insisted that fans everywhere should practice good sportsmanship and shouldn't have the right to boo the visiting team.

By the end of the 1961 season, it had been three years since McGuire added Dean Smith to his staff. Smith watched McGuire closely. Smith learned many useful tips from McGuire. He also learned from McGuire's mistakes. It was McGuire who first told Smith to always wear a coat-and-tie to the office and to games.

"You never know who is going to drop in on us, or when we might get called across campus to the chancellor's office," McGuire told Smith.

One day in 1961, the chancellor called for Smith. Dean grabbed his coat, tightened the knot on his tie, and rushed over to William Aycock's office to learn he was being offered the job that McGuire was leaving behind. He readily accepted.

"I realize I have some big shoes to fill," Smith said upon accepting the job, which meant a raise in salary from $8,000 as McGuire's assistant to $9,500 as head coach.

Smith was thirty years old and facing a challenge. The program would be on probation again in 1962 thanks to the point-shaving scandals, limiting him to a seventeen-game regular-season schedule, no postseason tournaments, and restricting his recruiting for the year to the ACC area only.

Years later, Frank McGuire would return to the ACC as coach of the South Carolina Gamecocks, where he experienced enormous success but never matched the singular magic of the 1957 miracle season. When McGuire passed away in 1994, Lennie Rosenbluth attended his funeral. Several of his former Carolina teammates were there.

"You know, we were really surprised at his funeral," Rosenbluth said. "We always had thought of him as Carolina basketball. Then it dawned on us that he spent more years and won more games at South Carolina. That was a surprise to us. We didn't picture him that way."

His former players thought of McGuire as legendary. As McGuire passed the North Carolina torch to Smith—the quiet, introspective, and little-known assistant—everyone wondered what kind of future lay ahead for the Tar Heels.

6

D'EM BONES,
D'EM BONES

As EVERETT CASE and Frank McGuire began to fade from an ACC scene they had dominated for nearly a decade, Bones McKinney and Vic Bubas stood poised to wage some great battles of their own. Wake's success centered on McKinney's greatest recruiting class ever—the class of 1959 that included Len Chappell and Billy Packer. Bubas quickly perfected some of the same recruiting methods he developed under his mentor, Everett Case, and then added some touches of his own that would soon vault his program past his former boss's.

Packer originally wanted to play baseball and basketball at Duke, not Wake Forest. But Duke waffled on giving the diminutive Packer, who stood only 5 feet, 9 inches, one of its valuable scholarships.

Growing up, Packer had never even heard of Wake Forest. As a kid, he had dreamed of going to Duke after reading a *Life* magazine article about Dick Groat, Duke's great baseball and basketball standout who later went on to become a major-league baseball star. Billy Packer envisioned himself following in Groat's footsteps all the way to the major leagues. Packer's father coached baseball and basketball at Lehigh University, and his teams had played at Duke and Wake Forest back before Wake had moved to Winston-Salem. But Tony Packer only spoke about his visits to Duke.

One day during his senior year of high school, Packer received a letter from McKinney, who had circled Packer's name in a hoops magazine.

"I had never heard of him," Packer said. "Back in those days, you never saw teams play. You didn't know anything about them. The Atlantic Coast Conference meant nothing to me. It was like Duke, the school, meant something, but not the conference or any of the other teams in it. I didn't know anything about Everett Case or anything like that. Even though Carolina had won the national championship in 1957, the conference didn't have national recognition yet as far as being looked upon as being one of the premier deals. Kentucky was big and San Francisco, and the East was monstrous. LaSalle and St. John's were more prominent basketball schools than anything the ACC had at the time in my mind.

"I was being recruited by a bunch of Ivy League schools, too, and my mother really wanted to see me go to Princeton or Penn. Hell, the Ivy League was considered the equal of what the ACC was."

McKinney's letter was nice, but it did little to change Packer's opinion of Wake Forest. Packer hadn't even known the school moved from tiny Wake Forest to Winston-Salem two years earlier. Packer wrote McKinney back and thanked the coach for the letter, adding that he had heard Wake Forest was a fine place to go to school, but that he had no intention of ever going there. He was headed to Duke to fulfill his childhood dream.

Then McKinney came to see one of Packer's high-school games. It would have been impossible for Packer not to take notice.

"You couldn't miss him," Packer said. "A tall, gangly guy wearing goofy-looking red socks."

One of McKinney's assistant coaches, Al DePorter, later came to see Packer in the state championship play offs and asked him to consider visiting Wake Forest. Packer agreed, but still had no intention of going there.

The visit went well nonetheless. A number of other fine players, including Len Chappell, Dave Wiedeman, and Frank Loeffler, visited the same weekend and talked about possibly playing together at the school. Even though Chappell was leaning toward accepting a scholarship to play at Duke, he thought about the benefits of attending Wake. He figured if he went there, he could play more right away and have an immediate impact on the team. Plus Chappell liked Bones. It was impossible not to.

Packer felt the same way, but he still wanted to go to Duke. When he returned home to Pennsylvania, Packer and one of his high-school buddies conspired to visit the University of Colorado—

not so much because they wanted to check the school out, but because they wanted to visit Colorado. The school was interested in them as potential scholarship basketball players and had offered to fly them out. It sounded like a fun trip.

But when Billy Packer told his father, Tony Packer hit the roof.

"You know you have no interest in going to Colorado," Tony Packer said. "You're not going to waste that man's money by flying out there. You know where you want to go to school. Why don't you just call them up at Duke and tell them you're coming?"

It sounded like such a great idea that the elder Packer took it upon himself to call Duke. He got Fred Schabel, a Duke assistant coach, on the telephone.

Billy Packer was eating dinner when the connection was made. He noticed his father getting a little agitated during the phone conversation. Finally, Tony Packer covered the receiver and motioned to Billy.

"They say they're still trying to decide between you and another kid (John Cantwell) for this scholarship," he told his son.

Billy suddenly became agitated.

"Just tell them to give the other kid the scholarship. I'm going to Wake Forest to play against him, and we'll see who the hell can play," Billy said.

Billy's father shook his head. He told Shabel that he would get back to him once Billy had really made up his mind, and hung up the phone.

"Let's make a decision on this and get on with it," Tony Packer said.

"I told you. My mind's made up. I'm going to Wake Forest," Billy said.

"No, no, no. You can't make a snap decision like that. Let's talk about it, think it over some more. There are other options. You still might even be able to get in at Duke."

"Shit no, I'm not going to Duke now. I'm going to Wake Forest. I don't know much about the place, but I know they play Duke. I know they play 'em."

Now Tony Packer was really upset with his son. He couldn't believe what he was hearing. Billy's mother was crying. Why, oh why, she wanted to know, couldn't her son take advantage of one of the Ivy League opportunities laying at his feet?

But Billy Packer was adamant. In that instant, he no longer wanted to attend Duke. He wanted to go to Wake Forest and kick the shit out of Duke and that other kid every time he played against them.

"I'm gonna call Coach McKinney in the morning and tell him that's what I'm doing," Packer told his parents.

Tony and Lois Packer were distraught. Lois still held on to the hope that Billy could be talked into going to an Ivy League school. She had no idea what kind of a school Wake Forest was academically. Lois insisted that Tony phone Jack McCloskey, the coach at Penn, to see if McCloskey would drive down from Philadelphia that instant to try and talk some sense into Billy. Tony Packer made the call and McCloskey obliged, arriving at the Packer home that very night.

"This is a ridiculous way to make a decision like this, Billy," McCloskey urged upon his arrival.

"I don't care. That's where I'm going," Billy replied, holding firm.

McCloskey eventually got annoyed and left, frustrated.

The next day Packer called McKinney.

"Coach, I've decided to come to Wake Forest," Packer said.

"That's great, Billy. All the other guys you were here with are coming, too. Even Len Chappell. We're going to have the greatest team in Wake Forest history. This is great. I'm glad you're coming," McKinney replied.

There was one problem. McKinney already had signed five players. He only had five scholarships available. He didn't tell Packer at the time, but he was fresh out of scholarships.

It wasn't until one of the other recruits, Charlie Leonard, signed a pro baseball contract that McKinney was able to come up with the scholarship he had already promised Packer.

"I don't know what he would have done if that hadn't happened," Packer said later. "It wasn't like Bones could just manufacture a scholarship out of thin air. I didn't even find out about it until a couple of years later."

Once he arrived in Winston-Salem, Packer learned very quickly that McKinney was an unusual man. Like all players, Packer could not play varsity ball as a freshman, so he sat behind the bench to watch the games. One night, an ugly fight broke out between Carolina and Wake. As usual, Dave Budd, the rugged Wake forward, was in the middle of it. But this time the fight wasn't confined to just a few of the players. It was more like a riot, with fans rushing onto the court and throwing punches.

McKinney got knocked to the floor during the melee, North

1

Two men who put North Carolina college basketball on the map: N.C. State's Everett Case and Wake Forest's Bones McKinney.

Old Reynolds Coliseum: home of the N.C. State Wolfpack and home of the erstwhile Dixie Classic. Reynolds was large, loud, and very unfriendly to opposing teams.

2

Who could have guessed that Dean Smith *(left)* would have more success at North Carolina than his mentor, Frank McGuire?

3

Vic Bubas, the man who elevated Duke's basketball program to national prominence, calls for a play during a home game in 1961. Assistant coach Bucky Waters is to the coach's right.

4

5

Two important pieces to Duke's success under Vic Bubas were All-Americas Art Heyman (*above*, number 25) and Jeff Mullins (*left*, number 44).

6

7

8

9

Though Wake Forest is the only one of the Big Four that has never achieved a national championship, they helped set the stage for basketball greatness in the state of North Carolina by recruiting bona fide stars: *(From top to bottom)* Lenny Chappel, with coaching great Bones McKinney; Charlie Davis; and Billy Packer *(right),* with 1959–60 team captain Dave Budd.

North Carolina was the first of the Big Four schools to capture the national championship. Here, Tar Heel star Lennie Rosenbluth (number 10) and three other Carolina players successfully defend against Wilt Chamberlain in the 1957 NCAA championship game. UNC went on to win 54–53 in triple overtime.

A young Dean Smith adding to the Tar Heel dynasty that coach Frank McGuire started. Smith would go on to win two national championships and 879 games to become the winningest coach ever in all of college basketball.

11

One of Dean's disciples, Billy Cunningham—the Kangaroo Kid—coming down with a key rebound.

12

13

Two mainstays of the Final Four 1968 North Carolina team: Larry Miller (*left,* number 44) driving to the hoop, and Charlie Scott (*below,* number 33) playing typical tenacious defense.

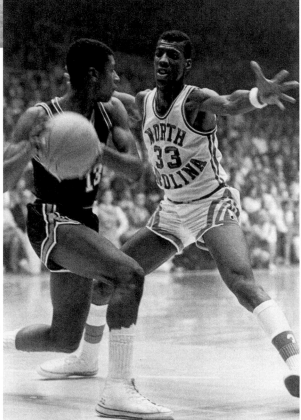

14

15

16

Three N.C. State coaching legends: *(above left)* Everett Case in his lucky brown suit, *(above right)* Norm Sloan in his outlandish plaid sports jacket, and *(left)* Jim Valvano in understated attire, but in typical dramatic fashion.

The 1973–1974 season was a magical one for Norm Sloan's Wolfpack. Here, Tommy Burleson (number 24) goes up against Bill Walton of UCLA in the NCAA semifinal game as State's David Thompson looks on. The Wolfpack beat UCLA, 80–77 in double overtime, before they went on to defeat Marquette in the championship game.

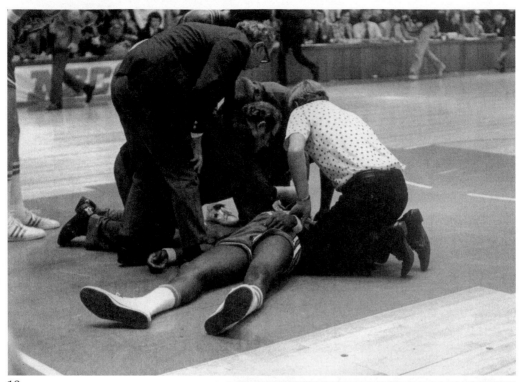

19

The Wolfpack had a major scare during their championship run. *(Above)* On March 16, 1974, against Pittsburgh, David Thompson, the team's star, crashed down hard on his head as he tried to block a shot. *(Right)* Fortunately, a heroic "DT" returned to the bench after receiving medical clearance from the local hospital.

N.C. State relived their past glory nine years later when the Wolfpack, under the guidance of coach Jim Valvano, captured the NCAA championship title again. A huge reason for that team's success: Numbers 35 and 25, Sidney Lowe and Dereck Whittenburg—roommates getting it done against Ralph Sampson and the University of Virginia.

21

Lorenzo Charles jamming it home against Houston in the 1983 NCAA championship game. Charles's dunk at the buzzer gave the Wolfpack a 54–52 victory.

22

23

N.C. State head coach Jimmy V sharing a happy moment with reporters after the Wolfpack's 1983 championship victory over Houston.

The man who preceded Mike Krzyzewski at Duke: Bill Foster, who left the school two years after guiding the Blue Devils to a Final Four appearance in 1978.

24

A fitting moment at Duke's Cameron Indoor Stadium: Beloved senior Gene Banks gets carried off the court by hundreds of the Cameron Crazies following the last game of his college career.

25

26

Two crucial members of the 1991 and 1992 national champion Duke Blue Devils: *(right)* Christian Laettner and *(below)* Bobby Hurley

27

28   Another member of the two-time national championship Duke team: Grant Hill. It was Hill's high-flying dunk off an alley-oop pass from Bobby Hurley against Kansas in the 1991 NCAA Finals that let everyone know that this Blue Devils team was truly special.

Coach K, Mike Krzyzewski, the mastermind behind Duke's success since 1980.

30

The single most memorable shot in Duke basketball history: Christian Laettner's buzzer-beating turnaround jumper against Kentucky in the 1992 NCAA Regional Championship.

29

31

Tim Duncan, Wake Forest's savior. The team's coaching staff wasn't really sure what type of player they had at first, but Duncan exceeded everyone's expectations and went on to earn 1997 Player of the Year honors.

Carolina's Frank McGuire got bopped in the head, and Carolina forward Doug Moe received a wicked black eye. In an attempt to get the fans to stop fighting, the Wake pep band broke into an impromptu rendition of the national anthem.

It didn't work. The fight continued.

Packer stepped around the brawls that were breaking out all over the place, and kept watching.

"This fight is humorous from our standpoint because Carolina has maybe ten fans there," Packer said. "These people were coming out of the stands and just beating the shit out of them. I was probably one of the few in the crowd of eight thousand that wasn't out there on the floor mixing it up."

Packer watched as his freshman teammate, the strapping Chappell, marched onto the floor. Chappell was sort of a gentle giant who never really knew his own strength. As Chappell walked onto the floor, he noticed York Larese, a Carolina forward measuring 6 feet, 4 inches and weighing near 200 pounds, grappling with someone on the floor. Chappell didn't notice that all Larese was doing was attempting to help one of his teammates off the ground. He picked Larese up by the waist and tossed him aside like a ragdoll.

"Lenny was so strong he didn't realize his own strength," Packer said. "And he didn't want to fight anybody. He was just trying to get a better look at what was going on. But I never forgot that."

Jim Weaver, the former Wake athletics director who was then commissioner of the ACC, was furious. Weaver phoned McKinney the following morning.

"I want to see the film of this fight," Weaver told McKinney. "We've had it with you guys. We've got to do something."

Bones was silent for a moment on the other end of the line.

Then he said: "I'm sorry, Jim. There is no film footage. We weren't filming this."

"Well, we're going to reprimand you anyway. But it would be easier to figure out who to blame if you had film of it," Weaver said.

"Sorry. There's no film footage," McKinney said.

"I'm not sure I believe you, Bones," Weaver said before hanging up.

At practice that afternoon, the players were laughing about the fight. They were in the middle of another bad season—one that would produce just 10 wins—and at least they could say they won a fight against Carolina, one of the top teams in the league.

McKinney strolled into the gym and made an announcement.

He wanted all players, varsity and freshmen, to meet that night at eight o'clock at the Monogram Club.

When everyone showed up, McKinney fired up a film projector so everyone could watch the fight in great detail.

McKinney worked the projector like a football coach. He would see an especially devastating punch thrown, stop the film, rewind it, and use a pointer to show everyone how the punch was delivered.

To outsiders, McKinney was the genial Baptist minister who also served as a basketball coach and builder of young men. In truth, he was a hell-raiser. It was almost as if he had a split personality: the one the public saw and revered, and the one his players knew.

When Packer first arrived at Wake, he thought Bones was as pure as the driven snow.

"When we were freshmen," Packer said, "you weren't even allowed to say, 'Aww, shit.' He would say, 'We don't need that kind of language here, son.' "

It was during his sophomore year in 1960, however, that Packer noticed a dramatic change in the way McKinney began conducting business on the court. Bones would work his team hard during Thanksgiving break, holding a light shootaround at eight in the morning, followed by a talk before lunch that outlined the objectives for the afternoon practice. A heavy practice would follow lunch, and then a third workout—actually an intrasquad scrimmage—would follow at night.

"That was the schedule during Thanksgiving and Christmas," Packer said. "He would detail strategy in the morning sessions, then you'd have your hard-working afternoon session where you worked on fundamentals, and at night you would scrimmage."

A good lunch, then, was something to look forward to. But one morning, McKinney started talking and kept on talking. And talking. His morning talk went past ten o'clock . . . then past eleven. Finally, it was eleven-thirty. One of the team managers knew that the nearby hospital cafeteria where the players ate would stop serving soon. He decided to interrupt the coach.

"Coach, you know, it's eleven-thirty. If the guys don't get over to the hospital, they'll miss lunch," said the manager, Tommy Vaughan.

Bones stopped talking. Then, he grabbed the manager's crotch and said, "Tommy, I've got your lunch right here."

Packer and the rest of the players were stunned.

"We didn't know what to do," Packer said years later. "Nobody laughed. Everybody's thinking, 'Did he really say that? God Almighty. This is Reverend Bones McKinney.'

"But then he started laughing. And we all started laughing. That was the beginning of his Dr. Jekyl-Mr. Hyde attitude. He reverted back to his hell-raising days. Half of the time he was the preacher; half of the time he was the coach.

"That was the first time we ever saw it. But he was a real hell-raiser in part of his life. He was a carouser and a heavy drinker. I say this now because I have so much love and admiration for him, but he must have been in a lot of personal crisis to realize that he wasn't this preacher that everyone in the public thought he was. It must have been tough for him to have that false image. That was basically what he had to be fighting internally all of the time. We knew as players that there were two sides to him. But the general public had no idea."

Packer, the unwilling Wake recruit, was starting to make some realizations of his own. He felt as if he was sitting on the verge of something big—something much bigger than he had ever imagined when he was trying to find his way onto the Duke baseball and basketball squads.

"My freshman year—that was the first time I had ever heard of the Dixie Classic, and yet, it was an incredible tournament," Packer said. "And I had never heard of the ACC postseason tournament, either. All of a sudden you realize, 'Hey, this stuff is bigger than life. This Christmas tournament was bigger than any damn tournaments that were being held anywhere, but it was kind of isolated to the region as far as people knowing about it. My freshman year was the year that Oscar [Robertson] played at Cincinnati and both Cincinnati and Michigan State, which also had a great team, played in the Dixie Classic. Suddenly I thought to myself, 'Hey, we're in the middle of something that is really amazing.'

"It was quite a deal. I had jumped into something that was much bigger than I had ever envisioned."

BY THE TIME Packer was a sophomore playing for the varsity during the 1959–60 season, Wake was beginning to project a new image as a basketball program. Packer was a feisty point guard who could score just enough to take the pressure off big Len Chappell, the team's emerging star. Dave Budd and George Ritchie were solid leftovers from the team that had struggled to win a total of 16 games the first two seasons under McKinney. Alley Hart and Jerry Steele were two other holdovers who would develop into dependable role players, while Dave Wiedeman and Frank Loeffler, two more from the Packer-Chappell recruiting class, also were added to the mix.

Suddenly, the team that had been a patsy the previous two years was very dangerous. For the first time in the storied history of the Dixie Classic, Wake emerged as the tournament victor—beating three national powers in Dayton, Holy Cross, and North Carolina to win the title.

Prior to the championship game against Carolina, McKinney began his pre-game talk in the locker room by turning to Budd and asking, "You can get the opening tap, right?"

"Sure, I can get it," replied Budd.

"Fine. Well, when you get the ball, I want it pulled out to half-court and we're never going to shoot the ball because they'll be in a zone," McKinney said.

Packer and his teammates were floored.

"I'm thinking, 'What's the theory here?'" Packer said years later.

As he was thinking that, McKinney was already answering him.

"We're a better team than they are, but the referees don't want us to be there yet and the crowd doesn't want us to be there yet, either," McKinney said. "The only thing is that they may have a little more depth than we do. So we're going to end up the game with our five on the floor just like their best five is on the floor. And we're better than they are with our starting five.

"So don't get upset, guys. I'm going to let you play the second half, but not the first."

So Wake won the opening tap and held the ball pretty much the entire first half.

"The score was nine to six or something like that at halftime," Packer said. "They thought we were afraid of them. It was just the opposite, though. The second half we came out and played a regular game and won [53–50]."

For McKinney, the championship would prove tainted. On New Year's Day, 1960, the day after beating Carolina to capture the Classic, McKinney's friend and coaching mentor, former Wake boss Murray Greason, was killed in an automobile accident near Greensboro.

McKinney tried to shove his grief aside by burying himself in coaching. For a long while, it seemed to work.

His strategy, at times, seemed brilliant. Other times it backfired on him. One such time was when the Deacons traveled to Dayton for a rematch of their Dixie Classic encounter. Dayton was nationally ranked, but had lost two straight to the Deacons.

"It was a big game for the state of Ohio," Packer said. "They were a top-fifteen team and we were ranked in the top ten at the time."

McKinney gathered his players beforehand.

"They're going to cheat us because they're going to get back at us for what happened last year," McKinney said. "They play zone, so we're going to do the same thing to them that we did to Carolina in the Dixie Classic. We're going to force the referees to call a technical to start the game for them not coming out of their zone to guard us."

So Wake won the tap and held the ball. And Dayton, predictably, just sat back in their zone. The referees did nothing.

McKinney started screaming and cursing at the officials. But still they refused to call a technical foul on Dayton.

"We held the ball for like twelve minutes and Bones went crazy," Packer said. "He cussed those referees out and told them they were yellow. The fans went ballistic. When we finally did start to play, the referees went crazy. They were fouling out guys. We didn't have any chance."

With about six minutes left in the game, a disgusted McKinney was so mad that he told all the reserves on the bench to head to the locker room. Then he followed them in, leaving only his assistant coaches and the five players on the court left amidst a very hostile crowd.

Then another Deacon fouled out. One of McKinney's assistants had to pull one of the reserves out of the shower just to put five players on the court to finish the game. Wake didn't get the reserve out of the locker room in time, so they were assessed a technical.

"Now Bones is going crazy," Packer said. "The referees are all upset. People are throwing stuff on the floor. And we're pissed at Bones because here we are a top-ten team and we're embarrassing ourselves out there."

When the game ended, the fans stormed the visiting locker room.

"I'm talking about five thousand of them," Packer said. "Their team won, but they came to see a great game and they saw this disaster instead, right? We can hear them. They're screaming, 'We want Bones! We want Bones!' They have pots banging on the door to our locker room. We have a bench against the damn door to keep them from breaking it down and coming in."

McKinney was in the locker room with his boys, shaking his head.

"I knew they were going to do this," he said. "I'll tell you what, boys, we're going to get the hell out of here."

One of Wake's players shook his own head in return.

"Coach, I don't think they want us; they just want you," he said.

Finally, some policemen arrived to clear a path through the crowd and escort the team to its bus. Fans were throwing everything they could get their hands on at the Wake team, aiming mostly at McKinney.

"We finally got on the bus, and the cops put us on the floor and told us to stay down until we got out of there," Packer said. "When we left the arena, people were throwing rocks, bottles, all kinds of things."

Most of the time during that season and the ones that immediately followed, McKinney did not produce such disasters. Fireworks, yes . . . but not disasters.

The Demon Deacons went 12-2 during the '59–60 regular season to tie North Carolina for the regular-season title in the ACC. They seemed poised to capture the tournament as well but Budd was ejected for fighting with N.C. State's Anton Muehlbauer with eighteen seconds left in Wake's 71–66 win in the semifinals. Budd had been on probation since the ugly fight a year earlier between Carolina and Wake in Winston-Salem. One more fight, the ACC office had warned, and Budd would be suspended for league games the rest of the season.

"Dave was on probationary status entering my sophomore year," Packer said. "And it never was a problem, because now we're a good team and Dave just has to play. He doesn't have to worry about fighting. We're a good team, and he's an NBA-caliber player.

"But we get over to N.C. State and Everett figures, 'I'll do anything I can to get this guy pissed off.' We would start games and guys would come up and spit in Dave's face at the opening tap or grab him by the balls. And he never fell for it."

But with eighteen seconds remaining in that semifinal game against State, after a full night of abuse, Budd could no longer take it. He exploded.

"They had been doing everything to Dave. They were spitting

on him, calling him names, and doing everything they could to get to him," Packer said. "And Dave, every time something happened, would have to put his hands up in the air to show that he wasn't doing anything wrong. He was not a bully. But he was a mean, tough son-of-a-bitch.

"All of a sudden Muehlbauer and this other guy do something, and that was it. Dave, before any of us could do anything to stop him, had taken both of those guys, flipped them on the floor, and knocked the shit out of them and was ready to kill them. It happened in a flash. He threw one guy on the floor, grabbed the other guy and threw him down. He was on top of both of them. Of course, they threw him out of the game and he was automatically suspended for the championship game."

McKinney appealed to Jim Weaver to have Budd reinstated, even though he later said he regretted it. His team was primed to win the championship for Budd, not with him.

"We didn't know until we went into the locker room that Dave was going to be able to play," Packer said. "That probably hurt us a little bit. We were like, 'We're going to win this damn game for him.' And all of a sudden, they announced he could play. In those days they would turn out the lights and guys would run out onto the spotlight in the middle of the floor. I'll never forget when they introduced him, the boos were unbelievable. Then the Wake fans started to cheer. It was an unbelievable, unforgettable moment in the [Reynolds] Coliseum."

Budd received a standing ovation before the opening tip-off. Duke, in its first season under Vic Bubas, already was fueled by the mystical power that sometimes allows overwhelming underdogs to overachieve. They had gotten to the championship final by upsetting a Carolina squad that had beaten them by 22, 25, and 27 points during the regular season.

"We were twenty points better than Duke. But that standing ovation for Budd made pussycats out of us. Pussycats," McKinney later said in disgust.

Wake lost 63–59 to a Duke team it had beaten by 17 and 19 points in two previous regular-season meetings.

Bubas was, naturally, ecstatic. The victory secured Duke's first championship of any kind since the Blue Devils had captured the 1946 Southern Conference tournament. Bubas took the moment to credit Case with helping him achieve his first major success as a head coach.

"I'm deeply grateful to Coach Case," Bubas told reporters. "No words can explain what he has done to make this moment possible. He's put so many pages in my book that I can never call it my own."

Duke's run wasn't completed until Bubas coached two more victories in the NCAA Tournament. After going just 12-10—including 7-7 in ACC games—during the regular season, Duke ended their season 17-11, and set the stage for future greatness under Bubas's guidance.

Wake ended the season at 21-7, but already, the Demon Deacons and their colorful coach were looking forward to the next season with great anticipation.

THE DEACONS began the next season as a favorite to capture the ACC title, a feat that seemed unthinkable a mere two years earlier. And even though they struggled in the beginning of the season, they regrouped in time to finish second to Carolina in the regular season with an 11-3 ACC record. Then they beat Duke to win the ACC Tournament and advance to the NCAAs, where they won two more games before St. Joseph's of Philadelphia, coached by Jack Ramsay, finished them off.

Playing in the postseason then was different. Proving that the ACC had yet to earn the lofty national status it enjoyed in later years, the champion of the ACC Tournament had to win a "play-in game" each year in the NCAAs after it won the conference tournament. Bigger conferences had a bye in the early rounds, giving winners of those conferences a decided advantage in the tournament.

In 1961, for instance, Wake beat South Carolina, Maryland, and Duke in a span of three days to win the ACC Tournament, which ended on a Saturday. The Deacons then had to board a train bound for New York the very next day, so they could play Tuesday in a triple-header at Madison Square Garden for the right to come back to Charlotte and play in the NCAA East Regional.

"We had to play St. John's at Madison Square Garden," Packer said. "They had a great team, ranked number three or four in the nation, and the Garden was basically their home court. But we beat them. We were down twelve and we ended up beating them by twenty-three.

"Then we got back on the train and came back to Charlotte and played St. Bonaventure, which was a great team ranked number six or something like that, and we beat them. Then the day after that we had to play St. Joe's (of Philadelphia), the ECAC winner. And while we were doing all that, St. Joe's was waiting on us in Charlotte. Not to make excuses, but I think if they had to go through what we had to go through before they played us, I don't think we would have had much of a problem. But they beat us and then they went on to the Final Four."

Wake Forest had tasted success and liked it. The stage was set for what would turn out to be a wonderful season, the best in school history. But like any other magical season, it did not take place without its difficult moments.

Packer was now a senior, and so were Chappell and Wiedeman. Others such as Bob Woollard and Frank Christie and Bill Hull were the kind of role players necessary to surround the main talent.

Chappell was coming to the end of one of the most spectacular careers not only in Wake Forest history, but also in the brief history of the ACC. Decades later, he would still be looked upon as one of the league's true great centers. In 1961 he averaged 26.6 points and 14.0 rebounds. No one in school history had ever averaged more points, and only the great Dickie Hemric—who played from 1952 to 1955 and as a senior averaged 19.0 rebounds—had pulled down more boards in a season.

But in 1962, Chappell topped his incredible junior season and helped lead Wake Forest to places it had never been before. The Deacons made a clean sweep of the ACC—winning both the regular-season championship and the tournament, where Chappell scored 87 points in wins over Virginia, South Carolina, and Clemson. Then they began a relentless march to the Final Four.

Chappell was 6 feet, 8 inches, weighed 255 pounds, and was incredibly strong. It seemed he could move mountains. Opposing players were not a problem.

"Lenny was a very unusual player for that era," Packer said. "He was six-foot-eight and unbelievably powerful. It was all natural. As a matter of fact, if you think of the history of the league, there probably hasn't been a more powerful interior player than Lenny Chappell. He had very good straight-away speed. He was not a gifted ball-handler, but he had great hands. So he could catch anything. And he had an incredible shot facing the basket, and great range. Today he would be a major three-point factor."

One of Wake's favorite plays was to have Chappell set up in the post. Then a forward would come down and screen for him, and Chappell would step out and hit the jump shot. It helped Chappell average 30.1 points as a senior, which still remains the highest in school history. He also got his share of second-chance points, averaging 15.2 rebounds.

"It made it difficult for people to play us," Packer said. "Lenny couldn't put the ball on the floor from out there and go by people, but you had to come out and play him because he was a great shooter. He was a tremendous rebounder because he had great hands, a powerful body, and he was a better-than-average jumper who loved to score.

"He had a great attitude about scoring. He was even a more-than-adequate defender. His approach was relatively simple. He had a workmanlike mentality where he would go out and just kick your ass every night."

Chappell and Packer became close friends, and they were almost inseparable during their playing careers. Having Packer do his talking for him was not unusual for Chappell, even in 1962. Packer would go on to become an assistant coach at Wake Forest and later would gain fame as a college basketball analyst for C. D. Chesley's ACC network and then on a national level for CBS-TV.

"He did all the talking. I did all the work," Chappell once joked.

Chappell and Packer used to take the laundry money given to them by the team to wash their uniforms, throw all of their clothes together in one load, and then use the money left over to go to the movies. Chappell was a big man with a big heart who rarely felt compelled to use his size and strength to abuse an opponent.

McKinney, however, did implore Chappell to get more physical on occasion.

"State always had an enforcer and so Bones decided he was going to have an enforcer, too," Packer said. "When we first got to Wake, Dave Budd was basically the enforcer. But he was also a great player. You didn't really want your enforcer to be a great player, too, because he might just get in a fight and get thrown out of the game. So Bones developed Jerry Steele to play that role for us next, and he filled it pretty well.

"But one night Lenny was getting pushed around over at State. Bones wasn't too happy about it."

McKinney called Chappell over to the bench.

"Just go out there and smack somebody! Knock the shit out of them if you have to!" McKinney said.

Packer had the ball out front and was looking to make a pass into the post to Chappell when the big guy did exactly what his coach told him to do. He turned and punched the State defender right in the face, then turned back toward Packer and called for the ball.

"He hits the guy right smack in the face," Packer said. "There was no foul called. I passed it in to him, he caught the ball and scored."

As they ran back down the court together, Packer turned to his good buddy.

"What in the hell did you do that for?" Packer asked.

"Coach told me to hit him, so I hit him," Chappell shrugged.

Packer laughed. He was still laughing years later when he thought of the incident.

"That wasn't what Bones meant. He didn't mean for him to go slap a guy or punch him in the face," Packer said. "He just wanted Lenny to play more physical. But Lenny was kind of that way. If you told him something, he took it literally."

Chappell was the star and Packer was a fine player, but McKinney ran the show. During the 1960 Dixie Classic, McKinney objected to a call by an official and broke a chair. State officials billed him $14.33 for the chair. Instead of buying a new chair, he had the broken one repaired and painted Wake gold-and-black on top and State red-and-white on the bottom. Then he proposed that whichever school won the most games in the year-to-year rivalry should get to keep it. It was Everett Case's kind of idea. It promoted sportsmanship between the schools and got both schools some ink in the local newspapers.

Another time, league officials sent down word that coaches would not be permitted to leave their seats during games. It was a short-lived, silly rule aimed at controlling the wild sideline antics of McKinney. His response was to show up at the very next game with a seat-belt strapped to his chair.

As the 1961–62 season progressed, and Wake overcame some early struggles against obviously inferior teams (the Deacons began the season by splitting their first 14 games and losing 8 of their first 17), McKinney knew he was sitting on something special. By February they were rolling, and Bones predicted they would win the ACC. He had good reason. A win at North Carolina and subsequent routs of Virginia and Duke at home by the combined total of 67 points started the team on a winning streak that would carry them through the rest of the regular season, the ACC Tournament, and all the way to a Final Four semifinal date with Ohio State, one of the teams that beat them earlier in the year. By then Wake's win streak was at 13 games.

The biggest scare during the stretch came in the play-in round of the NCAA Tournament against Yale, a team Wake underestimated. Just as Bones was at his best in the big games, he was at his worst in the little ones. And it almost cost his team against the Ivy League school.

"We kind of laughed about facing an Ivy League school and said to ourselves, 'They can't play against us,' " Packer remembered.

McKinney was as guilty as his players. When the teams were going to share a practice facility the day before the game, McKinney wouldn't let his players on the court until all the Yale players had left.

"I'm not going to let you guys watch them practice because they're so bad," McKinney said.

The result was a very poor game by Wake Forest the following day.

"We went in with a very poor attitude, and the next thing you know, we're in a dogfight," Packer said.

The score was tied with a few seconds left. Wake had the ball out on the side opposite its bench about sixty-five feet from the basket. McKinney angrily called a time-out and turned to Packer, who was going to take the ball out of bounds.

"Just get the ball in and run the time off the clock. Maybe now we've woken up enough to kick their ass in overtime. You guys know we're the better team," McKinney said.

"Wait a minute, Coach. I think I can throw the ball to Lenny and I think they'll foul us," Packer said. "Let's at least take that chance to win in regulation."

McKinney thought about it for a moment. Then he reluctantly agreed.

Packer threw it in to Chappell. But as he did, he saw Chappell blatantly push off on a Yale defender to make the catch. The nearest official blew his whistle. The foul was on Chappell, sending one of Yale's best free-throw shooters to the line.

Another time-out was called.

"I remember walking back across the floor to our bench," Packer said. "I'm thinking, 'Can you believe our careers are going to end with this damn stupid idea I had?' So I get over there and there is nothing we can do. There's no time left. There's no defense or offense for us to call."

Well, there was one thing McKinney thought he could do. As

the players spilled onto the court, he called yet another time-out. Then Bones motioned for the team chaplain, Dr. L. H. Hollingsworth, to join him and the players in the huddle.

"Holly, I watched that guy who's getting ready to shoot a free throw for them and that guy blessed himself," McKinney said. "He must be a damn Catholic. I want you to start praying. We're going to find out if the Lord likes the Catholics or the Baptists."

Packer, the Catholic in the Wake Forest huddle, had to smile to himself.

"That was the whole time-out, praying that the Catholic misses so the Baptist school can win," Packer said. "So the guy bricks the free throw; we go on to overtime and dump them."

McKinney, still considering himself at least a part-time preacher, decided to call on divine intervention yet again before departing for the Final Four. He phoned Billy Graham, the great evangelist and a friend, to ask him to speak to his team before they left Winston-Salem to play Ohio State.

As practice was winding up on the day of their departure, McKinney told the players to report to his office, which was a small room measuring maybe fifteen feet by fifteen feet in old Memorial Coliseum. When the players filed in, they saw Billy Graham sitting behind Bones's desk.

"Now the Billy Graham that we know of today is a world-wide guy, and at that point he was already pretty famous. It was amazing to see him sitting there," Packer said.

Graham had already spent considerable time talking with McKinney about possible strategy against Ohio State and other basketball-related matters. Now he turned his attention to the matters of the players' souls, and how God related to their current endeavors. He talked about how life presented certain opportunities, and about how it was important to seize them.

"I remember he was a very riveting person to me. I'm Catholic, but still, I'll never forget him sitting there talking to us about opportunities in life. I was fascinated," Packer said.

Not all of his teammates felt the same way.

Shortly after Graham began talking, Dave Wiedeman leaned over to Packer and said: "What the hell does this got to do with us beating Ohio State?"

Packer was mortified.

"I thought lightning was going to strike. Thank God he didn't say it too loud," Packer said.

As McKinney boarded the bus afterward that would take his

team to Louisville for the Final Four, he turned to Graham one last time.

"Billy, I hope you will be praying for us," he said.

"I will, Bones," replied Graham, "but you better find a way to play good defense against Lucas and Havlicek."

Jerry Lucas and John Havlicek, the two Ohio State stars, proved to be too much for whatever defenses McKinney tried. Wake lost, 84–68.

The next night, Wake faced UCLA in what McKinney assumed was a meaningless consolation game. Finally, after months of feeling almost unbearable pressure, he could relax a little. The boys had given him an incredible ride, but it was over. He sank down in his seat on the bench before the game and felt almost serene, despite the lingering disappointment of the previous game's loss.

But Bones was dead wrong. The game did mean something. The NCAA Tournament at the time included twenty-five teams, including fifteen conference winners. First-round byes, which were coveted by all for obvious reasons, went to the seven conferences with the best cumulative records in past NCAA tournaments. The ACC at the time didn't have a bye because its 20-15 record was second to the Middle Atlantic Coast Conference.

It turned out that McKinney's boys could change that. Just before tip-off, McKinney felt a hand on his shoulder as he sat there brooding about the loss to Ohio State. When Bones turned to see who was bothering him, he saw Everett Case standing behind him.

"Bonesy, you know what you're carrying?" Case asked. "You've got the whole ACC riding with you on this one. If you win this game, we get the bye next year."

Hated as State and the rest of his ACC rivals were during the season, they still were members of the same conference. Besides, Wake might need the bye themselves the following season.

"I might have known I would never get through a game without sweating off ten pounds," McKinney later said. "All of a sudden this 'nothing' game became one of the most important ones in my life. We didn't want to let the conference down."

When Chappell fouled out with two minutes left after scoring 26 points, it looked bleak. But Packer guided the Deacons to victory, scoring 22 himself and using his outstanding ball-handling and play-making skills to break UCLA's full-court press.

McKinney was drained. He joked with reporters that he wanted to "play a little golf, preach a sermon or two, and check on our six kids."

Years later, he admitted: "I was tired. It had been a long season and I needed to hug my players, prop up my tired old feet, relax, and drink a Pepsi."

The demands of the season and of his dual role as coach and preacher had driven McKinney to a habit of drinking more than Pepsis. Worse yet, he became addicted to amphetamines. His schedule was so intense during the season that a doctor friend handed him a bottle of the pills to help him keep going. McKinney had gradually gone from taking one or two at a time to downing handfuls.

During one late-night film session, McKinney sat with Charlie Bryant, who was getting bleary-eyed.

"No, no, no. Don't go to bed yet," McKinney pleaded.

Then the coach dug into one of his bags and pulled out a vial of pills.

"Here, take one of these," he told Bryant, throwing him the vial. "Then you won't even think about going to sleep."

Bryant was reluctant. He knew McKinney sometimes took the pills. But Bones wanted to watch more film, and Bryant couldn't keep his eyes open. So he took one of the pills and swallowed it.

He regretted it and never did it again.

"I took one of those damn pills and, hell, I couldn't sleep the rest of the weekend," Bryant said. "Bones was taking them by the handful—and then he couldn't sleep at night, so he would have to take a handful of sleeping pills."

"We thought he was under control," Packer said. "It turned out that by our senior year he was totally out of control in his personal life with drugs and alcohol. But we didn't know that."

McKinney was doomed as a coach at the school he had grown to love. In time, he would come to realize that he had to take some time away from coaching and decide exactly who he was—a preacher or a basketball coach. He couldn't be both.

7

DEAN BEFORE DEAN

As BONES McKINNEY struggled privately to regain control of his personal life, he remained the toast of the town in Winston-Salem. He was in constant demand as an after-dinner speaker and he even spoke at churches, where he would deliver sermons with such gusto that even his own inner demons were held at bay for those glorious few moments when he spoke from the pulpit.

After the Wake team returned home from its Final Four appearance, the university honored McKinney and his players at a dinner hosted by Dr. Harold Tribble, the president of the school.

"Bones, you and your fine team and your fine staff have brought such great recognition to this school and this community. I just don't know how we can thank you enough," Tribble said.

The Wake president barely had the words out of his mouth before McKinney rose from of his seat and reached for the microphone. He grabbed it from Tribble's hands.

"Dr. Tribble, ever since the Phoenicians invented money, finding a way to thank me has never been a problem," McKinney said.

The crowd roared with laughter.

About a week later, McKinney played golf with Charlie Bryant.

"Bones, I got a question," Bryant said.

"What?"

"Did the Phoenicians really invent money?"

McKinney smiled.

"Hell, I don't know. But it was a damn good story, wasn't it?"

McKinney enjoyed telling good stories and pulling practical

jokes. One day a freshman, Bob Woollard from Bloomville, New Jersey, walked into Bones's office and asked if he could borrow the coach's car. McKinney decided to humor the kid.

"My car? What do you need to borrow my car for?" McKinney asked.

"Well, I want to go home for Halloween. It's a big event in Bloomville," Woollard said.

Inwardly, McKinney was thinking this was pretty funny stuff. But he knew Bryant had just purchased a brand-new station wagon, so he decided to play the straight man.

"Gee, Bob, I can understand that. But I'm going to need my car. You're in luck, though, because Coach Bryant just bought a new station wagon and he told me that he wanted to make it available for some of the kids to use on occasion. Why don't you go ask him for the keys?" McKinney said.

Bryant was sitting at his desk shuffling through some papers when Woollard walked in.

"Coach Bryant, sir, I was wondering if I might borrow your station wagon to go home for Halloween?" Woollard began.

McKinney doubled over in laughter, listening just outside the open door as Bryant exploded in anger and chased the naive freshman from the room.

"At the time, I was making about five thousand dollars a year and that car was the greatest thing in the world to me," Bryant said. "I looked up at Woollard and ran his ass out of my office. When I walked out the door behind him, Bones was sitting on the floor laughing. He knew damn well what I was going to do to the poor kid."

Bryant loved McKinney, like most of those who came in contact with the colorful coach did. But he had his worries—about McKinney's health, about the general state of the sport of basketball in North Carolina, about his own future. In Bryant's mind the point-shaving scandals, as they widened to include more and more players and programs, threatened to shake the very foundation of the game in the early 1960s.

"It was a very scary time. I had trouble sleeping at night, thinking about it. I wondered if it might not lead to the end of college basketball as we knew it. That's how serious it was," Bryant said.

"The one man whose integrity often is overlooked in all of this is Everett Case. I mean, he turned his own team in. He called the district attorney and told him that something suspicious was going on. Sometime around then, I went to Duke to scout. Back then you didn't have the tapes to swap and all that. We swapped tickets for scouting purposes. So I scouted the Duke-State game, and Duke just wore them out.

"State guys came down and were just throwing shots up that I knew were unusual. [Anton] Muehlbauer, who turned out to be one of the guys involved, just flat-out missed a layup. It was unbelievable. It was an uncontested layup. They were throwing the ball all over the place. And Stan Niewierowski, another one of the guys who was involved, he was throwing the ball up every time it got in his hands. He wasn't even close to the basket."

Bryant reported back to McKinney and told him what he had seen.

"If ever there was a game that was fixed, that game was fixed," Bryant told Bones.

It turned out later that the game had indeed been fixed.

"The sad thing about it was that these really weren't bad kids," Bryant said. "The way the fix worked was that someone would befriend you. They'd take you out to dinner or do something for you—and become your best buddy, which is easy to do when you're eighteen or nineteen years old. And then they'd say, 'Look, I've got a little problem, right? I've got a bet on this game tomorrow night. Now I don't want you to lose it. I just want you to make sure your team doesn't win by too many points.' The young kids usually didn't realize what was happening. Then as soon as you do it one time, you're hooked—because then they say, 'Look, these guys I'm working for are tough. You'd better just keep doing exactly what we say or we're going to turn your butt in.' "

Sometimes it was even worse than that. Bryant received a report after the 1960–61 season that frightened him.

"We had played St. Joe's in an Eastern Regional championship game in Charlotte," Bryant said. "One of the guards, and they had some great guards back then when Jack Ramsay was coach, was supposed to put the fix in on that game. He got so wrapped up in the game that he forgot about it, and they beat us for the Eastern Regional championship. He got back to Philadelphia and they took him out on the docks and put a gun to his head and threatened him. That's how bad it was."

It was bad enough that the Dixie Classic, the Christmas tournament that had been the pride of Southern basketball and Case's beloved brainchild, was canceled as a result. University officials from the Big Four schools didn't want to worry about gamblers trying to get to the kids in an attempt to fix those games.

"It was a sad period," Bryant said. "When they cancelled the Dixie Classic, that's when I thought basketball was done. That tournament had been the epitome of college basketball. That was the most prestigious tournament in the country at the time. Even the NCAA Tournament didn't have the mystique of the Dixie Classic. Schools were just begging to get in there. It was a Christmas tournament where basketball got publicity from all over the country."

BRYANT HAD SEEN at close hand the devastation that a point-shaving scandal could bring to a school. When Billy Packer was among many players investigated for possible wrongdoing (he was cleared), Bryant had accompanied Packer to New York for a series of interviews with the district attorney's office and had seen a number of players who had done wrong break down and admit their sins. Programs were being devastated.

None in North Carolina had been devastated more than Everett Case's at N.C. State. Following the Final Four season, Bryant spent just two more seasons as an assistant under McKinney. Then he left to become, he thought, freshman coach and an assistant under Case at State for the 1964–65 season. Part of Bryant's reason for leaving was his belief that McKinney's addiction problems were worse than ever, and his good friend would not listen to pleas to take a break from coaching and preaching to get his own life in order by entering a rehabilitation program.

Another reason Bryant left Wake was because he wanted to work with Case, who was getting up in age and was beginning to have some health problems of his own. Case knew the end of his coaching career was imminent. So like everything else, he tried to prepare for it by controlling every variable he possibly could to make certain there would be a smooth transition to the next era. Case had hired Press Maravich two years earlier and made it known that he wanted Maravich to eventually succeed him as State's coach. Press's son, Pete, was already beginning to make a name for himself as an outstanding and unusually flamboyant young high-school player. Case envisioned Pete eventually joining his father at State.

There was a time when Case was into recruiting and all that went with it. Once, he even traveled to Indiana with long-time assistant Butter Anderson to recruit a prospect in the early years at

State. After talking with the kid and his mother about why State was the best choice for him, the mother interrupted Case.

"Well, we're going to have to pray over this," said the mother, who was obviously quite religious.

Case, who according to Bryant "hadn't been to church six times in his life," abruptly dropped to his knees and said solemnly, "I think we should, too. Let's pray."

After several minutes with their eyes closed, Case screwed one eye open and turned to the mother.

"What did He tell you?" Case asked quietly.

"Well, I feel like He was getting ready to tell me something. But nothing that I can make out for sure yet," the mother replied.

Case beamed and threw his arm around the mother.

"Well, He told me. He told me that He wants your son to attend N.C. State! Praise the Lord!" Case shouted.

The boy ended up signing a letter of intent to attend State that night, after which Case and Anderson piled back into their car and Anderson started driving back to Raleigh. They were about ten miles down the road from the recruit's house when a jubilant Case yelled: "Stop the car! Open the trunk. We're going to have us a drink and celebrate!"

They stopped the car, pulled some Imperial Whiskey out of the trunk, and celebrated.

Those were the good old days as far as Case was concerned. Since the point-shaving scandals broke in 1961, Case's teams struggled. State was still playing a shortened schedule in 1963–64 as a result of their probation. But after finishing 8-11 that season—Case's worst record—he seemed to be looking forward to the '64–65 campaign. The probation would be lifted, a full schedule was posted and Case liked his club's chances.

Maravich, however, noticed that Case did not look like his usual energetic self. For years Case had made one concession to age, and only one. He would work in the morning out of his office in Reynolds Coliseum, then have lunch and drive home for an early afternoon nap. Then he would drive back for practice and the rest of the day's work.

"He never drove anywhere while I was here except from Cameron Village [where Case lived] to Reynolds and back," said Les Robinson, who played at State from 1961 to 1964. "He only had to make two turns to get here and two turns to get home. He would go home and take a nap, so he had to make the trip twice a day. But his maroon Cadillac had to have been low-mileage."

Case, by this time, had plenty of mileage on his body, and it was beginning to show. But it seemed to Maravich that something more than just old age was creeping up on Case. Like many Case associates, he felt the Old Gray Fox hadn't been the same since the point-shaving scandal broke. He thought maybe it was time for Case to get out of coaching the game he so loved. He approached Case discreetly and told him so before the '64–65 season began.

"Coach, I don't want the head-coaching job as long as you're here," Maravich said. "But I don't think you're going to be here very long the way you're feeling. You're letting this game kill you, and it's not worth it."

Case listened and nodded. But kept right on coaching.

As it turned out, his club's chances were fine. Case's health was not. Just two games into that season, right after an 86–80 loss to McKinney and Wake Forest, Case called Bryant and Maravich into the shower room at Memorial Colisuem in Winston-Salem. Steam swirled around them, creating an almost eerie mist. Case wiped his brow as he fell into a seat in the corner. His breathing was heavy, almost as if he were panting and struggling to take in the necessary gulps of air.

"Fellas, I'm sorry. But you're going to have to do it alone. I can't go on," Case gasped, gesturing to his assistants.

This time it was Maravich who listened and nodded. Then he told Case to sleep on it before making the call for good.

The next morning at 6:00 A.M., Maravich's phone rang. It was Case.

"What's the matter, Chief? Are you all right?" Maravich asked.

"Press, I just can't take it anymore. I've got to step down," Case said.

Case was finished. After seventeen years and 377 victories in 511 games, his storied State coaching career was at an end. He would soon be diagnosed with bone-marrow cancer.

The Wolfpack, perhaps spurred on by the resignation of their beloved coach, played great that season under Maravich. They lost only four more games the rest of the way, finishing with a 21-5 record that included a huge upset of Duke, then ranked eighth nationally, in the ACC championship game. The hero of the tournament was Larry Worsley, a reserve, who scored 30 points in the win over Duke. Case watched the game from press row, and afterward, the players rushed over to hoist him on their shoulders so Case could cut the championship nets. It would be his eleventh and final time. It was an emotional scene played out, appropriately enough, at Reynolds Coliseum.

A year later, State lost to Duke in a rematch of the 1965 championship. About seven weeks later, Bryant was eating dinner at home when he told his wife that he hadn't visited Case in awhile, so he thought he would drop in on the old coach.

Case was sitting in his wheelchair watching television when Bryant walked in the door.

"How you doing, you old reprobate?" Bryant asked, expecting the usual Case jibe in return.

Instead Case turned and said, "Charlie, I feel like hell."

Bryant was stunned.

"With all the physical problems he had, that was the first time I heard him say he felt bad," Bryant said. "He always had a positive outlook—which was amazing because that type of disease, malignancy of the bone marrow, is extremely painful. The doctor told me after they did surgery on him a year or so earlier at the hospital that the strongest medicine Everett ever took was Darvon, which was nothing but a glorified aspirin."

The doctor told Bryant, "I've never seen a man as physically tough and as tolerant of pain as Everett."

That night Case could tolerate it no longer. Joining Bryant briefly was Fred Jones, an attorney and neighbor friend who recently had been asked to make some changes to Coach Case's will. Case tried to hold up his end of the conversation, but surprised his two visitors when he couldn't.

"Listen fellas, you go in the kitchen there and fix yourselves a drink if you want. But I've got to get my housekeeper to put me to bed," Case said.

Bryant stayed for another twenty to thirty minutes, talking with Jones about how unusual it was for Everett to behave in this manner. Then Bryant went home. The next morning he was driving to a State fund-raising function in Clinton, North Carolina, when he heard the news: Coach Case had slipped into a coma during the night and was not expected to survive.

Case died April 30, 1966. Etta Blanche James, a sister, was his only surviving relative. He left her nearly $200,000. In his will there were also cash provisions provided to the members of the coaching staff, arrangements for an originating scholarship fund to N.C. State, and distribution plans for his vast array of trophies. But the ninth and last paragraph of the recently revised will was the most unusual:

it divvied up the remaining $69,525 of his estate amongst fifty-seven of his former players.

All the dinners former and current assistant coaches had purchased him were rewarded tenfold. All the former players who had laughed about his twenty-five-cent tips for running to Merrill Lynch were suddenly in position to visit Merrill Lynch and make investments for themselves. It was a fitting and lasting tribute left by a man who had made his mark on basketball not only in North Carolina, but across the nation.

Case left his mark in other ways as well.

"He was a genius in marketing," Bryant said. "He was the first guy to make the pregame introductions a big deal, and then every school in the ACC started doing it. Everything was a promotion with him, and it was all designed not for his personal gain, but for the promotion of basketball. He made the Dixie Classic and the ACC Tournament an experience."

In one of the final tributes to Case's abilities as a showman, one of the most moving statements at his eulogy was made by Frank McGuire, the man who supposedly hated him. McGuire again stated that the much-publicized, long-running feud he had staged with Case in the ACC's formative years was largely an act. He professed a deep-held respect for what Case had done for the game.

Yet Case died a sad, disillusioned man. He never fully got over the fact that some of his players betrayed him in the point-shaving scandals that broke in 1961.

Bryant recalled that the coach spoke often of the pain brought on by the betrayal. "It bothered him until the day he died. I was pretty close to Everett. Other than his housekeeper, I was the last person to talk to him before he died. And I know he was hurt by it," Bryant said. "He loved basketball with a deeper passion than any other man I have ever known. He never fully recovered from that."

Les Robinson, who joined the State coaching staff as freshman coach when Case resigned, took the theory one step farther. He arrived in Raleigh as a player right about the time the point-shaving scandal became public, and over the next five years saw a dramatic change in the Old Gray Fox.

"It hit my first year. And I think, personally, it really contributed to Coach Case's illness," Robinson said. "They talk more about it today, about how stress and problems can sometimes create illnesses and disease. I really think that was the beginning of his end, the point-shaving scandal, and his health just started sliding. I saw it. His next-to-last year, he started missing a lot of practices and things like that. And then his last year, he just couldn't do it anymore.

"To have that happen to him just killed him, literally and figuratively."

CASE WAS GONE and would be missed throughout the ACC. McKinney's star was fading fast along with his own health, and his last season at Wake would be 1964–65, when school officials asked him to leave and get help for his addiction. Press Maravich, who would have been a Big Four coaching star, signed a five-year contract to become the coach at Louisiana State University just hours after Case's death.

Maravich left State mainly because his son, Pete—who over the previous two years had often stopped by Reynolds Coliseum after school and defeated State players in one-on-one matchups while playing in his socks (even for the coach's son, dress shoes were a no-no on the court)—could not qualify academically to get into the school. Otherwise, Pete Maravich would have played for the Wolfpack and his father would have remained the coach. They both headed to LSU instead, where Pete proceeded to smash all NCAA scoring records by averaging 44.2 points during his three-year varsity career.

So the coaching landscape in the Big Four was undergoing a dramatic change. Suddenly Vic Bubas, who at age thirty-one had taken over at Duke, was the dean of the Big Four coaches. The other "veteran" was Dean Smith of North Carolina, who had taken over for McGuire at thirty years old just two seasons after Bubas assumed the reins at Duke. Smith had met with mixed success his first three seasons—going 8-9, 15-6, and 12-12 overall. His 6-8 finish in the ACC in 1963–64 marked Carolina's first losing record in the conference since a decade earlier in the ACC's second season of existence. It was also the school's worst-ever conference mark.

After a particularly embarrassing 107–85 defeat at Wake Forest in early January 1965, the Tar Heels returned to Chapel Hill on the team bus to find that students had hung Smith in effigy on campus. Billy Cunningham, the Kangaroo Kid who was the team's star and later would achieve greatness as a player and coach in the NBA, charged off the bus and angrily ripped down the likeness of Smith from the tree where it hung. But only victories on the court could soothe the mob that put it there.

Billy Packer remembers that it wasn't just North Carolina alumni who were openly questioning Smith's competency at the time.

"It was like, 'Who is this guy?' Frank McGuire was considered next to Everett Case—and probably even the equal of Everett Case —as the greatest coach in the world at the time. And they turn the job over to this guy? It was like, 'Who the hell is Dean Smith?' It's not like he came on the scene as some Superman," Packer said.

While Smith struggled to gain a grip at Carolina, two of the other Big Four programs were in a state of rebuilding: State under Norm Sloan, who had replaced Maravich; Wake under Jack McCloskey, who replaced Jack Murdock, the coach who lasted only one season after replacing McKinney. That left Bubas at Duke standing as the one true power in the mid-1960s.

Starting with his second season, 1960–61, Bubas coached a string of smashing 20-win seasons. The Blue Devils went 22-6 that season and then rattled off consecutive finishes of 20-5, 27-3, 26-5, 20-5, and 26-4 through the 1965–66 season. The real breakthrough year came in '62–63, when they won 27 of 30 games and advanced to their first Final Four while earning a number two national ranking. The next season they made it to the NCAA championship game before losing to UCLA, 98–83, and they also made a trip to the Final Four under Bubas in '65–66, losing to Kentucky in the semifinals.

Bubas achieved these stunning successes through tireless recruiting, careful choosing of an all-star staff of assistant coaches, and brilliant organization. Among his assistant coaches were Chuck Daly, Hubie Brown, Bucky Waters, and Fred Schabel. Having spent years on the road as Case's ace recruiter, he knew what it took to go after players. Many credit him with taking recruiting to a new level.

"In terms of what a coach is today and what a typical coach was and what a typical program was in 1959, when he took over at Duke, Vic Bubas was more ahead of his time than anyone I've seen," Packer said. "If you followed the way he put together a staff, the way he recruited, the organization and all the things that he brought to the table in 1960, and followed that exactly, you would not be that out of touch in 1998. He was that far ahead of his time in terms of how he would do things for the betterment of his basketball program. I can't think of anybody else in the history of college basketball who has been as far ahead of the times as he was.

"He was a real gentleman and a great competitor. But more than anything, he was the greatest at figuring out, 'This is the format, this is how it's done.' And then he would do it exactly how he plotted it out."

Bill Hensley, a close friend of Bubas's, said that Bubas was the first coach to send potential recruits information about Duke while the recruits were still juniors and seniors in high school.

"Vic would send them newspaper stories of games, with a note attached saying, 'Thought you would like to see what we did to North Carolina last week, or Boston College, or whatever.' That may seem like small stuff now, but he was the first one I know of who started sending kids stuff like that," Hensley said.

When Bubas targeted a recruit, he usually landed him. He expanded Duke's recruiting base to include the entire country, for the first time challenging the likes of Case and State for top players in Indiana and New Jersey, and Carolina for players in New York City and elsewhere. He didn't always win in these head-on battles, but he won enough to make a huge difference in the talent level at his school.

One of Bubas's early recruits was Jay Buckley, an intelligent young man who boasted an IQ of around 160 and spent one summer attending Columbia University on a special grant from NASA.

"Jay, one of these days I'll be reading about you being the first man on the moon," Bubas told Buckley once.

Buckley disagreed.

"No coach, you'll be there first, looking for ballplayers."

Taking much of what he had learned during his years as Case's top assistant, Bubas carried forward the ideals of Case in a way that surely would have made the old man proud. In a way, Case continued to live on in ACC hoops through Bubas. His background worked for him in the job but worked against him in the eyes of many Duke alumni, who couldn't believe their alma mater had hired an assistant coach from North Carolina State.

Bubas worked quickly to silence critics by literally working the city of Durham. He would drive all over the city, getting gas at different service stations throughout, to meet people and shake hands. He upgraded parking facilities for home games and, based on his belief that folks did not want to watch games with coats in their laps, arranged for smiling coeds to check garments at the door. He was the first to have the last names of his players stitched onto the back of their uniforms, saying that he believed it would help the fans keep track of who was playing. He catered to women fans like no coach in the ACC had done before, upgrading the women's restroom facilities and encouraging women to come onto the court following home games to mingle with players, get autographs, and take pictures. He was a big fan of major-league baseball owner and promoter Bill Veeck, and he took many of his ideas from Veeck's autobiography, *Veeck As In Wreck.*

Bubas's best players on his first two Final Four teams were Art Heyman and Jeff Mullins. Taking Eddie Cameron's advice the day he was hired, Bubas wasted no time hitting the recruiting trail. Twenty-four hours after the news conference in which Cameron had introduced Bubas to the local media, Bubas met with Heyman in New York's Manhattan Hotel. Heyman, then a highly coveted senior from Long Island, was impressed and quickly agreed to attend Duke.

Mullins wasn't quite so easy. Mullins was playing his high-school ball in Lexington, Kentucky, home of the University of Kentucky. Adolph Rupp, Kentucky's legendary coach, wanted Mullins to play for the Wildcats, but Rupp had made a mistake a year earlier when he attempted to play hardball with Jon Speaks, Mullins's close friend and high-school teammate.

Rupp was the featured speaker at an athletic banquet at Mullins's school at the end of Mullins's junior year. Afterward, Rupp approached Speaks, a senior.

"Jon, I would like to speak to you," Rupp said.

Mullins, who knew that Speaks was being actively recruited by North Carolina State, Kansas, and Kansas State, started to move away. Rupp motioned for him to stay.

"No, I want you to hear this, too."

Then Rupp turned to Speaks and grinned.

"Son, I'm offering you an opportunity to come to Kentucky and play for Adolph Rupp. But if you don't say yes right now, I'm giving the scholarship to someone else. What do you say, son?"

Speaks was a little stunned. Rupp hadn't even hinted that he was interested in him to that point. He told Rupp that he would have to think about it, that he couldn't give him an answer right then.

Rupp got angry and stalked off. Mullins never forgot it.

"It really turned me off because I was standing there watching the whole thing," Mullins said years later. "They never recruited Jon again, which I felt bad about. I said to myself, 'I don't know if I want to play for this guy.' I think Rupp knew how I felt. He was very nice to me my whole senior year."

Rupp also knew how to apply pressure in other ways. The coach arranged for Mullins to meet with Bert T. Combs, the governor of Kentucky, not once, but twice.

The second time, Mullins already had signed a letter of intent to attend Duke. But back then, you could break a letter of intent if you wanted to. Mullins was working as a lifeguard at a local pool during the summer when one of his co-workers approached and said he had a phone call.

"I'm working. Take a message and tell whoever it is I'll call them back," Mullins said.

"Well, it's the governor," the co-worker said.

Mullins decided he had better take the call.

"Son, I'd like you to come and talk with me again about maybe staying in our great state and playing basketball for the University of Kentucky. How about breakfast tomorrow? I'll have a limo at your house at eight o'clock tomorrow morning."

"Well, sir, I've got to work tomorrow," Mullins told the governor.

"That's already been taken care of. See you tomorrow morning."

Click.

There was a limo waiting at Mullins's door the next morning, and he went to have breakfast with the governor.

"Jeff, I just want you to know—from someone who played basketball—of all the opportunities you have in this state. You should stay in the state and play for Kentucky. You won't regret it," the governor said.

Mullins politely nodded and listened. But he was going to Duke to play for Vic Bubas.

MULLINS MADE HIS DECISION to attend Duke based largely on the recruiting experience of his good friend, Jon Speaks. Mullins not only watched as Rupp tried to intimidate his friend, but also observed how Speaks was treated by Bubas, who successfully persuaded Speaks to leave the state of Kentucky to attend North Carolina State instead.

But Speaks was part of the last State recruiting class that Bubas helped put together for Everett Case. He soon thereafter accepted the head-coaching position at Duke, met with and secured Art Heyman's services (who like Speaks, was one year ahead of Mullins), and continued to recruit Mullins—except now he was recruiting him for a different school. Mullins was more impressed with the man than the school at first.

Kentucky, despite the pressure from the governor and Rupp, was no longer an option as far as Mullins was concerned. The Rupp incident with Speaks had turned him off. The limo rides to the governor's mansion were nice and breakfast with the state's leader was something he would never forget, but it obviously wasn't the place for him. The legions who assisted in Kentucky recruiting had made one other mistake.

"The other thing that got on my family's nerves was that UK had this booster club, The 101 Club, and a member was going to come by every day at about five before dinner. They did that for about three days and my dad put an end to that," Mullins said.

Bubas was different than the Kentucky gang, whose methods seemed to be about as subtle as hitting a recruit over the head.

"He was a very warm guy, yet very businesslike," Mullins said. "I've since heard Dean Smith and others say that he really wrote the textbook on recruiting; that the evolution of recruiting started with Vic Bubas. From letters to organized visits, he was very structured as to who he saw and visited on the road. All those things were new to recruiting. I just felt like I could play for Bubas."

Mullins also considered attending Maryland, State, or Purdue. The Big Ten had just passed a rule—one that would be short-lived —that said freshmen couldn't play at all, not even a freshman schedule. They could practice with the varsity and move up to varsity as sophomores, but that was it. That ruled Purdue out. Mullins wanted to go someplace where he could play right away, and that meant the ACC.

Once Mullins visited Duke's sprawling campus, however, the rest of the competition was dead. What caught his eye the most was his first visit to Duke Chapel—a magnificent structure that sits in the middle of campus at the end of a circle driveway, just a short walk from the arena where the Blue Devils play basketball.

"I visited over Thanksgiving and it was a very dismal weekend. It was raining. I'll never forget driving from the airport and doing that circle loop and then looking up the drive toward the chapel," Mullins said. "They have those lights shining on it. It's just such an impressive sight. I think that sold me right away."

But that wasn't all. Mullins's parents were sold as well.

"Back then you could visit a school more than once. In fact, my parents came back with me in the spring. The rule was that there had to be a booster who would fly over in a private plane to pick you up and fly back over with you. One of the local businessmen flew over and met my mom and dad in Lexington. I had talked about the campus a lot and they wanted to see it."

They loved it immediately.

But young Jeff Mullins had another reason for wanting to go back to Duke for a second visit. He wanted to get a better feel for what Art Heyman was all about.

"Everybody and their brother was bad-mouthing Art. They were saying, 'You don't want to play with Art,' " Mullins remembered.

Everybody except Bubas, of course.

"If you're going to come here, you're going to play with a great player in Art Heyman," Bubas told Mullins. "He's going to be the next Jerry West or Oscar Robertson, and I want you to come down and meet him."

During his first visit that gloomy Thanksgiving weekend, Mullins had visited and watched Duke practice. He was anxious to see Heyman on the court.

"Then I saw this kind of chubby guy with this big old rear end and, well, Jerry West was my high-school hero. And so I'm thinking, 'They're comparing this guy with Jerry West? C'mon,' " Mullins said.

Now Mullins didn't know what to think. But after the practice he had met Heyman and thought the guy seemed nice enough.

"That first visit was during November, and then during the winter recruiting period a lot of coaches from other schools started bad-mouthing Duke to me because of Art. So I said I wanted to go back to get to know him better. And I did," Mullins said.

During his second visit, the introspective Mullins hit it off with the bold Heyman, who once was described by a sports writer as wearing his modesty like a loud sports coat.

Heyman was one of the game's great characters of his day. And despite his deceptive physical appearance, he could play. For the freshman team in 1959–60, Heyman averaged more than 30 points a game with a high of 47. In his first varsity season, '60–61, he became the only sophomore in the nation to earn All-America honors, averaging 25.7 points and 10.9 rebounds for a team that went 22-6.

Heyman was 6 feet, 5 inches and a rock-solid 205 pounds. He was so intense and got so worked up before every game that his stomach churned until he threw up. "I remember even through my pro years that Art was the only player who was literally sick to his stomach before every game," said Mullins, who went on after his Duke career to play twelve seasons in the NBA. "You'd hear him in the restrooms before a game. That's how emotionally involved he was."

Sometimes those emotions ran away with him.

Heyman was also so strong that once, at the end of a time-out, he grabbed Bubas's hand and shook it so hard he dislocated the coach's thumb. His specialty was driving to the basket, a move that best utilized his amazing strength. He could get fouled and still make a shot with defenders hanging all over him. And he was a devastating offensive rebounder for his size, using that "big ol' rear end" and his strength to clear a space underneath the basket.

"I've always said this, and I still believe that next to Elgin Baylor, he was probably the best 6-foot-5 offensive rebounder I've ever seen," said Mullins. "Art had that knack. Whenever he went up for a rebound, people on both sides of him tended to fall away. He threw his body at the ball like all great rebounders do. He was an outstanding offensive rebounder.

"He was a great driver and he could shoot in traffic and get fouled. He was very good at getting to the line. And he had a good understanding of how to pass. Like most good scorers, he could pass well, too. I got a lot of points early in my career because of his passes. But if I had to pinpoint one thing that made him so great, it was that he was extremely strong."

Chuck Taylor, the man from Converse shoes who first had recommended to State officials that they hire a man named Everett Case as coach back in 1946, was by the early 1960s known as "Mr. Basketball." He saw Heyman play and raved about him.

"Art Heyman is one of the great drivers in the game today. He bulls his way toward the basket like Elgin Baylor and Tom Heinsohn. He just overpowers the defense," Taylor said. "Not many drivers can make the shot with defenders hanging on their shoulders. He's a lot like Bob Cousy and Oscar Robertson."

Heyman got such a kick out of the comparison that one time he checked into a hotel in Myrtle Beach, South Carolina, with a girlfriend and registered as Mr. and Mrs. Oscar Robertson. He didn't even seem to mind when the story got in the local newspapers and he was charged with transporting an underage girl across state lines. Although the charges eventually were dropped, Bubas was furious with him. It was one of many incidents that landed Heyman in Bubas's office.

Sometimes Mullins was invited in to hear Bubas chew Heyman out, perhaps in an effort to keep Mullins from following Heyman's wild path. One day Bubas was particularly harsh on his star forward.

"If you're going to continue to act like this, you can pack your bags and get out of here," Bubas seethed. "We're sick and tired of this."

Bubas continued to rail on Heyman for several more minutes. Heyman listened, his head bowed.

Finally Heyman had a chance to speak.

"Coach, you're right about everything you said. I did do everything you said, and I was wrong to do those things," Heyman said. "But do you ever have to get me ready to play? Am I always ready to play a game? Am I always ready to carry this team?"

Mullins watched as Heyman carried on for several minutes. He wasn't sure how Bubas would react.

"Art wouldn't quit, though. It finally got to the point where Vic just started laughing and told him to get out of the office," Mullins said.

Heyman didn't take long to establish himself as a young man who wouldn't take much of anything off of anybody. During a game against Carolina in the last Dixie Classic, Carolina began the game with Jim Hudock guarding Heyman. Heyman scored Duke's first eight points before Coach Frank McGuire of the Tar Heels called a time-out.

McGuire wasn't very fond of Heyman, and neither were Doug Moe and Larry Brown, Carolina standouts who knew Heyman from playing against him in New York City. Brown and Heyman were from the same Long Island neighborhood, and had once been friends.

Their tenuous friendship ended when Heyman broke a verbal commitment to attend North Carolina. The recruitment of Heyman had been intense, and Bubas didn't really enter the game until late. Heyman later claimed he had been offered ten thousand dollars to attend the University of Cincinnati. He said that was enough to get him there, but his parents protested. So he turned to McGuire and Carolina via the Tar Heels' New York City pipeline. But when Heyman made it to Chapel Hill for his official recruiting visit, Heyman's stepfather became embroiled in a shouting match with McGuire. Heyman had to step between the two men to prevent it from escalating into a fistfight.

So when McGuire called time-out early in that Duke-Carolina game during the 1960 Dixie Classic, he motioned with disgust toward Heyman and gave Moe a simple command.

Moe walked over to Heyman after the time-out and said, "Art, I'm sorry. But Frank gave me the word."

"What are you talking about?" asked Heyman.

"You're not to touch the ball anymore," Moe replied.

And for the rest of the game, Moe frustrated Heyman by over-playing him, denying him the ball. Heyman scored just 3 more points, finishing with 11.

Heyman was in shock. No one held him to 11 points. No one.

When the two teams met five weeks later for a regular-season ACC battle in Durham, Heyman was still fuming. He came out smoking against the Heels and torched them for 36 points as Duke avenged the earlier loss. Back then the benches for both teams were located under the baskets. Late in the game, Brown was driving and Heyman fouled him hard. Both players went down, falling to the floor right in front of the Carolina bench.

Four Carolina players immediately jumped off the bench and started grabbing Heyman. Truth be told, Heyman wasn't about to get much help from the Duke seniors. They had been pretty good the year before without this brash sophomore. So they started to sidle back toward the Duke bench.

Mullins, then a freshman, was watching from the stands as Heyman started throwing the Carolina guys off him. Soon Heyman was free. He staggered to midcourt and everyone thought that would be the end of the brief scuffle.

Everyone but Heyman.

"He gets to half-court and most guys would have said, 'Whew, I'm out of there,' " Mullins said. "Not Art. He realizes he's away and immediately he turns around and runs back and tackles about two of those guys who had jumped him. That's when the fans erupted and everything else."

It took ten Durham policemen to help restore order. Heyman was suspended from Duke's final three ACC regular-season games, while Brown and Donnie Walsh of Carolina were suspended for the Tar Heels' last four ACC contests.

The trouble from that particular game didn't end there for Hey-man. At halftime that same afternoon, a Carolina male cheerleader had patted Heyman on the back as he headed for the Duke locker room. In a typical knee-jerk reaction, Heyman swung at the cheer-leader. Blackwell M. Brogden, a Durham attorney who was an alum-nus of North Carolina, witnessed the exchange and later swore out a warrant charging Heyman with assault. When the Carolina cheer-leader refused to testify, Brogden had him subpoenaed. The case eventually was dismissed, but not before a circus atmosphere developed and a crowd of three hundred jammed a Durham courtroom to see what was going to happen.

The real action worth watching, however, wasn't in the courtroom. It was on the court. And over the next several seasons, Coach Vic Bubas would take Duke and their fans on a ride they would never forget.

ONE YEAR AFTER Wake Forest's magical run to the Final Four, it was Duke's turn. Heyman, a senior, and Mullins, a junior, gave the Blue Devils a terrific one-two scoring punch that was difficult for other teams to defend. The two high-scoring forwards were surrounded by a group of smart, efficient complementary players who knew their roles. Two of the members of the starting five—guard Fred Schmidt and center Jay Buckley—were on the Dean's List as students. Their intelligence was evident in the way the team worked for good shots in games. Buckley ended up leading the ACC in field-goal percentage, hitting 60 percent of his shots, and the Blue Devils ended up becoming the first team in league history to shoot better than 50 percent from the field for the season.

Bubas was the main reason for that. Organized and disciplined, the team became a reflection of their coach. Even the ball boys took notice.

"He was Dean Smith before Dean Smith was Dean Smith," said Steve Luguire, who was a ball boy for Duke for four seasons and later in life served as a vice chairman on the committee that brought the Final Four to Charlotte in 1994. "I mean, he was the man. He was the coach of the sixties.

"When he ran the basketball team at Duke, he was more like a CEO than anything else. You would see the other coaches, and you knew he was different. That stood out in my mind."

Bubas even had Chuck Daly sit up at the top of Duke Indoor Stadium in what they called "the crow's nest" and call down to the bench whatever insight he gained from being able to see the whole floor. Bubas communicated with Daly via a telephone that was located right next to Bubas on the bench.

"You would just hand him the telephone," Luguire said. "But I always thought what was funny about that was it was in Indoor Stadium, and you think to yourself, 'What in the world can you see up there that you can't see down on the court?' It was only about twenty-five rows up."

With Daly up in the crow's nest and Bubas on the bench, Duke won their first 6 games in 1962–63, before suffering upset losses at Davidson and at Miami of Florida. The loss at Davidson was a difficult one for Bubas to take, even though the Blue Devils had opened the season at home a few weeks earlier with a victory over the same team. The reason: Davidson was coached by Lefty Driesell, the colorful former Duke player who had interviewed for the head-coaching position at Duke before Bubas eventually was hired in 1959.

The loss at Miami was, in the final analysis, much easier to swallow. It was somewhat of a fluke, influenced by a questionable call by a questionable official at the end of the contest.

"When we played a big nonconference game, we could get one ACC official to do the game," Mullins said. "We usually liked Charlie Eckman. He was one of the premier officials in our league. He really seemed to like us and we liked him. So he's doing the game at Miami. But the other guy, we didn't know him. We called him the Lifeguard because he had a great tan."

Duke was up by a point and had the ball with just a few seconds remaining. Fred Schmidt was holding the ball, waiting to get fouled, running some time off the clock—when all of a sudden, the official with the great tan whistled him for an offensive foul.

"Lifeguard calls an offensive foul on Fred and they get the ball with four seconds left, down only one. We couldn't believe it," Mullins said.

Neither could Eckman. He ran by the Duke huddle during the subsequent time-out and shouted, "The Lifeguard screwed us. Worst call I've ever seen."

When Miami scored to win by one, Eckman's sympathy made little difference. Suddenly a team that had been ranked number two in the nation had lost two games in a row.

The Blue Devils didn't lose again that season until the national semifinals in the NCAA Tournament, ripping off 20 wins in a row. That included a perfect 14-0 record in the ACC regular season.

Mullins remembered a rare TV game against West Virginia at Duke Indoor Stadium. It was billed as a showdown between Heyman and Rod Thorn, the great guard for the Mountaineers. Both were candidates for National Player of the Year honors. But in the early going, it was Mullins who was hot and scoring most of the points for the Blue Devils. Heyman had only 7 points in the first half.

As they came out onto the floor for the second half, Heyman grabbed Mullins.

"You son of a bitch, you're making me look bad. You're not going to touch the ball in the second half," Heyman said.

Mullins laughed at Heyman, thinking for sure his teammate was joking.

"Yeah, I laughed at him," Mullins said years later. "But then, sure enough, I got four points in the second half and he scored eighteen."

Heyman finished off a tremendous career with a great senior season. Eventually he was named Player of the Year. He capped his outstanding career with a performance to remember in his final outing at Duke Indoor Stadium, scoring a career-high 40 points and grabbing 24 rebounds in a 106–93 victory over Carolina.

When Bubas removed Heyman from the game with twenty-two seconds remaining and victory assured for the Blue Devils, the crowd roared its appreciation for the special career Heyman had given them. The standing ovation lasted a full three minutes.

Bubas told reporters afterward that for the first time in his coaching career, he had given a player, Heyman, the green light to do all the personal damage he could to the other team. Heyman responded in a manner that made Bubas beam with pride.

"Everyone talks about what a great player Dick Groat was here at Duke. Groat was a great basketball player, without a doubt," Bubas said. "I guarded him and he's a good friend of mine. But Heyman is bigger and stronger than Groat was. Art has got to be the best player who ever put on a Duke uniform."

Heyman continued his magic in the ACC Tournament, as the Blue Devils swept past Virginia, State, and Wake Forest. In the championship game against Wake, Duke led by only 4 at halftime and was struggling to stretch its lead early in the second half when Heyman suddenly called for a time-out.

When his teammates joined him in the huddle in front of the Duke bench, Heyman had a simple message.

"Give me the ball and get out of my way," Heyman said.

Bubas didn't argue with him, and Heyman went on to finish with 24 points and 11 rebounds in a 68–57 victory. Bubas said afterward that he believed his boys could keep on winning until they won the national championship, and they almost did. This time it was Mullins who was hot, scoring a total of 49 points in wins over New York University and St. Joseph's to earn MVP honors in the East Regional of the NCAA Tournament.

Heyman, dogged by the latest rumor that he had been married secretly during the season, struggled at first in the tournament, hitting only 9 of 35 shots against NYU and St. Joe's. In the Final Four semis against a Loyola of Chicago team that symbolized changing times in America and in college basketball, Heyman rebounded to score 29 but Loyola, who started four black players, had its way with lily-white Duke. Loyola won 94–75 and went on to beat defending champion Cincinnati for the national championship.

Mullins remembers watching the championship game between Loyola and Cincinnati with his father. During an early time-out the 6-4 Mullins turned to him and said, "You know Dad, I've been watching this game for the first five minutes and I don't think the ball has come down low enough for me to touch it."

Times were definitely about to change in the world of college basketball.

Heyman, meanwhile, ended his career by scoring 22 in Duke's 85–63 win over Oregon State in the consolation game. He became one of only four players in NCAA Tournament history to be named Final Four MVP despite not playing in the championship game.

AFTER GOING 27-3 and nearly winning it all during Heyman's senior season, the question for Duke the following year was what could they do now?

Mullins was back for his senior season. Backcourt men Danny Ferguson and Buzz Harrison were also back, as was Buckley and Hack Tison, a pair of 6-10 trees who now started on the front line along with the smooth-shooting Mullins. Another shooter, newcomer Jack Marin, was added to the mix.

For the first time, Duke sold out many of its home games. Mullins got the fans going every time he went to the free-throw line, and by the end of his career they would loudly count out each of the 13 dribbles he took before attempting every foul shot.

The Devils were ranked number four in the nation at the beginning of the season, and they played a difficult nonconference schedule that produced losses to two teams ranked number one at the time, Michigan and Kentucky. But the losses did not come often. Duke lost only one ACC game, 72–71 at Wake Forest, en route to back-to-back regular-season and ACC Tournament championships.

The tournament had by then become a hotter ticket than ever before. Steve Luguire, who was Duke's ball boy, did not have a coveted participants' pass to get in the back entrance at Reynolds Coliseum.

Hack Tison said to Luguire, who then measured no more than 5 feet, 2 inches, "We'll get you in. Don't worry about it."

"But how?" Luguire asked.

Tison held up the ball bag, which actually was an oversized laundry bag. He dumped out several basketballs that were in there and motioned for Luguire to climb in. Then Tison threw the ball bag —and the ball boy—over his large shoulder. Teammates scooped up the loose basketballs and carried them to the back entrance, where they knocked on the door and began entering, showing their passes one by one to the doorman, a crusty old soul named Dorsey Poole who had been watching the entrance for years.

All of a sudden, Luguire felt himself getting punched through the bag.

"That doesn't feel like any damn basketball in there to me. Put that bag down," Poole ordered Tison.

Luguire felt like crying. He thought for certain he was headed back to the team bus, where he would have to sit and wait for about five hours by himself.

But Poole just smiled at him and shook his head.

"Son, if you want to get in the basketball game this bad, you just knock on the door and ask for Dorsey. I'll let you in."

After winning the 1964 ACC Tournament by whipping North Carolina State, North Carolina, and Wake Forest by the combined total of 68 points, the Blue Devil players gathered in the winning locker room at Reynolds Coliseum to sing an off-key rendition of Wilbert Harrison's "Kansas City." That's where they figured they would soon be headed for their second straight Final Four appearance. With their first two NCAA Tournament games on the same Reynolds Coliseum court where they had just romped to the ACC championship, they disposed of Villanova 87–73 and Connecticut 101–54 to earn the return trip.

Physically getting to Kansas City proved to be more difficult than they had envisioned—not so much because of the games they had to win, but because the eighty-five-seat chartered airplane they arrived on almost crashed upon landing.

"We were landing during a storm," Mullins said. "We came down on one wheel and we spun off the runway. Thank goodness it was one of those things that happens so quick that you don't think too much about it."

Then the Blue Devils walked into the airport terminal and one of the first things they saw was a banner welcoming the ACC champions to the Final Four. It read: "Welcome to Kansas City, Tar Heels."

The chaos continued when the team got to its hotel and the rooms weren't ready.

"Then we got to the arena where we were playing, and they told us our locker room was the only one they were still painting. So everything got off to a bad start from the very beginning," Mullins said.

It briefly got better in the semifinals when the Blue Devils avenged their earlier loss to Michigan, making it to the national championship game for the first time in school history. But they lost to UCLA—a team that went 30-0 that season despite not having a single starter taller than 6 feet, 5 inches. The Bruins' battle cry all season was "Tall Ain't All."

Mullins said he and his teammates simply put too much energy into beating Michigan and had little left for UCLA.

"It was one of those deals where we put all our eggs in one basket," Mullins said. "We played very well against Michigan. I remember saying afterward that I couldn't think of a time when any of us had played any better. Then we went back to the hotel at something like eleven-thirty and we still didn't know who we were going to play next. Kansas State was up something like six points on UCLA with something like fifty seconds to go. We thought we were going to play Kansas State."

When it became UCLA instead, the Bruins' full-court pressure caught Duke off-guard. UCLA won 98–83. Mullins's career at Duke was over.

"It was hard to have it end that way," Mullins said. "I'll tell you what it was like: you play in the ACC Tournament, which was magical, the Regional, which was kind of magical, and then the Final Four. Even though we were sad, it was kind of like a magic ride that didn't quite make it to the end."

TWO YEARS LATER, Bubas would experience the same sort of unfulfilling magic ride when Duke again made it to the Final Four and fell just short of winning it all.

Jack Marin and Steve Vacendak were solid seniors, but the real star of the team was Bob Verga, a high-scoring junior. Another key player was 6-7 sophomore Mike Lewis, a rough-and-tumble center from Missoula, Montana, who had supposedly trained for the rebounding rigors of the ACC by wrestling broncos back in his home state.

Lewis had been heavily recruited by other schools, including UCLA.

"Yes, we were after Lewis," UCLA coach John Wooden admitted at the time. "We called him up several times, but every time we did, Bucky Waters answered the phone."

Waters was, of course, Bubas's trusted assistant coach then before going on to become a head coach himself at West Virgina.

Duke blasted UCLA 94–75 in Charlotte earlier that season, but Wooden complained that playing the Blue Devils in Charlotte hardly constituted a neutral site.

"A neutral court? That was sort of like our football team playing Notre Dame in Rome," Wooden said.

Duke attained a number one national ranking early in the 1965–66 season and kept right on winning, no matter who it played or where. The Blue Devils stumbled some during the middle of the season, including a game in which they blew a big lead to lose at West Virginia to Waters, who was in his first season with the Mountaineers. But by the end of the year they were rolling again.

A 103–73 victory over Wake Forest in the opening round of the ACC Tournament set up a second-round showdown with North Carolina. Duke was heavily favored, but Carolina opened the contest in a delay game, holding the ball. The Heels took only five shots in the first half and actually led 17–12 with ten minutes remaining in the contest.

Then Duke rallied to win, 21–20.

"I didn't want a good game. I wanted to win it," Carolina coach Dean Smith told reporters afterward. "We thought we could win it playing this type of game."

They almost did. The next night, Duke played in its sixth ACC championship game in the seven years Bubas had been coach. The Devils beat State to win their fourth title, and then beat St. Joseph's and Syracuse in the NCAA Tournament.

But bad luck struck again at the Final Four. Bob Verga came down with a nasty case of the flu. Both Verga and Larry Conley, a senior forward at Kentucky, were hospitalized for the entire week leading up to the Duke-Kentucky semifinal matchup that everyone thought would determine the national champion. Verga tried to play in the game, but wasn't himself.

"Verga was sapped," Steve Luguire said. "He had no energy. He was like a different ballplayer. He had been the go-to guy, but he just wasn't able to play.

"He never made a jump shot in that game, and he was the purest shooter I had ever been around. Jeff Mullins was a great shooter, but there was no one who had played at Duke up until then who compared to Verga. But he couldn't throw it in the ocean that night. He was very weak."

Verga made only 2 of 7 shots and scored just 4 points, playing limited minutes. Kentucky won 83–79.

The next night, Duke beat Utah in the consolation game.

"Third place in a country as large as ours isn't bad," Bubas said.

But Kentucky, the heavy favorite, did not win the national championship. Texas Western did. Texas Western started five black players who did things Duke and the rest of the Big Four schools were not accustomed to seeing.

"Texas Western was kind of the unknown going into that Final Four," Luguire said. "They were sort of the odd team out, or so everyone thought. The thinking was that they would lose to Utah in the semifinals. Everyone was thinking our game (Duke-Kentucky) was going to decide the national champion.

"But that very first night, before they beat Utah, they came out for layups and they didn't do layups. They did dunks. Both nights, you could see the other teams looking at Texas Western and thinking like 'Ohhhhh. This is different.' You had large, powerful African American athletes out there playing. That was something that was just happening in our country [at the established, predominantly white schools] and we hadn't seen that in the South and the Atlantic Coast Conference yet."

It was time for a dramatic change in the ACC and Big Four basketball.

8

BREAKING THE BARRIER

CHARLIE DAVIS never considered himself a groundbreaker for the civil-rights movement in the South. He just wanted to play basketball. But when he arrived at Wake Forest in 1967, he was part of something much bigger than he or anyone else could have realized at the time. Times were changing, and life as it was known on the basketball courts of the Big Four would never be the same again.

Davis wasn't the first black player recruited by Wake Forest. He wasn't even the first to play for them. Nor was he the first great African American player to open eyes in the Big Four arena; that was Charlie Scott from North Carolina. But Davis's story illustrates many things: how education can make a difference, how opportunity must be afforded and embraced regardless of the color of one's skin, and how the ignorance and arrogance of others can be transformed through sport.

Rail-thin, pigeon-toed, and barely stretching an inch over 6 feet, Davis arrived at Wake during a tumultuous time. Jackie Murdock—who had starred for the Demon Deacons in McKinney's first years as coach and later served as McKinney's assistant—had eventually replaced McKinney as head coach. But after only one disastrous season Murdock was out. The 1965–66 season was the first post-Bones campaign and the team lost 18 of its 26 games. Jack McCloskey, the former Penn coach who once tried to talk Billy Packer out of attending Wake Forest, was hired to replace Murdock for the '66–67 season.

Packer, who would have much to do with recruiting Davis and other African Americans to Wake Forest, always had been a little different. As a sophomore during his playing days at Wake, Packer kept hearing and reading about a great player who was enrolled right across town at Winston-Salem State.

"I had been reading about this guy Cleo Hill. I heard he was a hell of a player, but I had never seen them play," Packer said. "So one night I hitch-hiked over to Winston-Salem State to see them play. It was almost crazy in those days for a white guy to go into the black side of town. But it wasn't to me. I was just going over to watch a basketball game. I wasn't into breaking the color barrier and all that kind of stuff."

Once there, Packer ignored the fact that he was the only white guy in the building and eventually struck up a conversation with Clarence "Big House" Gaines, the legendary Winston-Salem State coach. He also came to admire the play of Hill, and the two developed a friendship together. Later the great guard Earl Monroe would attend Winston-Salem State and lead the school to a small-college national championship.

"I used to take our guys [from Wake Forest] over and we would play against the Winston-Salem State guys in the spring. We would go to Atkins High School and play," Packer said.

After finishing up his career at Wake and going into private business, Packer still kept tabs on the Winston-Salem team. McKinney knew this. So toward the end of his run as coach he started recruiting black players. Schools up north had been doing it for years, and by the mid-1960s even some in the South had started doing it.

Billy Jones from Towson, Maryland, had become the first black to play in the ACC when he suited up for Maryland in 1965. Coaches from the Big Four schools had long been aware of the ability of some black players, but either couldn't or wouldn't recruit them.

Jesse Arnelle, a black player from Penn State, received a standing ovation for his play in the very first Dixie Classic in 1949. Oscar Robertson from the University of Cincinnati and Jumpin' Johnny Green from Michigan had wowed the crowds and the coaches at the 1958 Dixie Classic. Robertson's play prompted Everett Case to say: "Great Scott! I know a lot of southern coaches who would like to pull a Branch Rickey with that boy." Despite Case's interest, it would still be eleven more years before North Carolina State landed its first black recruit: Al Heartley of Clayton, North Carolina. Another ACC school, the University of Virginia, did not have an African American play for the team until 1972.

Truth be told, Carolina almost began the recruiting process for black players by accident in 1953 when Coach Frank McGuire sent a letter and a recruiting form to Don Byrd, a center for the Fort Belvoir Army team in Virginia. The team was coached by former Duke star Dick Groat, who told reporters that Byrd was good enough to start for any college team in America. McGuire sent the letter not knowing Byrd was black—or that Byrd had not yet earned a high-school diploma. He backed off as soon as he found out those facts.

By the mid-1960s, most coaches wanted to begin recruiting blacks. The question was how to go about doing it. Most coaches were worried that many blacks would not make the test scores necessary to qualify for their schools.

McKinney called Packer one day in 1965 and told him, "Hey, I want you to help me recruit a player."

At first Packer wasn't interested, but McKinney called him again.

"I really need your help recruiting this guy. Will you help me?"

"Who is he?" Packer asked.

"He's a kid by the name of Herm Gilliam," McKinney replied.

Packer was surprised. He knew Herm Gilliam, and Herm Gilliam was black.

"Well, Herm goes to Atkins," said Packer, who didn't need to add that Atkins High was an all-black school.

"Yeah, I know," McKinney said. "He's going to be the first Negro in our league."

Packer was intrigued by that thought and agreed to help. He went over to Atkins and met with Gilliam's coach, George Green.

"I wasn't there for breaking color lines," Packer said. "The kid was a good player. So I looked at his grades and found out they were good enough that he could get into school."

Packer met with Herm Gilliam and instantly liked him. The only obstacle left to face was the Scholastic Aptitude Test, for which Gilliam needed to score a minimum of 800. This was about the time that Pete Maravich, who was white and the son of State coach Press Maravich, was having difficulty making the same score. Packer arranged to have Gilliam tutored in the spring and summer. He took the test shortly after and then waited to hear if his score would meet the mark.

Even then Packer thought the 800 rule, as it was called, was stacked against minorities.

"Many people feel that's why it took so long for blacks to break into the ACC," Packer said. "There was the cultural thing, but there was also the educational thing. You've got to remember that a black kid went to a black school. He had no chance. He wasn't even recruited."

The schools blacks attended used mostly second-hand books that had been discarded by the white schools. Most of the teachers had gone to all-black high schools and all-black colleges that often were victimized by the same lack of opportunities, creating a vicious cycle that made passing a test created from the current books used by all-white schools a virtual impossibility for most blacks.

And that wasn't the only bias working against the black athlete of the day.

"I'll never forget this," Packer said. "Herm was the best player in the state of North Carolina in 1965, bar none. He was the Michael Jordan of his day. So one day in May of that year, I picked up the paper and saw something about the North Carolina high-school all-star game."

Packer scanned the list of players who had been invited to participate and didn't see Gilliam's name. He couldn't believe it.

"So I called him up and said, 'Herm, when is the all-star game? How come you're not on the list?' I look back now and you realize how courageous a black kid had to be in those days, or even a black parent," Packer said. "A white guy like myself was so naive about the real world and the lack of opportunity for them.

"He was polite beyond reason. Instead of Herm saying, 'I'm black. I can't play in this thing,' he just kind of ignored it. Then I called George Green and said, 'Coach, how come Herm didn't get nominated for the all-star game?' And George was the same way, very polite. But by that time George and I had a good relationship and he said, 'Billy, blacks don't get a chance to play in the North Carolina all-star game.' "

Packer was furious. He called the North Carolina High School Athletic Association to complain.

"This is ridiculous. The kid is the best player in the state. How can he not play in your game?" Packer added.

"Don't you understand? He's a Negro," the stoic official on other end of the phone said. "He has to play in the Negro game."

"That's crazy," Packer said.

"Yeah, well, that's your opinion. That's the way it is."

After he hung up, Packer felt even more helpless and confused. More than anything, he was angry. He hadn't even known that there were separate all-star games for blacks and whites. He vowed to get Gilliam into Wake Forest; or if not Wake Forest, at least some school where Gilliam would receive the opportunity he deserved to display his remarkable talents before people who could appreciate him for what he was—a gifted basketball player and a decent person, regardless of the color of his skin.

One day Packer and Gilliam were sitting around talking.

"Herm, where would you like to go to college if you can't get into Wake?" Packer asked.

"I'm only going to Wake. If I can't get into Wake, I'll just go to some small school around here or I won't go at all," Gilliam replied.

"Oh, no. You're too good of a person and too great a player to be denied going to a big-time place," Packer said. "I'll see that you get in somewhere. Is there anyplace else you can think of that would make sense?"

Gilliam told Packer he had an aunt who lived in Indianapolis. He had heard of Purdue University in the Big Ten. Maybe that would be a place?

Packer took it upon himself to find out. He called Coach Bob King at Purdue.

"Coach King, you probably don't know me, but I'm Billy Packer," he started out.

"Oh, I know you. You played for Wake Forest just a couple of years ago, right?"

"That's right. Well, I'm working with this kid in Winston-Salem who is a great player and a great kid. He can play for anybody in the country. I want you to give him a scholarship."

King hesitated.

"Well, we'll come down there and take a look at him."

"No, you're not going to look at him. I'm just telling you that he can play for you or anyone else in the damn country. Here's the deal: he wants to come to Wake Forest, but I don't know if he'll score high enough. If he can't come here, he wants to come to your place. I want to know that you'll give him a scholarship if he can't get the 800 he needs to get in at Wake."

King was taken aback. He didn't really know Billy Packer. Just who in the heck did Billy Packer think he was, anyway?

"You're asking an awful lot, Billy. I'll think about it and get back to you," King said. Then he hung up the phone.

Packer wondered if he had laid it on too thick. "It was an out-landish request, really," Packer admitted years later.

But King called back.

"Billy, if you say he's that good a player and a person, I'll take your word for it. You've got the scholarship," King said.

Gilliam came close, but didn't make the 800 score on the SAT that he needed to get into Wake Forest. So he went to Purdue, where he became an All-American and a member of the Boilermakers that went to the Final Four in 1969. They lost in the championship game to UCLA. Then, Gilliam went on to play eight seasons in the NBA. It was all about receiving an opportunity.

EVEN THOUGH Packer didn't get Gilliam into Wake Forest, it was by then only a matter of time until he found a black recruit who could play and find a way into the school. McKinney had been so impressed with Packer's enthusiasm and attention to detail with Gilliam that he offered the former player a position on his staff as an assistant and recruiter.

Packer readily accepted. He packed his family into his car and took off for more than a month to recruit along the East Coast. It didn't take him long to find a neighborhood in the Harlem section of New York City where some of the best black talent seemed to be centrally located. It was there that Packer found Norwood Todmann, who became the first African American varsity basketball player at Wake in 1968. Todmann played his high-school ball at Power Memorial, where he was teammates with Lew Alcindor. His best friend, who lived just down the street, was little Charlie Davis. Charlie Scott lived nearby, too, and all three used to play with and against each other in neighborhood games.

Todmann, once he was at Wake Forest, started telling Packer about Davis.

"There's this kid in my neighborhood—you need to see him play," Todmann said.

Packer agreed to go. He was unaffected by going into Harlem and Brooklyn and other predominantly black areas in New York to see kids play.

"In those days I was more naive than tough or smart," Packer said. "I used to go into Harlem and go to kids' houses and playgrounds and be the only white person around. Other coaches would say, 'How do you go up there? Aren't you afraid?'"

Packer just shrugged and went about his business. One time he was preparing to scout a game at a high school in Harlem when Bill

Miller, then the coach at Elon College, asked if he could tag along. Packer said sure, he didn't mind.

The game they scouted was in a packed gym, and the temperature inside was soaring. As the night wore on Packer noticed that although beads of sweat were beginning to appear on Miller's forehead, his friend still had his hands thrust in the pockets of his heavy winter trench coat.

"Why don't you take your coat off?" Packer asked.

"I don't want to take my coat off," replied Miller, staring straight ahead.

"Why not?"

"I don't want my gun to fall out of my pocket," said Miller, still looking straight ahead.

"Are you out of your damn mind? Did you really bring a gun in here?"

Miller nodded, then said, "Yep. And I still might need it. I'm going outside."

Miller turned toward Packer before walking out.

"And you know something, Billy? You're crazy for coming to places like this."

Packer didn't think so. He wanted to go where the best players were. So he went to New York with Todmann to track down Charlie Davis and take a look at him. It was not as easy an assignment as it sounded.

"I went out to find Charlie, and I couldn't find him," Packer said. "He played in a league in the morning, in the afternoon, and at night. We finally tracked him down in the midnight league in a YMCA."

At first glance, Packer was disappointed.

"I finally see this kid and he's like six foot one and a hundred and thirty pounds," he remembered.

Packer turned to Todmann and expressed his frustration.

"You've got to be crazy, Toddy. What the hell are we going to do with this kid?" Packer said.

"Just watch him play. That's all I ask," Todmann replied.

Packer watched, and it took him about five minutes to realize Davis was a special player. Despite his slight build, Davis could score at will. He could drive to the basket and score, or he could bomb away from the outside. One thing was obvious: no one had figured out a way to stop him. The next day Packer took Todmann and some other players to see an all-star game in the area. He asked Davis to come along.

"We stopped on the way back to get something to eat, and he ate like a little bird. He didn't eat any food. He didn't say two words the whole day," Packer said. "Charlie's teeth were all messed up and he was so shy. He was maybe a little ashamed of where he lived and so forth. He and Toddy lived in the same neighborhood and they were about as close to poverty as you can be.

"Charlie had on his game jersey and his pants and his sneakers. And I'm starting to realize that's all the clothes he has. The reason these guys played on all these league teams was to get shirts."

Davis didn't say much then, but later he admitted that he was impressed with all the attention Packer gave him. Besides, Todmann was his best friend. If Toddy said Wake Forest was okay, then it was okay.

"I was one of the easiest recruits ever," Davis said. "Todmann was at Wake Forest already, and I got along great with Billy Packer. So with the combination of Todmann and Packer, I came to Wake Forest sight unseen. I had never been any farther than Philadelphia all my life when I agreed to come to Wake Forest."

But first Davis had to finish high school. His grades were fine. He was quiet, but intelligent. He was one of only 124 African Americans who were enrolled at Brooklyn Tech High School. The school was made up of several thousand students, and had an outstanding academic reputation. But Davis was a little short of the credits he needed for a high-school diploma so he agreed to finish up at Laurinburg Institute, the same North Carolina school Charlie Scott had attended a year earlier before enrolling at the University of North Carolina. Not long after Davis arrived at Laurinburg in February 1967, the Ku Klux Klan held a rally, firing rifles toward the Laurinburg campus. A half-mile down the road from campus, Davis witnessed his first cross burning.

But whenever someone asked him if he was apprehensive about coming down south to play college basketball, he shook his head and grinned. Then he would tell one of his favorite stories.

"Man, there's no great big difference between the South and the North. I remember going halfway across the Harlem River bridge into the Bronx when I was twelve years old. I was chased back across the bridge by grown white people telling me, 'Nigger, I'm gonna throw you off the bridge!' " Davis said.

"The only difference was that in New York I knew exactly where I could go and where I needed to be. But there was no need to be apprehensive or nervous about coming down South. I always figured that if I didn't like it, hey, I could just go back home."

Even after he arrived on the Wake Forest campus, it wasn't like he and Todmann were thrust into the white mainstream of local society.

"The great thing about Winston-Salem in nineteen sixty-seven and the early seventies was the black community," Davis said years later. "It was a community that really understood what was taking place. I have guys today who still come up to me and say that they used to sit there in the stands and cheer, and how they were so proud to see me play here. But I lived on Winston-Salem State's campus. My wife is a graduate of Winston-Salem State. That was the community that opened up its arms to us—from the black community leaders to individual families. There were homes where we were readily accepted. This was a thriving black community, between Winston-Salem State and [North Carolina] A&T [located in nearby Greensboro]. What I did was go to class on the Wake campus, and practice. After that, we'd pile into a car and be gone."

When he did hang around the Wake campus, he took note of the attitude most white people exhibited toward him.

"You had those who wanted to try to do the right thing. And then you had a few unadulterated jerks who weren't going to accept you. But once again, you learned very quickly where you wanted to be and where you didn't want to be," Davis said. "Even in this great city of Winston-Salem, there were places where you weren't going to get served something to eat unless some great white man came in and said, 'Hey, Joe. Serve these people.' We would go some places where we would stand and wait for forty-five minutes until we got served. But that was just a part of the times."

One of the great white men in the South who had tried to do the right thing was Dean Smith, who was finally beginning to make a name for himself as the coach at North Carolina. Smith was only twenty-eight and in his second year as Frank McGuire's assistant at Carolina in 1959 when Dr. Robert Seymour, the pastor at Binkley Baptist Church where Smith was a charter member, asked for his help in a delicate matter.

When a black theological student came to spend the summer with Seymour's staff, the pastor decided it was time to test the area's accepted way of life when it came to segregation. He called Smith and told him he wanted to take the student to a segregated restaurant. He told Smith that he was pretty certain they would all be served if Smith came along.

Smith eagerly agreed. He wanted to make a difference. (In fact,

Smith later tried to recruit the ACC's first black player during his first season as Carolina's head coach. But the player, Lou Hudson from Greensboro, chose Minnesota instead before going on to a career in the NBA.)

Seymour, Smith, and the young black theological student walked into the Chapel Hill restaurant that night and sat down. Some people stared, but no one made a scene. The three men were served dinner without incident. Though Smith would later downplay his role in the exchange, it is widely regarded as one of the first known steps toward integrating Chapel Hill.

But while Seymour and Smith showed courage that night, it was nothing compared to the courage shown by the black theological student—or by later black athletes like Scott at North Carolina or Heartley at North Carolina State or Todmann and Davis at Wake Forest. Duke's first black player, C. B. Claiborne of Danville, Virginia, enrolled in 1967. (Although Scott was UNC's first black varsity player, he wasn't the first black player recruited by Smith. In fact, in the early '60s, Willie Cooper, recruited by Smith, attended UNC briefly, but then left the school without playing any basketball. Scott would arrive on the scene a few years later.)

"What was so different about the times back then as compared to now is that guys like me, Scotty, Todmann, and all the [black] football players knew we were having an opportunity that most other people didn't have," Davis said. "We were still among a group that believed that when you left the neighborhood, you were going to represent your family, your neighborhood, and your people as well.

"All of that played a really big part in your desire to not only be successful, but also to hang in there regardless of what happened. You had the opportunity that no one else had, and you realized it. That made for a different mindset, plus so many different things were starting to open up for us. As you realized that, I think you were kind of proud that you were playing a part in it."

CHARLIE DAVIS began hearing about Charlie Scott when he was twelve or thirteen years old. Scott's legend and reputation grew until people just felt like they had to see him play. Davis certainly felt that way.

"I kept hearing about this cat who was six-foot-three who played guard and was maybe thirteen or fourteen years old. And I kept hearing so many good things about him that I said to myself,

'Yeah, right,' " Davis said. "In New York, you played with different teams and you played all year long. You played in a tournament here and a tournament there, and you played with this guy here and that guy there. You might play with a guy one time and against him the next.

"I was playing with a Baptist church one time and Scotty was playing with a group called St. Joe's. Well, St. Joe's was big-time then. They had nice uniforms, their coach would take them out to eat. They wore real nice shoes, while we wore Brand X's."

Davis knew of St. Joe's and wanted to see them, mostly Scott, play. He even dreamed of playing against him. One day some of Davis's buddies told him St. Joe's was playing over at a place called Bradhurst on 145th Street. He decided it was time to check this guy out, to see if he was for real.

Davis was not disappointed.

"Oh my goodness," Davis said to himself. "He really is six three. He really can handle the rock like everyone says. Wow! This dude can play."

Years later, Davis still marveled at the memory of his first look at Charlie Scott on the basketball court.

"That was the first time I ran into Scotty—and the guy you saw at Carolina was the same guy I met when he was thirteen, fourteen years old," Davis said.

Davis and Scott found ways out of Harlem and into the wonders of ACC basketball. Some of their Harlem teammates didn't. One, a kid named Kenny Bellinger, was considered the equal or even better than Scott at age fourteen. But a year later, he was shot to death by police who suspected Bellinger had broken into someone's house.

"When the cops come in Harlem, you can hit the roof or hit the basement and run all over the city. He hit the roof. He was going to make a jump from one building to another, and he didn't realize they would shoot him halfway between," Davis said. "They did—and he took an eight-story fall."

"I always thought Kenny Bellinger was the baddest dude up there. There were a host of dudes who could play, and certainly Scotty was among the baddest of them. And as time went on, I was, too. If you go through that spectrum of time, within a year or two older than me and a year or two younger than me, I think eleven of us ended up going to the pros. You're talking about Kareem [Abdul-Jabbar], Scotty, Tiny Archibald, Dean Meminger, myself, and a bunch of others. We all grew up together, so you couldn't have too big an ego because you were going to run into somebody who was going to put a smokin' on you. But there were a host of guys who made it out, and a host of guys who didn't.

"Kenny's was the worst of the stories. The others who never made it out just became drug addicts or drunks—or big-time dope dealers who pulled so much money out of their pockets that they never thought about going anywhere else."

When Packer arrived in Harlem to recruit Davis—one year after Carolina and Davidson and other schools had swooped in to fight over Scott—the skinny little guard with bad teeth was presented with the opportunity to get out. But it wasn't something he jumped at right away.

"I'd love to sit here and say that was the case," Davis said thirty years later. "But I was a kid growing up in the streets. I wasn't that smart. Those were the lives that we lived. You lost some dudes. Other things would happen to others. You would fight to survive. We survived. What was normal for us, well, I didn't realize that other people lived the way they did. I was a kid from New York City who survived."

By the time Davis arrived at Wake Forest, Scott was doing more than surviving at North Carolina. He was thriving. A year earlier Dean Smith had finally broken through and established the school as a power, taking them to the Final Four behind the fine play of Larry Miller. Scott became eligible to play varsity ball in 1967–68, and he immediately became the perfect playing complement to Miller—averaging 17.6 points while Miller poured in 22.4 a game.

If critics thought Smith's 26-6 finish that included regular-season and ACC Tournament titles in '66–67 was a fluke, Scott and Miller helped prove that it wasn't the following season. This time the Tar Heels went 28-4 and advanced all the way to the NCAA tournament championship, losing to UCLA 78–55.

The story of Scott's recruitment to Carolina was well-publicized. He had already committed to Davidson, where Coach Lefty Driesell was drooling at the thought of adding him to a team that was already potent. But Scott had an unpleasant experience at a Davidson restaurant—even though he was with Driesell's assistant coach, Terry Holland—and Miller and several of his future Carolina teammates basically talked him out of going there.

"We've got something good going here. Come with us. Let's see what we can do together," Miller told Scott.

Miller assured Scott that race would not be an issue with the Tar Heels.

"Listen, Charlie, when you come here you are part of the program and there's nothing I won't do for you or nothing the guys on this team won't do for you. We'll protect you. You are part of our family," Miller said.

Driesell didn't take the news that Scott was switching schools lightly. One time after he had made it clear to the Davidson coach that he was going to play at Carolina, Scott was walking to a movie in Laurinburg when a large man startled him by jumping out from behind a bunch of bushes. It was Driesell, who then proceeded to plead with Scott to change his mind again and attend Davidson.

Scott's mind was made up, and he never regretted his decision.

Likewise, Davis never regretted his decision to attend Wake Forest. He and Scott would stage some terrific scoring duels during their careers. Those are the good memories. But they also had some bad ones. Both on and off the court, the two continued to fight prejudice.

Scott's college career ended on a bitter note. He thought he should have been named ACC Player of the Year over South Carolina's John Roche, and didn't hide the fact that he believed the color of his skin had everything to do with the vote going the other way. Roche was white. Many neutral observers agreed with Scott. One newspaper cartoon depicted media voters of the award going to the polls dressed in Ku Klux Klan outfits.

Throughout their careers, Scott and Charlie Davis attempted to match each other point for point and word for word on the court. But they rarely guarded each other.

"Both coaches were too smart for that," Davis said. "I couldn't guard him. He was too big and too quick. He would have eaten me alive. And I would have had him in foul trouble real quick if he had tried to guard me."

Yet on those few occasions when fate dictated that they ended up on each other, they loved it. One time Scott was mouthing off to Davis at Memorial Coliseum in Winston-Salem.

"What you tryin' to do? You can't guard me. Come on, Charlie. Bring it on," Scott taunted.

"This is my place," Davis responded. "You're not winning here, sucker."

He didn't. Not his senior season anyway. Davis and Wake Forest, despite being the inferior team, beat North Carolina both times they met during Scott's senior season. It wasn't Scott's fault, but Davis can claim the victories in their ongoing verbal warfare even today. That hurts Scott, who was a trash talker before it was fashionable to be one.

"He would be talkin' trash while he was smokin' you," Davis said. "He would just wear you out with that trash talk."

That wasn't all he would use to wear out opposing players.

"A lot of people talk about Scotty, but the only thing he ever wanted to do was win," Davis said. "He's been that way since I first knew him. He didn't care if he got forty points or fourteen. I can honestly say that. If I was picking a team, and I wanted to win, Scotty was the first dude I would pick every time. He would do everything possible to win. He might piss you off sometimes. He might be arrogant and run his mouth too much sometimes. But if you wanted a dude on your team who was going to do everything he could to help you win, he was the dude."

But he wasn't the first African American player to win ACC Player of the Year honors. That went to Davis a year after Scott's career ended. That year, Davis averaged 26.5 points for a Wake team that finished 16–10. It was one more thing Davis could use to needle his friend from the old neighborhood forever more.

Davis had come a long way from when Billy Packer first discovered him in New York. Legend has it that Packer later put the skinny kid on a bananas-and-beer diet to put weight on him, but Packer denies it.

"That's legend. I didn't do that. I wouldn't be smart enough for that," Packer said. "You could try anything with Charlie as far as food. He never has been a big eater. To this day, he doesn't have any damn weight on him. But he was so wiry as a player that it was a big part of what made him great."

Davis, however, insisted: "The bananas-and-beer diet was Packer's idea. He wanted me to put some weight on, and I got up to a hundred and sixty-two, too. But you talk about being bloated. I felt fat as a pig. The fact of the matter was that I was a hundred and forty-five-pound basketball player. I couldn't play as well at one sixty-two. I got off that diet real quick."

He got off it quick enough to make history. But he credits Scott with helping him win ACC Player of the Year honors. He saw how Scott rubbed many people the wrong way and tried not to follow in those footsteps.

"Charlie Scott was a great basketball player, but he had a tendency to irritate people. I was more low key," Davis said.

And he could shoot. Davis regularly bombed away—and sank —shots from well beyond where today's 3-point arc is painted.

"The three-point line would have given me, I have no doubt, another five or six points a game. I mean easily," Davis said. "As a matter of fact, I find the three-pointer today in college sports disgusting. It's nothing but a regular jump shot in college."

RECRUITING THE BLACK ATHLETE was by the late 1960s becoming much more sophisticated, much more the focus of the Big Four programs. Playing alongside Davis during his Wake career was another African American named Gil McGregor, who had grown up near Dave Odom's hometown of Goldsboro, North Carolina, in a place called Pikeville.

McGregor and Davis were two among a growing number of African Americans who were beginning to find their ways into predominantly white schools. In 1965, McGregor was one of nineteen blacks to integrate Hoke County High School in North Carolina. Prior to that, he had played only one year of basketball despite obviously having the physical build for the game.

Before transferring to Hoke, he played as a freshman at all-black Upchurch High School in Raeford, North Carolina. The school couldn't afford warmup suits for its ninth-graders, so McGregor, the grandson of a sharecropper who had spent his earliest years helping his grandfather pick cotton, would warm up for games wearing bib overalls over his uniform.

McGregor's proudest moment in high school was followed almost immediately by his saddest. Shortly after scoring 38 points in a losing cause for the basketball team, two white male students stopped him in the hallway at the school.

"We're so glad you decided to transfer here. We're very happy to have you here at our school," the students told him.

McGregor thanked them.

He thought, "I'm making a difference here. We're building a bridge of race relations here because of my presence."

Then McGregor turned the corner, and a black co-ed walked past him going the other way. The two white males could no longer see him, but they saw the girl coming and McGregor remained close enough to hear them snort, "Here comes the nigger."

Years later, McGregor still remembered the incident with distaste.

"It made me at that moment feel very low," McGregor said. "I realized that they called her a nigger in a very negative way, but they dealt with me differently only because I was a basketball player who helped their school win games. I guess it was at that moment that I started to reevaluate why I was there and what it meant to be there. I started becoming a little more cynical about the relationships I had there."

When it came time to choose a college, all of the Big Four schools came calling. Duke backed off after recruiting another big man, Randy Denton, but Wake Forest, North Carolina, and North Carolina State all remained interested.

McGregor visited Norm Sloan at State. But as he was sitting in Sloan's office, the coach took a call from his wife that concerned a planned cookout at Sloan's house that night for McGregor and some other recruits.

"He talked to his wife about the arrangements, and it came up that no one had bought the charcoal," McGregor said.

Sloan lost his temper.

"He became a little agitated at that situation," McGregor said. "When I sat across his desk and saw what was happening, I knew he was too volatile to play for. To be quite honest, I made my decision not to go to N.C. State based on that conversation about charcoal."

He made his decision not to attend Carolina based on a conversation he had with Charlie Scott. McGregor was supposed to make his official visit to Chapel Hill the same weekend he had a prom date, so he called the Carolina coaches to tell them he intended to arrive on campus Saturday instead of Friday as originally planned. A couple of days later, the phone rang. It was Charlie Scott, who was playing for Carolina at the time.

"You've got to quit jerking our coaches around," Scott told him. "They've shown strong interest in you. If you don't want to come to Carolina, you should just stop wasting their time."

Again, the sensitive McGregor was offended. He called Coach Dean Smith and canceled his visit to the school altogether. McGregor just didn't feel he could play with Scott after their conversation ended with heated words. But when Smith asked McGregor why he was canceling, McGregor didn't tell him the truth.

"There had been a student at Carolina who had jumped off a balcony or something and committed suicide, and I told him that any school that could put that kind of academic pressure on you, I didn't think I could handle it. I didn't think I should come," McGregor said.

"But Dean Smith is a very wise man. The last thing he said to me was, 'One day, will you tell me the real reason why you're not going to come to Carolina?' "

Wake Forest remained a front-runner because of Billy Packer,

Bones McKinney, and Norwood Todmann. McKinney had run into McGregor in the hallways at Upchurch High School back in 1964 and told the gangly young freshman then that someday he should consider attending Wake Forest. McKinney even went so far as to check McGregor's grades. By the time he was ready for college, Bones was no longer the Wake coach, but Packer was one of Jack McCloskey's assistants, and McGregor was impressed with the way Packer brought his whole family with him on recruiting visits. He also took a liking to Todmann, the first black in the Wake program.

But while Todmann and Davis were street kids from New York City, McGregor represented the new breed of the Big Four black recruits. He was a country kid from Carolina. Prior to the mid- to late-1960s, their only options if they wanted to play college ball were to head north or play in some lesser program in the South, like Winston-Salem State or Guilford College or High Point College. McGregor grew up watching High Point and Western Carolina and Catabwa College.

"They had the black players that you saw on TV, not the ACC," McGregor said. "So I was thinking about going to a Carolinas Conference school, so I could be seen on TV."

He ended up at Wake Forest, and became a decent player. When McGregor was a freshman at Wake, a crowd of about seven thousand turned out for the freshman game against Artis Gilmore (who actually thought about transferring to Wake) and Gardner-Webb. About five thousand of them went home before the varsity game after watching Gilmore lead Gardner-Webb to a 2-point victory.

One summer, Gilmore hung out with McGregor in Winston-Salem. They worked in the mornings together in a program called Experiment on Self-Reliance, which was designed to help kids in low-income neighborhoods begin to fend for themselves in a structured society. In the afternoons they would play pickup ball together and talk of someday becoming teammates.

Gardner-Webb was at the time a two-year junior college, but was planning on becoming a four-year institution. The school didn't want to lose its prize basketball recruit in the middle of this process.

Coming out of high school in Alabama, Gilmore could not make the 800 required SAT score to get into an ACC school. But if he had a two-year diploma from a junior college, the 800 rule could be waived. Packer knew about this and he set his sights on getting Gilmore.

Packer went to Gardner-Webb to see Gilmore play and found

his path to the locker room blocked afterward by a fiesty little man who did not identify himself.

"You're not welcome here. You're not going into that locker room," the man told Packer, who was stunned.

"Listen, I'm going in and you're not going to stop me. If you don't get out of my way, I'm going to knock the shit out of you," Packer said.

Packer didn't know it at the time, but he was talking to the president of Gardner-Webb College. The next day, the president called Dr. Tribble, his counterpart at Wake Forest.

"He said you were completely out of line, Billy," Tribble said.

"I was. I was going to slap the shit out of him. But I didn't know he was the president. He didn't identify himself."

"Tell me something, Billy. The Gardner-Webb president said that Artis Gilmore has no academic ability whatsoever to do the work at Wake Forest. Why are we recruiting him?"

"With him," Packer responded, "we will win the national championship. If we bring Artis Gilmore into this program to join this other group of guys, we will win it all."

Tribble was not impressed.

"Billy, he can't do the work academically," Tribble repeated.

"Look, the first year he has his [two-year] degree [from Gardner-Webb]. So he'll be eligible to take classes. He can't become ineligible the first year. By the second year, we can have him in enough courses where we can get two years out of him. After that, he'll be playing in the pros anyway," Packer said.

Tribble frowned at the thought.

"Dr. Tribble, who is the most famous person to ever come out of Wake Forest?" Packer asked.

"I don't know what you mean," Tribble answered.

"Who is the most famous Wake Forest person? How about if I say Arnold Palmer? He never got a degree. And he's the guy we brag about all the time," Packer said. "How can we fault Gilmore? He'll do a great job for us. And we'll do a hell of a job for him."

Packer's argument won Tribble over for the time being. He went back to recruiting Gilmore.

But in January of that year, the ACC voted to require all incoming recruits—whether they owned a two-year junior-college degree or not—to score a minimum of 800 on the college boards. Packer didn't even find out about the rule change until two months later.

"Why are you messing around with Gilmore?" Bucky Waters

(then Duke's coach) asked Packer. "You can't get him. He doesn't have an eight hundred and he can't get one."

"You know, Bucky, you're new to the damn league. You've got to understand that a junior-college graduate doesn't have to have the eight hundred," an indignant Packer replied.

"No, Billy. They changed the rule back in January," Waters said.

Packer got on the phone to his boss, Jack McCloskey. At first McCloskey said he was sure there was no such rule change made. But after Packer insisted he double-check, McCloskey came back on the line and told Packer to come back home. The rule had been changed, and there was no way now to land Gilmore.

Packer was fuming. He was sure North Carolina was to blame for the rule change. If they couldn't get Gilmore, they didn't want any school in the ACC having him. But when he arrived back in Winston-Salem, he learned a disturbing fact. The vote for the rule change had been tied at 4–4 when Dr. Jack Sawyer, a Wake Forest professor, cast the deciding vote that killed the school's chance of getting Gilmore.

The 7-2 center went on to transfer to Jacksonville, where he proceeded to lead that team to the Final Four. Then he played seventeen seasons as a professional in the ABA and NBA.

"We could have been contenders for the national championship, too," McGregor said. "We were so close."

But even then, playing for a big name school was no easy task. Black players were constantly fighting racism at the schools in the South.

The worst place to play in the ACC for a young black man, in Davis's opinion, was Blacksburg, Virginia, home of Virginia Tech. In the visiting locker room, there was a shower stall marked "Whites Only."

"I wanted no part of Virginia Tech after I played against them there my freshman year," Davis said. "I said, 'Get me out of here, please.'

"I remember going up in the stands there. I always explain to people that racism isn't necessarily what you say or do. It's really a gut feeling, and I think black people have this extra sense. It's a gut feeling you have that you are in the wrong place. That's the feeling I had at Virginia Tech."

It didn't help that Davis thought he saw a woman in the stands wearing a "KKK" pin.

While Blacksburg may have been the worst, Clemson wasn't far behind.

"Clemson was just obvious. They would play Dixie and wave Confederate flags," Davis said. "But you realized where you were. You were in the environment of Frank Howard."

Howard, the legendary Clemson football coach for whom the school's football stadium is named, was not very fond of black folks and didn't care who knew it. The first time Davis remembered going there, Howard made sure the skinny black kid was within earshot when he bellowed to Doc Martin, the Wake Forest trainer: "Why'd you bring these niggers into my building?"

Other schools would throw chocolate candy bars or hot coins on to the floor. They would shout vulgar insults and laugh derisively every time a balck player got called for a foul. As time went on, the young black men learned a few basic survival techniques they had not learned in Harlem: ignore the insults and play, and don't stop to eat at a local restaurant on your way out of town.

"We always ate box lunches on the bus," Davis said. "And that was probably pretty wise."

Davis left Wake Forest without a degree in 1971 to pursue what became a brief career in the NBA. It took him eighteen years to gather the courage to return to school and make up the eighteen hours he needed to get his undergraduate diploma, which he finally received in 1990. Then he went on to earn a master's degree. By the mid-1990s, Davis was running a successful program at Wake Forest geared toward preparing student-athletes for life after sports. He encountered his own personal struggles before moving back to Winston-Salem.

"I've got the story to tell," Davis said in 1998. "I tell our athletes all the time, 'Hey, you're no bigger than me. I don't care how big you think you are; you're no bigger than I was. The biggest mistake I made was not getting that piece of paper [in 1971]. So I tell them, 'Let's go ahead and get that done and prepare you to get a job in the real world.' We do a whole litany of things to prepare them for that."

Norwood Todmann, Davis's boyhood friend, chose a different path and ended up getting mixed up with drugs. When Davis and Billy Packer last heard of his whereabouts in the mid-1990s, Todmann was homeless and still battling a drug addiction. It was all about receiving opportunities—and then either doing something with them, or throwing them away.

9

DEAN EMERGES

WHEN BILLY PACKER RETURNED from his first extensive recruiting trip as a Wake Forest assistant coach, Bones McKinney was no longer his boss. The pressure of trying to maintain his image as a Baptist minister while living the life of a high-profile basketball coach had taken a heavy toll, physically and mentally.

Drug and alcohol abuse had taken a toll, too. McKinney needed help. The university asked him to step down as coach and get it. It was all done quietly so the popular coach would not be embarrassed in front of his adoring public.

"I never got to work for him. He had to step down," Packer said grimly years later.

Packer was torn. He knew there had been signs of McKinney's instability, but then again, the craziness and zany antics that were so much a part of his life were part of Bones's universal charm. He remembered one time when he played at Wake and the Demon Deacons traveled to Clemson for a road game. Harvey Gantt, who would later become mayor of Charlotte, was preparing to register as Clemson's first black student the day the second semester opened. That also happened to be the same day Wake arrived in town for their game against the Tigers.

As the Wake bus approached the outskirts of Clemson, McKinney stood up and addressed his players.

"I'll tell you one thing: there's going to be trouble," he said.

Then he turned to his assistant coach Jackie Murdock, the former player who soon would replace him as head coach, and added:

158

"We're staying at the Clemson House. You go in by yourself and get everybody's room keys, and then come back on the bus. Then everybody can get their room key, and I want y'all to go immediately to your rooms around the side entrance. Then stay in your rooms until I call for you."

The players nodded. They were beginning to get a little nervous, especially when the bus drew closer to their hotel. Suddenly, the streets were lined with armed national guardsmen.

"Oh shit," thought Packer and his teammates. "Coach is not kidding here. This is serious. Somebody's going to get shot here."

They pulled up to the Clemson House, and Murdock bounded out silently—and alone—as planned. The rest of the team stayed put.

Except for Bones.

The next thing the players knew, McKinney was out of the bus and standing on top of the vehicle, shouting at the national guardsmen.

"What do we have here, a state police convention?" McKinney yelled. "Yep, that's what it looks like, a state police convention. Christ, you could probably rob any bank you wanted in this state right about now because all of you guys are here!"

His players finally pulled McKinney off the bus and calmed him down, telling the guardsmen: "Just forget him. He's crazy."

McKinney used to go a little crazy in Clemson because he always figured the officials were screwing him. They usually were. Back then, Clemson was so bad in basketball that the officials had to attempt to slant the game a little in the home team's favor just to make it mildly interesting. What really drove McKinney nuts, though, was Frank Howard and his bigoted attitude.

Even before the days of Howard sitting behind the visiting team's bench and yelling racial slurs at young black players, Howard haunted McKinney. He knew McKinney's public image as a Baptist minister who happened to be a coach was a total farce. He knew McKinney drank. And he loved to let McKinney know that he knew.

Howard used to make it a point to try and greet McKinney as soon as the Wake coach arrived in the Clemson gym.

"Hey Bonesy, did you bring your Bible?" Howard usually asked.

During the games, Howard would sit right behind McKinney and taunt him until McKinney exploded. But as soon as McKinney stood up, three or four of Howard's football players who were sitting with him would push Bones back down by his shoulders. Nothing infuriated McKinney more.

"Bones hated Frank Howard," Packer said. "Frank would mock the hell out of him. Bones would cuss him out. It used to be brutal."

But as crazy and out of control as McKinney was by Packer's senior year, Packer still respected the coach. About a year after Packer was finished playing for Wake, he received a phone call from a reporter for the student newspaper, the *Old Gold and Black.*

"We're going to do a story that exposes Bones McKinney. He's drinking heavily and he's on drugs," the reporter told Packer.

"You've got to be kidding," Packer said. "There's no way."

"Those are the facts, and we're printing them. We wanted to see if you'd have a comment. If you don't, we're still running the story. It will be printed next Monday."

Packer was furious. He went to see Dr. Tribble, Wake's president.

"Do you realize the school newspaper is coming out with this article next Monday? It's ridiculous. Coach drinking and on drugs? Whoever heard of such a thing? Doctor Tribble, you've got to shut that newspaper down."

Tribble called the students who ran the newspaper into his office.

"That article will not be written," he said.

And it wasn't. But roughly eighteen months later, Tribble privately asked McKinney to step down and seek treatment for his addictions. It wasn't until Packer returned from his first Wake recruiting trip that he finally discovered the truth.

"I was defending coach not because of my respect for him, but because I thought it was all a lie. Then it turned out just a year or so later that it was all true," Packer said years later. "He just had to get out of the coaching business and get his health back and get his life back. It was very unfortunate.

"He was not ashamed of it. And I'm not by telling it—because he ultimately overcame it."

Charlie Bryant, who coached with McKinney and ended up leaving Wake Forest partly because he could not convince McKinney to get a grip on his personal life, had a similar reaction to Bones's getting out of college coaching. It helped that McKinney finally admitted to himself—and others—that he just wasn't cut out to be a Baptist minister.

"He finally gave up the ministry, which was creating a great conflict in his mind. In fact, the doctors encouraged that. It helped him. I don't believe he could have come out of this thing without

Dave Odom, the man responsible for rebuilding Wake's basketball program and bringing the Demon Deacons back to the glory days reminiscent of Coach Bones McKinney.

Led by center Tim Duncan *(left)* and guided by head coach Dave Odom, the Demon Deacons captured the 1996 ACC Tournament in Greensboro, North Carolina.

Phil Ford, point guard for the 1977 Tar Heels—who lost in the NCAA championship game to Marquette—calls for Dean Smith's tactical offense: the Four Corners.

North Carolina's Walter Davis hits a sweet jumper against South Florida during the 1977 season.

North Carolina great Sam Perkins, a member of the 1982 championship team.

37

One of the greatest players of all time: Michael Jordan. Yet Bill Guthridge, then an assistant at North Carolina, was the only ACC coach to recruit him as a high school junior.

Some things never change: Michael Jordan hitting a short jumper against Pittsburgh. Jordan's biggest college shot came in the waning moments of the 1982 NCAA championship game against Georgetown, securing Dean Smith's long-awaited first national title.

39

Jimmy V—in his capacity as an ABC commentator—during his "Never Give Up" speech at Reynolds Coliseum in 1993. Coach V passed away just two months later.

40

Two of coach Valvano's successors: *(above)* Les Robinson, who found it impossible to fill Valvano's shoes, and *(left)* Herb Sendek, who is only now beginning to try.

41

Playing against Duke at Cameron Indoor Stadium is hard enough without having to worry about the taunts and jeers of the Cameron Crazies, who sometimes camp out for days in front of the arena before big home games.

42

43

44

The heart and soul of the 1998 Duke basketball team: Steve Wojciechowski.

North Carolina star Antawn Jamison often gave Duke and their Crazies fits on his way to capturing the 1998 National Player of the Year Award.

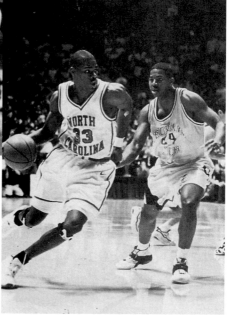

45

March 15, 1997, North Carolina vs. Colorado: Coach Dean Smith earns his 877th victory, breaking the all-time record for coaching victories formerly held by Kentucky legend Adolph Rupp. Surrounding Smith are assistant coaches Phil Ford *(left)* and Bill Guthridge *(right)*. Guthridge would take over for Smith seven months later and lead the Tar Heels to yet another Final Four appearance.

doing that," Bryant said. "I mean, he didn't lose his religion or anything like that—but he had been trying to project this image where he was too much to too many people.

"Bones and I ended up mending our fences and becoming very good friends again."

BY THE LATE 1960s, the Big Four stage Bones left behind was filled with some wonderful African American basketball players. The two Charlies, Wake's Davis and Carolina's Scott, were the best. They staged some scintillating scoring duels, including two games when Davis, a junior, and Scott, a senior, scored a total of 75 and 74 points respectively.

By then Carolina was beginning to replace Duke as the team to beat in the Big Four and the Atlantic Coast Conference. Scott was one of the main reasons for that, but certainly not the only one. The tide really began to turn two years before Scott's arrival, when Dean Smith landed his first real hotshot recruit in Larry Miller. Smith had coached some fine players before Miller—Billy Cunningham, the Kangaroo Kid, being one of them. But Cunningham, a New Yorker, was as much a McGuire find as a Smith recruit. He was yet another product of the Underground Railroad that helped stock McGuire's Carolina teams.

But Miller was different. For one thing, he was heavily recruited by Vic Bubas of Duke in an era when Bubas was accustomed to landing any player he really wanted. Bubas had just taken the '62–'63 Duke team to the school's first Final Four when he began recruiting Miller.

Also, Miller wasn't from New York City or anyplace close to that in terms of size and visibility. He grew up in Catasauqua, Pennsylvania, a town of about five thousand located on the outskirts of Allentown, a rough-and-tumble steel-mill town. Catasauqua was a place that featured as many bars as churches, and many young men growing up around Miller found themselves in reform schools after misguided pranks such as stealing hubcaps off cars or throwing rocks through store windows landed them in hot water with the law.

Miller and his parents decided that basketball was a way to keep him out of trouble. So he worked out every day on an isometrics rack built by his father and practiced running and shooting baskets while wearing both ankle weights and a heavy weighted vest his father had made out of an old hunting jacket. Their goal was to increase Miller's strength and leaping ability. It seemed to make a difference. By the eighth grade, Miller actually was playing with the Allentown Jets of the old Eastern Basketball League. As a senior in high school, Miller averaged 30 points a game, and 30 rebounds. He had by then grown to 6 feet, 3 inches, was a solid 210 pounds, and could jump high enough so that he could position both of his elbows over the rim.

Along with a center from Power Memorial High School in New York named Lew Alcindor, Miller became one of the top two or three college basketball recruits in the country. Michigan and UCLA recruited him. Harvard recruited him, too. Bobby Kennedy and Ted Kennedy, even took the time to write Miller to suggest that he might want to consider attending their alma mater. Other schools wrote to tell him what wonderful things they could do for him and his family. Many coaches visited to make their pitches in person. But no recruiter came after Miller as early or as hard as Bubas, who started the process when Miller was just a sophomore in high school.

"That was kind of unusual back in the sixties," Miller said. "It was usually late in your junior year when the recruiting started. But Vic and his wife came up to visit me in the Poconos when I was in high school, and I liked him very much. Vic and his wife and I became good friends during the recruiting process. We were real tight."

Yet when it came time to pick a school, Miller chose North Carolina instead of Duke. More than 30 years later, he said he still wasn't sure why.

"Duke was *the* program at the time. I think they had seven high school All-Americans that Vic had recruited," Miller said. "It's one of those decisions that you make once in your lifetime. I don't know what made me pick Carolina. I wasn't scared of playing with those guys at Duke, but there was something that turned me the other way."

Part of that something was Dean Smith. A bigger part of it, Miller said upon reflection, probably was the mere aesthetics of the lush, well-manicured Chapel Hill campus.

"I think what made me go to Carolina was that I just fell in love with Chapel Hill. I really did. There's no doubt about it," Miller said. "I think that's what drew me there more than anything."

Once Miller made up his mind, he couldn't bear the thought of telling Bubas. When he received a letter from Bubas in the mail shortly after he signed with Carolina, Miller found that he couldn't bring it upon himself to open it.

"I knew I would cry when I saw it. I'm an emotional type of guy," Miller said.

Miller quickly averaged 20.9 points and 10.3 rebounds as a sophomore during his first year of eligibility, developing a fast reputation for being able to hit clutch shots at the end of ball games. He was deadly with his left-handed jumper and he could leap out of the gym. But before he could become a bona fide star, Miller had to work out a few differences of philosophy with Coach Smith.

Shortly after arriving in Chapel Hill, Smith told Miller that he expected all of his players to go to church. Miller balked.

"Sorry, coach. I won't do it," Miller said.

"What? Why not?" Smith asked.

"I don't believe in the hypocrisy of religion," Miller said. "I grew up as a Catholic, but I have some problems with the Catholic religion. I'm in the process of redefining my religion, whatever it is."

Smith tried to explain that it was his policy as coach to have his players go to the church of their choice, then bring him a bulletin from the service to prove they had attended.

"It's not that I don't believe in God or the Holy Spirit," Miller said. "But at this point in my life, I don't think it's right for me to go to church just to bring you a brochure that shows you I went to church. I just don't think that's the right thing to do."

Again, Smith tried to explain that it was his belief that parents wanted their children to attend church while they were away from their homes, and it was Smith's intention to follow through on those wishes. No player to that point had fought him over it. But Miller wouldn't back down.

"Look, if I was home, my parents wouldn't make me go to church. So I don't think you should, either," Miller said.

Smith finally relented. He had his first star recruit and wasn't about to lose him over a clash of religious beliefs. Besides, he could take his time and help Miller find a religion that best suited the confused young teenager.

Carolina went 16-11 Miller's sophomore year, but reached new heights the following season when Scott arrived. In Miller's eyes, once Charlie Scott suited up, Miller's status as Dean Smith's best recruit ever was over.

"The truth is that Charlie Scott was the best recruit. Let's face it," he said.

Not that it bothered him. Miller and some of his teammates had helped talk Scott out of attending Davidson. Smith never made a big deal of Scott being black. He never told Miller and the others that someone different was about to join the program.

"Charlie was special because he was the first black kid to play at Carolina," Miller said. "But Charles knew we were on his side. He could look at us as friends. . . . We told him, 'You are a part of this program and there is nothing the guys on this team won't do for you. We'll protect you. You are a part of our family.'

"And that is when it became a family at Carolina."

Miller watched as Scott overcame all the racial insults at places like Clemson, South Carolina, Virginia, Virginia Tech, and occasionally even at Duke.

"I don't think Charlie ever got down. I've always told the young black kids I've spoken to that what happened back then was that a special individual came to Carolina," Miller said. "And it had to be that way."

Smith met with Scott during one of the new recruit's first visits to campus. The topic of religion came up in discussion.

"Would you like to go to church with me?" Smith asked.

Scott told him yes. But inside, Scott figured it would just be for show and that Smith probably would take him to an all-black church in some sort of pre-arranged deal. He was more than a little surprised—and impressed—when Smith actually took him to his own church. It showed Scott that he would be treated the same as everyone else if he decided to come to Carolina.

Smith also asked Scott what he wanted to be called. The player told him that his family members called him Charles. Most other folks called him Charlie. Smith began calling him Charles that day and never called him Charlie again.

One day Scott was late to practice. Like anyone else who was late to practice, he was ordered to put on a twenty-five-pound weighted vest and run the steps of Carmichael Auditorium. Usually this drudgery would last for about ten minutes. But Scott kept running the steps for fifteen . . . twenty . . . thirty minutes. Sweat was dripping off him and he was totally exhausted. Finally, he came down to ask Coach Smith how much longer he would have to run the steps.

"Oh, Charles, I'm sorry. I forgot about you. I thought you were out there practicing," Smith said.

"Coach, I'm the only black guy on this team. How could you not notice I wasn't out there?" Scott asked.

Smith just shrugged. He truly hadn't noticed. It was then that Scott thought to himself, "This man just doesn't see color."

□

SMITH'S DETRACTORS in Chapel Hill were seeing red going into the 1966–67 season. He had been in charge five full seasons since McGuire's departure and had little to show for it in the way of top finishes and milestone victories. It was true that he was showing some progress, coming off 15–9 and 16–11 seasons, but his overall record was just 66–47, and in the games that really mattered—against Carolina's Big Four foes—he was just 12–22.

That all began to change in '66–67, and no team paid a steeper price for Carolina's rise than Duke, which began to slide after reaching their third Final Four in four years the previous season. Miller arguably was the reason for all this. He was terrific. In the 1967 ACC Tournament final, he hit 13 of 14 shots en route to 32 points and 11 rebounds in an 82–73 victory over Duke. It gave Smith his first ACC championship.

Had Miller followed Bubas and gone to Duke, the basketball histories of both schools might have been changed forever.

Miller wasn't just an outstanding player. He was a unique, fiery competitor with an unsurpassed will to win. When his parents called from Pennsylvania to say they wanted to come down for the ACC Tournament one year, he told them to forget it.

"Mom, I've got enough pressure on me as it is. It's three days of hell. The ACC Tournament is three days of hell," he told his mother over the phone.

"Listen, you can come to the NCAA Regionals when we get there, but not the ACC Tournament."

Miller's thinking was that if he was at his best, then the Tar Heels would win every time. So much of the pressure he felt was placed upon him by himself.

"It's a hell of a philosophy and it works. But it's tough on your body," he said. "I paid hell for it on the inside. You can't sleep or eat for two or three days during the ACC Tournament. There was so much pressure. People just don't understand. I mean, I had to tell my parents no when they wanted to come down. My stomach couldn't handle it."

It was the beginning of an incredible run for the Tar Heels, who went on to beat Princeton in overtime and Boston College in the NCAA East Regional to make their first Final Four under Smith. They lost to Dayton in the semis and to Houston in the consolation game, but Smith's program clearly had arrived. After six seasons, and for the first time since McGuire's departure, no one wanted to run him out of Chapel Hill.

That same year, Duke became the first school since formation of the ACC in 1953 to accept a bid to the NIT, taking advantage of a rules change by the conference adopted prior to the season. The league still permitted only its tournament champion to represent the conference in the NCAA Tournament, but they at least relaxed their stance on not permitting any other school to participate in a postseason tournament. The ACC tournament runner-up was now allowed to accept an NIT bid if offered. Yet Vic Bubas and his players were well aware that the NIT was not for the ACC champion. Even though the NIT in 1967 still was considered a very prestigious tournament, it was a bittersweet consolation prize. They lost in the first round to a Southern Illinois team led by Walt Frazier that went on to win the NIT title.

With Scott added to the Carolina mix the following season, the Tar Heels followed with two more fine seasons. The 1967–68 team went 28-4, losing only its last two regular-season ACC games. The first, to South Carolina, which pitted Smith against his old boss, Frank McGuire; the second, to Duke in a wild, three-overtime epic at Duke Indoor Stadium. Another one for the ages followed in the ACC Tournament, when Smith won a close rematch against his mentor, beating South Carolina 82–79 in overtime in the ACC semis.

The other semifinal that year was not nearly as thrilling. Norm Sloan, who was beginning to bring the North Carolina State program back to life after a disastrous first season, decided the best chance his team had to beat Duke was to hold the ball. Wolfpack guard Bill Kretzer did so almost the entire first half, with Duke refusing to come out on him and apply defensive pressure. Both teams were booed by the crowd at Charlotte Coliseum, where the tournament was being held for the first time.

Bill Currie, announcing the game on radio, told his audience that the action was "as exciting as artificial insemination."

Afterward, Bubas defended his strategy.

"The truth of the matter is, we couldn't pressure a team of grandmothers," he said.

At halftime, Duke led 4–2. With 2:30 remaining in the game, it was tied at 8. But a missed free throw by Duke's Dave Golden opened the door for State's Dick Bruacher to sink a clinching free throw with three seconds left. State won 12–10. Their next opponent was Carolina in the ACC championship game.

State elected not to hold the ball again against Carolina. As a result, Carolina blasted them 87–50 for the widest margin of victory in a championship game in ACC history.

It wasn't until after this game that Miller finally opened the letter Bubas had sent him shortly after Miller committed to Carolina four years earlier.

In it, Bubas expressed regret that he wouldn't be able to coach Miller as a collegian, but added that he wished him the best of luck. He wrote, "Look, we love you and we wish you the best always."

As he suspected he would, Miller cried when he at last read the letter. Bubas came over after Miller's final ACC game and told him, "You're the greatest. Congratulations. Now keep this thing going in the NCAAs."

Miller still had tears in his eyes. He told Bubas about the letter.

"Coach, I couldn't open it until now," Miller said. "I'm glad I waited."

Carolina's second straight ACC title set up another trip to the Final Four for Smith and Miller. Playing at Reynolds Coliseum in the NCAA East Regional, the Tar Heels beat St. Bonaventure and then Davidson to secure a second straight Final Four berth.

Smith was finally coming into his own as a coach. He had proven he could beat McGuire's ghost. He had proven he could beat the best recruiters in the nation, snatching Miller from Bubas at Duke and Scott from Lefty Driesell at Davidson. Now all he had to do was prove he could win the big one.

But after beating Ohio State 80–66 in the NCAA semis, Smith made a colossal coaching mistake even before his team took the floor for the title game. He permitted his team to watch part of UCLA's 101–69 rout of Houston in the other semifinal. The UCLA-Houston game was a rematch of their nationally televised January game, where Houston and Elvin Hayes defeated John Wooden and his UCLA Bruins. That game probably did more for college basketball on a national level than any other game. Everyone wanted to watch the rematch. Smith later wished he hadn't let his team watch it at all. It was something he would never again allow his Final Four teams to do.

Even Smith left the Los Angeles Sports Arena that evening somewhat awed by the Bruins and their terrific center, Lew Alcindor. His players didn't have a chance. UCLA thrashed them 78–55 in what was the largest margin of victory in an NCAA title game.

The next season, Miller was gone. But Scott was back for his junior season and so was Eddie Fogler and the rest of Smith's best recruiting class—Rusty Clark, Joe Brown, Bill Bunting, Dick Grubar, and Gerald Tuttle.

This group, playing as freshmen in an intrasquad scrimmage in the fall of 1965, defeated a varsity squad that included Miller. Smith never held the freshmen-varsity scrimmage again—but by the time those freshmen were seniors, Smith knew he had something special.

So did Scott.

Scott took over the ACC championship game against Duke, scoring 28 of his 40 points in the second half to rally Carolina from an 11-point deficit to an 85–74 victory. Bubas tried everything to stop him, but couldn't find a way.

At one point, Bubas looked at the Carolina bench and thought he saw defeat written on their faces. Then he saw Scott, yelling to his teammates: "Give the ball to me! I'll win the game for us!"

Smith assured reporters later: "It was one of the great individual displays you've ever seen."

Playing in the NCAA East Regional again shortly thereafter, Scott and Carolina once again ran into Lefty Driesell and Davidson. The contest was held at Maryland's Cole Field House, and Driesell already knew that he would be leaving Davidson after the season to coach at Maryland. He did not want to go out at Davidson—and into the ACC—a loser to Smith and the Tar Heels again.

"I'd rather die than lose to North Carolina again," Driesell told reporters.

Scott almost killed him single-handedly. His basket with a minute, thirty seconds left in the game tied the score at 85. Then he hit the game-winning shot with two seconds left after Tuttle got the ball back for the Heels by taking a charge from Davidson's Jerry Kroll. Scott scored 32 points and secured Carolina a spot in the Final Four for the third straight year.

In the semifinal game against Purdue, Scott continued his scoring onslaught. But his 35 points weren't enough to overcome a well-balanced attack by Herm Gilliam and the Boilermakers. The Tar Heels lost badly, 92–65, and then got drubbed by Drake in the consolation game, 104–84.

Despite the twin season-ending defeats, Smith was feeling special. Following the second Final Four visit in 1968, appreciative Carolina boosters had rewarded him with a 1968 Cadillac convertible. It was reminiscent of the automobile N.C. State fans had given Everett Case as a reward for his coaching efforts a decade earlier. It was also symbolic because it confirmed that Smith was in the Big Four arena for the long haul. He wasn't going anywhere for a long, long time. All he had to do to put a cap on his skyrocketing career was win the Big One.

While Carolina basked in the glory of three straight trips to the Final Four, which was unprecedented for a Big Four and ACC school, Duke prepared to enter a dark age without the coach who defined their program. After losing out to Smith in intense recruiting battles for Miller and Clark and others, Bubas was becoming disenchanted with the whole recruiting process he earlier helped elevate. He just didn't have the energy to keep up the pace he set ten years earlier. He no longer had the burning desire to watch one more game film or scout one more kid to make certain he was giving himself and his beloved school the best chance to win a championship. A four-game losing streak to Michigan, Virginia, East Tennessee, and Wake Forest during the early part of 1968–69 season was the longest of Bubas's career at Duke.

Following the loss to East Tennessee, a somber Bubas addressed his players in the locker room.

"We have disgraced ourselves by the way we played. There will have to be some drastic changes made," he said.

On the afternoon of a December game at Virginia, Bubas called his assistant coaches, Chuck Daly and Hubie Brown, into a meeting.

"I'm going to retire at the end of the season," he told them bluntly. He wanted to move on to new challenges and he wanted to spend more time with his family. And he thought his coaching methods had started to slip.

Bubas informed his players and the general public of his intention to call it quits before a home game against Wake Forest in mid-February. The team responded with a rousing 122–93 victory.

His last game at home, fittingly, was against Carolina. For no apparent reason, Bubas decided to start a senior named Steve Vandenberg who was only averaging 8.3 points for the season. Vandenberg responded with 33 points on Senior Day to make Bubas look like a genius in his last game as Duke head coach. Duke pulled off an 87–81 upset.

"This one is precious to me because it's my last game in Duke Indoor Stadium. I'll always cherish it," Bubas said.

Years later, Smith credited Bubas in Ron Morris's book, *ACC Basketball: An Illustrated History,* for teaching all the coaches in the ACC the fine points of recruiting.

"Vic taught us how to recruit," Smith said. "We had been starting on prospects in the fall of their senior year, like almost everybody else. But Vic was working on them in their junior year. For a while all of us were trying to catch up with him."

By 1969, Smith had caught up in a big way. The Dean before Dean was done. The real Dean was just getting started.

NORTH CAROLINA's incredible and unprecedented run of three straight trips to the Final Four ended in 1969–70, Charlie Scott's senior year. That was the season marked by his memorable scoring duels with Charlie Davis. It was also the year Frank McGuire returned to center stage in the ACC. Though Scott averaged 27.1 points and 8.6 rebounds, McGuire's latest star at South Carolina, junior guard John Roche, won ACC Player of the Year honors for the second straight year. The Gamecocks finished a remarkable 14-0 regular season in the league. Only two other teams had finished 14-0 in league play—Bubas's Duke team in 1963, which went on to play in the Final Four, and McGuire's Miracle team at Carolina in 1957, which went on to win it all.

But South Carolina didn't get to play anywhere in the postseason in 1970. North Carolina State, the Big Four team that had been playing largely in the shadows cast by Duke and Carolina much of the previous decade, prevented South Carolina from advancing. N.C. State coach Norm Sloan had been hired because of his past ties to glory under Everett Case. But Sloan also brought some baggage. After playing on Case's first two teams at State, and helping the Wolfpack to a combined record of 55-8 and two Southern Conference championships, Sloan had angered Case by quitting the team midway through the 1949 season to play football instead. Sloan later explained his decision by pointing out that back then, if you wanted to get into coaching, you often had to coach football as well as basketball. He was recently married at the time and was about to become a father. He felt like he had to do it to best set himself up for the future.

The entire incident would prove to be indicative of Sloan's nature. He didn't always do what other folks thought he should, and he didn't really care who he happened to offend.

Sloan's return to Raleigh came one week after the death of Everett Case and the departure of Press Maravich to Louisiana State. Sloan soon discovered his predecessors had left the cupboard bare. The situation immediately worsened when Eddie Biedenbach, the lone returning starter from the previous season, suffered a back injury that would keep him out Sloan's entire first season. Even though Biedenbach was pictured next to a smiling Sloan on the cover of State's 1966–67 media guide, Biedenbach was unable to play a single minute all season. State finished with a 7–19 record as a result.

"When Norm first came here, the recruiting season was over. There was nothing left," said Charlie Bryant, a holdover from the Case and Maravich staffs who then served as an assistant coach to Sloan.

Realizing this, Sloan became frantic. He called Bryant into his office, which was actually an extension of his own in the bowels of Reynolds Coliseum.

"I know it's late. I know all the top recruits have signed with somebody. But is there anybody we can get? Anybody at all?" Sloan asked Bryant.

"Well, there's a young man at Pfieffer College who would give anything to come to N.C. State," Bryant answered. "I made a bad recruiting mistake once when I failed to take Rick Barry because I thought he was too thin. This kid is like Rick Barry. This kid also is too thin, but he's talented. His name is Vann Williford."

"Let's see what we can do," Sloan added.

Bryant phoned a Wolfpack alumnus who lived in Fayetteville and was close to the Williford family.

"You think Vann would be interested in coming to N.C. State instead of Pfieffer?" Bryant asked.

"I'm sure he would be. Let me call him and get back to you after he thinks it over," the alum said.

It took less than thirty minutes for the return phone call.

"You just made Vann the happiest boy in Fayetteville. He would love to come and play for State," the alum reported.

When they took their first look at Williford on the court, both Sloan and Bryant had doubts about his ability.

"When Vann came in his freshman year, well, he was just horrible," Bryant said. "During games, he would be looking around the crowd to see if his high-school friends were there. We were bad as a team and he wasn't any help at all."

After that season, Sloan called Williford into his office and read him "the riot act."

"You know, you could be a good basketball player if you worked at it. But you really have to work because there are so many areas of the game where you need to get better. I expect you to work hard at it, harder than you've ever worked at anything in your life," Sloan said.

Sloan then added: "If I ever catch you without a basketball in your hands, you're going to regret it."

Sloan, of course, was speaking figuratively, but Williford didn't care. Everywhere Williford went on campus, he took a basketball with him.

By Williford's senior season, the Wolfpack was respectable again, tying North Carolina for second place behind unbeaten South Carolina in the regular season. Then the Wolfpack pulled off a huge upset of South Carolina in the ACC Tournament championship game. Williford was named tournament MVP. As a senior, Williford averaged 23.7 points and 10.0 rebounds while shooting 50 percent from the field and 80 percent from the free-throw line. The Wolfpack lost in the first round of the subsequent NCAA tournament, but finished 23-7 and was heading for a promising future.

10

DT AND DESTINY

ONCE THE RACE BARRIER had been broken in the ACC and blacks started getting into the Big Four schools, the recruiting wars for the top minority talent in the state of North Carolina started heating up. The possibility of altering the academic requirements for students to get into all ACC schools was under close scrutiny in the early 1970s, as two schools in particular, Clemson and South Carolina, continued to vigorously oppose the 800 rule. Both threatened to leave the conference, arguing they should be able to recruit student-athletes based on the less-stringent NCAA guidelines that required only a projected 1.6 grade-point average for admission.

In early March 1971, the ACC made a small concession in an attempt to please the two schools. The conference voted to continue requiring the 800 SAT score and a 1.6 grade-point average, but added a provision for students who scored between 700 and 799 on the SAT. Those students could be admitted if they had a projected GPA of 1.75.

That wasn't enough for South Carolina. Before the month was out, the Gamecocks announced they were withdrawing from the league. Clemson decided to hold off on its decision. A year later, the ACC—faced with a lawsuit by two prospective Clemson soccer recruits—finally agreed to drop the 800 requirement altogether.

At first the loss of South Carolina appeared to be very damaging to the ACC's basketball reputation. In the league's first eighteen years, only Maryland in 1958 and South Carolina in 1971 had dented the Big Four's domination of the league by winning the ACC Tournament. In '71 star player John Roche and the Gamecocks had gained a measure of revenge for their failure to win the tournament the previous year by upsetting North Carolina 52–51 when Kevin Joyce, a guard measuring 6 feet, 3 inches, somehow managed to outjump 6-10 Tar Heel center Lee Dedmon with six seconds remaining in the championship game. Joyce tapped the ball to teammate Tom Owens, who laid it in for the game-winner.

Then, only a year later, South Carolina was out of the league.

But life went on. The Big Four schools continued to dominate, and they continued to scrap with each other over talent.

One player who drew interest from all the schools was young Robert McAdoo, an African American from Greensboro with an unorthodox jump shot and an interesting background. McAdoo was a member of his high-school marching band and he was also a terrific high jumper in track.

Billy Packer used to invite McAdoo over to Wake Forest on weekends to play basketball with some of the Demon Deacon players. Packer also kept an eye on McAdoo's budding track career. One day, he noted that the state AAU meet was being held at the Wake facility. At the same time, a young man by the name of Bobby Jones was being recruited by the Big Four schools to play basketball. The Charlotte native was also a fine high jumper, and even though it already looked like Jones was headed to North Carolina to play basketball, Packer made plans to talk with him when Jones was in Winston-Salem for the meet.

First, though, Packer met with McAdoo.

"Robert, are you going to get in the meet?" he asked.

"I don't know," McAdoo replied.

"I'll take you over Saturday morning. I think you should," Packer said.

McAdoo shrugged his shoulders and nodded.

On the day of the meet, Jones arrived in a state-of-the-art sweatsuit and real honest-to-goodness track shoes. Packer found McAdoo sitting underneath a tree near the track, dressed in blue jeans, an old jacket, and a pair of well-worn high-top sneakers.

"When are you going to go down and jump?" Packer asked.

"Well, they're starting off with the other guys. I'm going to go down when the bar gets to six-five," McAdoo replied.

Sure enough, McAdoo waited until the bar reached 6 feet, 5 inches. Then he peeled off his jacket and easily cleared that height, jumping in his T-shirt and jeans. Jones cleared the height easily as well. That started a battle that lasted until they both cleared 6-10¾ to break the national AAU high-jump record. By then McAdoo had finally shed his jeans to reveal a pair of shorts underneath.

Because of his performance, McAdoo qualified for the national AAU meet in Los Angeles. He was chosen to go over Jones because he had fewer misses.

But on the morning McAdoo was supposed to leave to go to Knoxville to train for the national meet, Packer's phone rang. It was McAdoo.

"Hey, can I come over and play basketball today?" he asked.

"Aren't you supposed to go to Knoxville today to train for the AAU nationals?" Packer asked.

"I'm not going to go," McAdoo said.

"What? Robert, what are you talking about? You have the highest jump in the country. You have to go. Why don't you want to?" Packer said.

"They told me I have to pay for my own bus ticket to get to Knoxville. So I'm not going."

"I'll get you a ticket. You should go."

McAdoo was adamant.

"That's not right. I won. They should get me a bus ticket."

So McAdoo didn't go. Jones replaced him and went on to win the AAU national high-jump title.

Less than three years later, McAdoo (who had transferred from Vincennes Junior College in Indiana) and Jones were teammates on a North Carolina squad that went 26-5, won the ACC regular-season and tournament championships, and advanced to the Final Four before losing to Florida State in the semifinals. The Tar Heels were heavily favored, but were hurt by the benching of starting forward Bill Chamberlain by Coach Dean Smith. Smith made Chamberlain sit out the first seven minutes of the game because Chamberlain had been seven minutes late to the pregame meal. The Heels quickly fell behind and never recovered. They lost 79–75.

"That was the longest night I've ever had in coaching," Smith told reporters afterward.

It turned out to be McAdoo's one and only season at Carolina. After averaging 19.5 points and 10.1 rebounds that season, Smith urged him to turn professional.

McAdoo took Smith's advice and left school to begin a long and lucrative NBA career.

□

As outstanding a player as McAdoo and Davis and Scott had been, the conference was about to see a player who would transform college basketball in the ACC. And he was going to do it in Raleigh, not Chapel Hill.

The player's name: David Thompson.

North Carolina State had begun the road back to respectability long before Thompson's arrival in 1972. Even though the Wolfpack had finished with a 13-14 record in 1970–71, they knew good things were on the horizon. Two years earlier, Sloan and assistant coach Charlie Bryant were stunned one afternoon when a very tall man walked into the State basketball offices at Reynolds Coliseum.

"Are you interested perhaps in a seven-foot basketball player?" the man asked.

"I have a nephew up in the mountains who is a sophomore. His name is Tommy Burleson," the man said, explaining that he was a graduate student at State and that he might be able to help convince Burleson to come there.

"My nephew is supposed to come down with his high-school team to see a Carolina football game. If you would like, I think I can get him to come over here and visit with you guys."

Sloan and Bryant looked at each other. Their jaws dropped. Could this be true? Could a 7-footer be about to drop in their laps?

"Well, sure," they answered in unison. "Bring your nephew over if you can. We'd like to meet him."

So the next weekend, while the rest of his high-school team went to Chapel Hill to watch the Tar Heels play football, Tom Burleson visited Sloan and Bryant in Raleigh. They immediately hit it off.

"After that, Norm and I spent the next two years driving to Newland, North Carolina," Bryant said. "To this day I believe I could drive up there blindfolded—because I don't believe we missed two or three games over the next couple years."

It seemed Burleson was a lock to come to State, but by his senior year in high school the 7-footer was no longer a well-kept secret. It's hard to keep a potential recruit under wraps when he's in the process of growing to 7 feet, 4 inches tall.

"Everybody kept telling us he would come to State, but neither he nor his family would tell us," Bryant said. "Tommy's reasoning was that he had a lot of friends who were Carolina or Duke people, and he didn't want to hurt their feelings. He was a typical wonderful mountain person.

"Well, when we got Tommy, everything began to fall into place. Then we started recruiting David."

So did everyone else.

David Thompson was a basketball legend in the state of North Carolina before he even played his first collegiate game. All the schools were after him. Sloan first learned about Thompson when he was just a sophomore in high school at Shelby Crest High, a small North Carolina school near Boiling Springs in western North Carolina. Thompson grew up in a cinder-block home and often spent as many as six hours a day playing basketball. It wasn't unusual to see Thompson shooting baskets late at night on a makeshift court at the family home, illuminated only by the burning headlights of his father's car. Boiling Springs was also home to Gardner-Webb College, and by the tenth grade, Thompson was playing and excelling in pickup games against the likes of Artis Gilmore.

Charlie Bryant hit the recruiting trail once again, watching Thompson play and taking him to dinner often during Thompson's sophomore and junior years in high school. Then Bryant quit his job and moved to Gastonia, which was only thirty miles from Shelby. He took a job with First Union bank, but essentially spent most of his spare time helping Sloan recruit Thompson.

"I went to most of his games," Bryant said. "I got to know him and I got to know his coach. Every time we saw some coach from another school come in, we would call and get Norm or Eddie Biedenbach [then one of Sloan's assistants] to come down and take David out to dinner again. Back in those days you could do that. It was legal. So we were there all the time."

Everything that went on during the recruitment of Thompson *wasn't* legal, and despite all the time and effort put in by the State folks, he wasn't a lock to head to Raleigh until some things sorted themselves out. Thompson was a quiet, introspective sort who didn't necessarily enjoy all the attention he was getting. He was impressed that Duke and North Carolina and North Carolina State were coming after him so hard, but he was seriously considering attending Gardner-Webb. It was by then a four-year institution that offered black students a good education.

"I had mixed emotions," Thompson admitted even years later. "I knew Coach [Eddie] Holbrook from back when I was in the eighth grade. I had gone to summer camps there. I knew the players. And of course, it was home to me. As one of eleven kids and not having traveled a lot, I was pretty much a homebody. That was one of the things I was most concerned about—leaving home. I had never really been very far from home at all."

Thompson eventually received more than a hundred letters

from colleges who wanted him to come and visit. He came to realize that as comfortable as he would have been playing at Gardner-Webb, he probably would be better off in the long run going to a larger Division I school.

"As I got older, I guess more people heard about me," he said. "By my senior year in high school I was one of the top players in the country. A lot of the schools came in real late—and by then, my mind was made up. Regardless of who called, UCLA or whatever, my mind was made up to play in the ACC.

"When it came right down to it, I always was committed to the ACC. My thinking was that ACC basketball is the best. That was where my heart was."

Thompson had narrowed his choices down to three of the Big Four schools—North Carolina State, North Carolina, and Duke.

Carolina was the early frontrunner, but Thompson soon tired of hearing everyone talk about him like he was the next Charlie Scott. He didn't want to be the next Charlie Scott. He wanted to be the one and only David Thompson. Bryant said he remembered the time a Carolina player promised to come and see Thompson, but went to Charlotte to meet up with some friends instead.

"David remembered that," Bryant said. "That's how David was. Well, he didn't get mad. That wasn't his nature. But he sort of soured on Carolina after that. And then, of course, our people jumped into it big time. It was one of those things where he was such a great kid and such a great athlete that everybody wanted him."

Thompson said years later that he didn't recall the specific incident, but did admit that "Carolina was one of the top teams."

Duke remained in contention because an alumnus of the school was vice president of a mill near Shelby and knew Thompson and his family. The Duke alum had never been involved in recruiting at all—and probably should have stayed out of it on this occasion—but the lure of landing Thompson was enough to cloud the judgment of anybody. So after visiting the Thompson family and "seeing that the boy didn't have any clothes," the Blue Devils booster invited Thompson and his high-school coach to come to Charlotte to attend the ACC Tournament. He provided transportation to the game and tickets, and he bought Thompson a sports jacket and a pair of pants. These recruiting maneuvers were all illegal actions under the NCAA guidelines.

Meanwhile, back in Shelby and Boiling Springs, the rumors swirled that Thompson was receiving a whole lot more than tickets to basketball games and a few items of clothing. When the dirt access road that led to the Thompson family home was suddenly paved, along with the driveway leading to the house itself, it was alleged that North Carolina State boosters had gotten together with some legislators from Raleigh and arranged to have it done. Robert James, the ACC commissioner at the time, later investigated the charges and determined that "the road was almost impassable" and that Daniels Construction Company, for whom Thompson's father worked, had bulldozed the road and worked on it for a full day at the request of Thompson's father.

"Mr. Thompson arranged for the work and paid the one-hundred-and-twenty-dollars cost over twelve months," James reported.

That hardly silenced the rumors. Ten dollars a month over one year seemed an incredible bargain to have so much asphalt laid.

It also was rumored that one school offered Thompson a Cadillac, and another offered his father a lucrative new job. Others charged that State, in particular, had offered him "under-the-table bait" that included cash, clothes, and cars. One investigator later reported that one of the local persons interviewed said "he had seen David driving Coach Dean Smith's Cadillac, and that Coach Smith had told David he could keep the car if he came to UNC." It was merely a wild rumor, and investigators found nothing to it. Even tiny Gardner-Webb stood accused of offering cash and extra illegal incentives to lure away Thompson.

While the rumor mill churned, Thompson finally made his decision. He would attend N.C. State.

It was partially for events that occurred after this decision was announced that the Wolfpack would later be placed on one-year's probation for NCAA violations. One of the incidents involved Bryant giving Thompson a free ride to Raleigh for freshman orientation; another involved Thompson staying for free on two separate occasions in the dormitory room of Larry and Jerry Hunt, who were longtime friends of Thompson and counselors at Sloan's summer basketball camp. The NCAA said that Thompson should have paid a total of eight dollars for his four-night stay with the Hunt brothers, and that Sloan, knowing the Hunts and Thompson were "lifelong friends," should have "taken every precaution to insure that David did not stay with them."

Bryant said he remembered getting a call from Sloan one day, asking about having Bryant bring three other "black kids" from the

Gastonia-Shelby area to Raleigh. When he and his daughter arrived in their station wagon to pick the other kids up, Thompson was with them.

"Can you take me to school for orientation?" Thompson asked.

Bryant thought for a moment, but only a moment. Thompson already had committed to State, but still could change his mind if something went wrong.

"Sure, I'll take you to orientation," Bryant said.

It was a blatant violation of NCAA rules. Then, when Thompson arrived in Raleigh, he discovered he wasn't yet eligible for orientation. So he hung around campus for five more days—again staying free of cost in the dormitory room of Larry and Jerry Hunt. To keep the boys out of trouble, Biedenbach (the former State guard who was one of Sloan's assistants) provided tickets to a Jackson Five concert for Thompson and the Hunts.

Finally, there was the matter of some alleged illegal pickup games when Thompson played along with Biedenbach. At least twice Biedenbach had participated in pickup games that involved Thompson, Tom Burleson, and others. The NCAA classified one of these games as "an illegal tryout."

"Why would they have to try me out?" Thompson asked. "I was the top player in the state and I had already signed. Why would they try out a player who had already signed? What good would that do? And it wasn't like I had to prove I could play. Everybody already knew I was a good player. That just doesn't make any sense. The whole thing was kind of silly."

Nonetheless, the ruling stood.

Years later, a reporter called the NCAA office to ask about the wild circumstances surrounding Thompson's recruitment.

"Oh, yeah, we've got a whole drawer filled in a file cabinet on that," said the NCAA spokesman. "We've got thick files on what N.C. State did, what Duke did, what Carolina did—and then this real thick file on some school in Boiling Springs. Some school called Gardner-Webb. Their file might have been the thickest of all."

Yet the majority of these charges were never proven. Thompson insists to this day that what subsequently landed both North Carolina State and Duke on one-year's probation for their recruitment of him was "ticky-tacky stuff" that could have landed any school that went after him on probation. Boosters at both schools were annoyed with the ruling; particularly so at Duke, where they had nothing to show for it. At least State got Thompson.

The NCAA ruling did not come down until after Thompson was already enrolled as a freshman at State. It hit Sloan doubly hard. For years, the coach had been lobbying unsuccessfully to have freshmen be eligible to play varsity. Thus, the fabulous Thompson would be unavailable for varsity play his freshman season, and State would be unable to participate in the NCAA Tournament Thompson's sophomore season because the one-year's probation wouldn't go into effect until the 1972–73 season.

THOMPSON'S FRESHMAN SEASON coincided with Burleson's first season on varsity. Most of the interest in the school that year was in the freshman team with Thompson. They averaged 108.3 points and lost only one of 16 games—to hated North Carolina, nicknamed "the Tar Babies" by State fans. State fans were still bitter toward Carolina because they believed the rival school had something to do with turning them in for the recruiting violations involving Thompson. On the court, Thompson was everything Sloan imagined he could be and more. He averaged 35.6 points for the freshman team and set a Reynolds Coliseum record with 54 points one night.

It was, however, his varsity career that everyone anticipated. DT did not disappoint.

His surrounding cast was completed when Sloan recruited point guard Monte Towe, a solid player who only stood a mere 5 feet, 7 inches. Sloan knew what he had in Burleson, Thompson, and others like Rick Holdt, Joe Cafferky, and Tim Stoddard (who later would gain fame as a major-league baseball pitcher). That alone was a solid cast. But he needed a ball-handling whiz to direct the attack.

He tried to sign hotshot recruit Baron Hill, but Hill elected to go to Furman. Then Sloan picked up the phone and called former State great Dick Dickey to ask him to check out a prospect near Dickey's home in Marion, Indiana. Sloan and Dickey had been teammates and roommates at State under Everett Case.

Dickey agreed, and traveled to Oak Hill in northern Indiana to scout the guard Sloan had mentioned. By the second quarter of the game he turned to his wife and said: "We should be watching that little guard for Oak Hill, not the other guy."

The little guard from Oak Hill was Towe.

"This guy can really play, Norm," Dickey later told Sloan. "You've got to give him a chance."

"There is no way a guy five-seven can play guard in the ACC," Sloan said.

"Yeah, well, remember when I tried to get you to recruit John Mengelt and you didn't? You don't want that to happen again, do you?" Dickey said.

Dickey had Sloan's attention. Just a couple of years earlier, he had attempted to interest Sloan in Mengelt, an Indiana kid who had not been all that heavily recruited. Sloan declined and Mengelt went on to earn all-Southeastern Conference honors at Auburn before forging a decent ten-year NBA career. Mengelt had reminded Sloan of State's recruiting oversight by pumping in 40 points during Auburn's victory over State during the 1970–71 season.

When Mengelt was a senior, Sloan mentioned that Dickey had recommended him.

"Well, one phone call would have done it, Coach. I would have come here," Mengelt told Sloan.

Sloan, still sick over missing out on Mengelt, decided to offer Towe a scholarship. But he still worried about other teams taking advantage of Towe defensively. Even after Towe arrived and proved to be a rare and exceptional leader who could direct the offense with ease, Sloan still worried about it. Sloan was committed to playing man-to-man defense. He didn't want to switch to zones, even though the 7-4 Burleson was available to patrol the middle. So he had his staff keep statistics on when opposing guards posted up Towe and how often they scored on such plays.

The results surprised him. Thanks to the presence of the towering Burleson, who provided great help defense, the opposing team usually failed to score when Towe got posted up. Sloan found that 50 percent of the time, it resulted in a blocked shot and a recovery of the ball by State. Even if the other guys made 50 percent of their remaining shots in such situations, they would only score 25 percent of the time when they posted Towe.

Despite weighing a mere 145 pounds, Towe was tough, too. In a game against Virginia his sophomore season, he took a charge from Cavaliers forward Wally Walker that left him with a broken, bleeding nose. He stayed in the game for more than a full minute before Sloan realized he was badly injured. Immediately after having the team trainer stuff his bloody nose with gauze to stop the bleeding, Towe began pleading with Sloan to let him return to the game. Sloan relented, playing Towe thirty-four of a possible forty minutes that night. Towe also played during his career with a broken bone in his left wrist, a broken finger, a pinched nerve in his leg, black eyes, and a gash above his brow.

"I don't believe a platoon of Marines could keep him away from the court when we're scheduled to play a game," Sloan told reporters.

Jim Pettit of the *High Point Enterprise* wrote: "Towe doesn't play a basketball game, he dictates it. Calling Towe a team leader is like calling Castro an administrative coordinator. When Towe is on the floor there is no doubt about who is in charge."

Maybe so, but Towe was smart enough to know as the player in charge that the man he needed to get the ball to most was Thompson. Together, they reinvented a play that would come to be recognized as revolutionary in the history of the game of basketball—the alley-oop pass. Versions of it had been done previously, but not involving someone like Thompson, a glider with a shooting guard's body and a forty-two-inch vertical leap. Thompson had the athleticism and body control to first catch, then lay the ball through the basket before coming back down to earth. That became their signature play.

It is difficult to put into words how great a player Thompson was, or the impact he had on those around him. He once walked onto the North Carolina State track and recorded a 47-0¼ triple jump after only one day of practice. The leap set a school record and was a qualifying distance for the NCAA Track and Field Championships, even though assistant track coach Charlie Galloway noted, "David did everything wrong as far as we were concerned and still got that kind of distance. He even started a foot-and-a-half behind the takeoff line."

Thompson was more than a leaper, though. He had charisma and he could do it all. He could score inside and out. He could pass the ball and even could handle it when needed. He rebounded and played defense and scored almost at will. He wanted to take the biggest shots at critical times, and he usually made them. At 6 feet, 4 and one-half inches and a sleek 195 pounds, he could play every position but center if required.

No matter how great Thompson was, though, the Wolfpack could not go anywhere his sophomore year. They were on probation because of him. Knowing that going in, they set different goals for themselves.

"Since we couldn't play for a national championship that year, the championship for us was to win the ACC and go undefeated. That was our goal," Thompson said. "At the beginning of the year, we didn't know if it was possible. But we knew we had a great team."

A year late as far as Sloan was concerned, the ACC began permitting freshmen to play varsity ball during the 1972–73 season,

Thompson's sophomore year. Maryland had a great freshman guard in John Lucas and teamed him with the formidable front line of Tom McMillen, Len Elmore, and Jim O'Brien. They also had considerable depth in Tom Roy, Owen Brown, Darrell Brown, and Mo Howard. The Terrapins—not North Carolina's Tar Heels, Duke's Blue Devils, or Wake Forest's Demon Deacons—quickly established themselves as State's toughest opponent in the league during the Thompson era.

On Super Bowl Sunday in 1973, it was showdown time between the two undefeated teams. Maryland was ranked second in the country, North Carolina State third. Television guru C. D. Chesley arranged for the game to be nationally televised prior to the NFL's championship game. It proved to be another stroke of genius for the man who had introduced the ACC to the wonders of TV years earlier. Providing the color commentary was one Billy Packer. An estimated audience of 25 million watched as the two teams battled to an 85–85 tie with twelve seconds left.

This was the time when Thompson was at his best, and he did not disappoint. He soared high above the taller McMillen and Elmore to tip in Burleson's miss at the buzzer for an 87–85 victory.

Packer, who was broadcasting his first game ever, cornered Maryland coach Lefty Driesell after the game for an interview.

"I learned a hell of a lesson. After the game they asked me to go down and do a postgame interview with Lefty," Packer said. "I had never interviewed anybody. I had never been on television in my life. So I go down and say something stupid."

What he said was something to the effect of, "Lefty, most of us don't think about you being much of a coach, but you had a hell of a night tonight, huh?"

The next day Packer got a call from Big House Gaines, the legendary Winston-Salem State coach, who scolded him fiercely.

"Billy, let me tell you something: you're okay as an announcer, but don't ever say something like that again," Big House said. "You can't be bigger than the game. Always show respect."

Packer later admitted: "He gave me a hell of a lecture."

Meanwhile, the Wolfpack kept rolling. Maryland, North Carolina, and Virginia were the only teams to really threaten them as they rolled to an unbeaten season in the league, joining the 1957 North Carolina and 1970 South Carolina squads as the only teams to earn that distinction.

State finished the season 24-0, with only the ACC Tournament left to play. Knowing they had no chance to go on to the

NCAAs, the Wolfpack placed a high priority on finishing out the perfect season and winning the tournament. Predictably, it came down to another showdown against Maryland in the championship final. The Terrapins, despite playing without an injured Elmore, went into the game already knowing they would represent the conference in the NCAA Tournament—but they wanted to beat State badly.

Thompson and Burleson refused to let it happen. Thompson hit two free throws with ten seconds left for a 76–74 victory. And Burleson earned tournament MVP honors, going for 14 points and 14 rebounds in the final. The Wolfpack finished 27-0 and were primed to do it again the following season, when they could finally contend for the national championship. Thompson and his teammates set their goal: repeat the perfect season and dethrone seven-time defending NCAA champion UCLA, led by center Bill Walton.

THE 1973 NORTH CAROLINA STATE squad may have been better in the minds and memories of some, but the '74 team gained far more glory. Although they didn't finish the regular season undefeated, this '74 Wolfpack team surpassed all expectations, even though they suffered an early season defeat to UCLA in just the third game of the season. The Bruins brought an astounding 78-game winning streak into the contest. The Wolfpack was on a 29-game win skein. The two met on a neutral court in St. Louis, and UCLA promptly drubbed State. Thompson suffered a rare off day and got outplayed by UCLA forward Keith Wilkes. UCLA cruised to an 84–66 victory.

"At that time, we weren't playing our best basketball," Thompson said. "Early in the season we played a couple of lightweight teams, and we weren't ready for that type of competition. When you're playing against UCLA, not only are you playing against the seven-time defending national champions, but you're also playing against a tremendous veteran coach [in John Wooden]. It was a great team. They had one of the greatest centers to ever play college basketball and about seven guys in all who went on to play in the NBA.

"We played them well for about three-quarters of the game, but once they took the lead it was difficult for us to catch up. We got behind for the first time. We weren't used to that. You can't get behind to a great team like that. We knew we had to play our best game to beat them, and we didn't come close to doing that."

They did, however, learn from the defeat. Using the loss to UCLA as motivation, the Pack started rolling again. When UCLA's

88-game win streak was snapped by a loss at Notre Dame, and the Bruins lost back-to-back games at Oregon and Oregon State in mid-February, State earned the nation's number-one ranking for the first time since the glory days of Everett Case in 1959. They celebrated by continuing to win.

State's regular-season home finale at Reynolds Coliseum was a tribute to Burleson, the lanky senior who was the perfect complement for the flashy Thompson. Burleson was presented the game ball by teammates after registering 19 points and 9 rebounds in an 83–72 victory over North Carolina. That victory marked State's sixth straight triumph over the Heels since the 1971–72 season. It also marked the Wolfpack's 29th consecutive ACC win, surpassing the record of 28 established by Vic Bubas's Duke teams in 1963 and 1964.

While State continued to dominate the ACC, Duke had fallen on hard times. Bucky Waters had found following the Bubas legend difficult—almost impossible. Despite a 63-45 record during his four seasons as coach, students and alumni repeatedly called for his ouster. He quit suddenly in September 1973, leaving assistant Neal McGeachy to coach a thin, undermanned team. McGeachy got the job only after an attempt to lure retired Kentucky coach Adolph Rupp to Durham failed.

McGeachy's claim to fame during what would be his one and only season as coach was a disastrous collapse against North Carolina just a few days after Burleson's big game against the Tar Heels in Raleigh. In Carolina's regular-season finale at Carmichael Auditorium, the Tar Heels rallied from an 8-point deficit in the final seventeen seconds of regulation to force overtime against McGeachy's Blue Devils. Carolina went on to whip them in overtime for a 96–92 victory.

Trailing 86–78, North Carolina started the rally with two free throws by Bobby Jones. Then Duke's Bob Fleischer, having used up four of the allotted five seconds to throw the ball in, tried to throw it off the legs of Carolina's Ed Stahl. But he miscalculated and fired the ball right through Stahl's legs to Walter Davis, who passed to John Kuester for a basket that made it 86–82 with 13 seconds left.

Next Fleischer tried to inbound the ball to teammate Tate Armstrong, who lost the ball out of bounds to give it back to Carolina once again. Davis then missed a shot, but Jones rebounded and laid it in to make it 86–84 with six seconds left. Duke's Pete Kramer was subsequently fouled by Kuester, but missed the front end of a one-and-one and Stahl rebounded for Carolina. Three seconds now remained.

Smith called timeout to plot strategy.

McGeachey called another timeout to plot strategy.

Advantage Carolina.

Mitch Kupchak inbounded to Davis, who grabbed the pass near midcourt and took three quick dribbles before launching a shot from 28 feet. Davis had no intention of banking it, but the ball inadvertently slammed into the backboard and then the basket at the buzzer to complete the miracle comeback and force OT. Duke went up by 3 points early in overtime, but fate assured Carolina's 96–92 victory.

"I didn't try to bank it. I always try to swish it unless I'm right underneath the basket," Davis later admitted of his incredible shot. "I'm just glad I shot it hard enough for it to get there and bank in."

A day later, during practice at Carmichael, Smith was joking around with Davis.

"Hey, Walter. Let's see if you can do it again," Smith told his shooting star as he tossed him a basketball and directed him to the same spot on the floor.

Davis tried to recreate the shot, but he threw up an air ball.

The improbable and devastating defeat for Duke sealed McGeachy's departure. He was replaced by Bill Foster, then the coach at Utah, shortly after the season.

With the rest of the Big Four struggling, State landed a spot in the ACC Tournament finals. Their opponent, yet again, was the University of Maryland. The two hooked up in an epic battle that has often been described as the greatest game ever played in conference history.

Norm Sloan knew how to push just the right buttons to motivate his team. Earlier in the week, Burleson thought he had been slighted when Maryland's Len Elmore had beaten him out for a spot on the All-ACC first team. Elmore also won the ACC rebounding title, wresting it away from Burleson for the first time in three years.

After a game earlier in the season where Burleson made only 3 of 19 shots against Elmore, the boastful Maryland center had told a reporter to tell Burleson: "I'm the best center in the ACC." When the quote appeared in the newspaper the next morning, Sloan clipped it out and tucked it in his wallet, knowing there would come a day when he would be able to pull it out again and use it to fire up Burleson. On the morning of the championship game against Maryland, Sloan taped the clipping to Burleson's locker.

That wasn't the only thing Sloan did to stir Burleson's soul. When the team gathered at four o'clock for a pregame meal of steak and potatoes, Sloan continued a season-long tradition by placing a can of Ken-L Ration dog food on Burleson's plate. Strange as it might have seemed to outsiders, it was the ultimate compliment from the coach. It meant that Sloan deemed Burleson's 15-point, 11-rebound performance against Virginia in the ACC semifinals the most valuable on the team. It was an obvious ploy to motivate Burleson, since Thompson had poured in 37 during the 87–66 rout.

Curry Kirkpatrick of *Sports Illustrated* magazine had unintentionally started the dog-food tradition by writing prior to the season that the Wolfpack deserved the "Ken-L Ration Award" for scheduling the nation's worst "dog" of a nonconference schedule. After that, Sloan began handing out cans of the dog food at pregame meals to the most valuable player of the team's previous game. In truth, Thompson could have garnered enough of the stuff to feed 101 Dalmations, but Sloan was careful to spread the credit around as much as possible. By the season's end, the Ken-L Ration company sent a case of the stuff along to Sloan, as well as a trophy for the team MVP.

Driven by all this controversy, Burleson responded with a terrific game against Elmore and the Terrapins this time out. He hit 18 of 25 shots, scored a career-high 38 points, and grabbed 13 rebounds.

Burleson bounced from locker stall to locker stall in the State dressing room afterward, shaking hands with each teammate and telling them: "Thanks, you helped me make another $100,000 tonight." After this performance, Burleson figured his NBA draft stock could soar to a cool $1 million if State kept winning and captured the national championship.

Burleson even silenced Elmore, who mumbled to reporters afterward: "Nobody has ever done that to me. I just can't believe it."

But what most people couldn't believe was Mo Howard passing up an open eighteen-footer at the end of regulation. Instead of taking the shot, he kicked the ball back out to John Lucas, who could only heave a desperation twenty-five-footer that had no chance at the buzzer. Howard was a fine shooter and had made 10 of 13 shots in the game to that point. The score was tied at 97 when Lucas found the open Howard as State's man-to-man defense was caught momentarily out of position. State's David Thompson figured Howard would drain the open shot.

"Oh, no. We're dead," Thompson thought to himself.

All the hard work. All the victories. They would have added up to nothing if Howard had taken and made the open eighteen-footer.

"To this day, I still don't know why he didn't take that shot," Thompson said. "That shows how much pressure there was."

State won in overtime, 103–100. The 203 total points set a record for an ACC championship game. It remains widely regarded as the most thrilling game ever played in the ACC.

"I still have the tape," Billy Packer said. "I have the original tape of that game. I don't know if anyone else in the country has it. That was a year when the ACC Tournament had arguably two of the best three teams in the country. There was UCLA, N.C. State, and Maryland. No one else in the country was better than those teams that season. And two of them went head-to-head in a game in which everything you've ever worked for is down the tubes if you lose.

"I remember sitting there watching that game, hoping it would never end. You didn't want to see a loser. You were happy for the winner, but you didn't want to see a loser."

Charlie Bryant added: "It was without question the best college basketball game ever. It was just unbelievable."

Norm Sloan agreed, telling reporters after the game: "That was one of the greatest college basketball games that has ever been played. And I think you saw us beat the second-best team in the nation."

Driesell was devastated by the defeat. The season was over for Maryland. With nothing else to prove, the Terrapins turned down an offer to play in the NIT.

"It makes me sick," Driesell told reporters after the game. "I see who is getting bids to this NCAA Tournament, and I know that we and Carolina and State are better than most of the teams. But only one of us is going. It's not fair."

Driesell was heartbroken, but he still had the class to climb onto the Wolfpack team bus afterward and tell the team: "You guys are going to win it all. And I'm going to be back on your bus when you do."

The NCAA East Regionals were held on N.C. State's home court, Reynolds Coliseum. For the first time since Thompson's arrival on the Raleigh campus, the Wolfpack were in the NCAA Tournament. It seemed the only thing that might possibly prevent the Wolfpack from going all the way and ending UCLA's stranglehold on the NCAA championship was some kind of injury to Thompson or Burleson.

Their first game was against Providence, a team that had advanced to the Final Four the previous season. State made quick work of them, winning in a 92–78 rout. Thompson scored 40 points and added 10 rebounds, setting up an East Regional championship encounter with Pittsburgh.

With ten and a half minutes left in the first half of that game, Thompson took a shot from near the foul-line and appeared to get hit on the arm. The shot fell well short of the basket, resulting in a rare air ball for DT. There was no whistle. Pittsburgh grabbed the rebound and moved to the other end. Thompson, who rarely lost his temper, was furious.

"David shot the ball and was obviously fouled," Bryant said. "The ball was about two feet short of the basket. David Thompson had never been short on a shot. Not like that.

"Then David got really mad and took off to the other end, determined to make up for it somehow. It was the only time I ever saw David lose his cool."

Thompson later admitted that he snapped.

"I went up for the shot and the guy slammed me pretty good on the arm. They didn't give us the call. It was an air ball. I got a little upset," he said.

Thompson took off like a jet and darted to the other end of the court, attempting to block a shot by Providence's Keith Starr. He soared so high that his foot caught the back of teammate Phil Spence's shoulder, sending Thompson flipping head over heels toward the floor. Thompson landed head-first with a loud thud.

Then . . . nothing. The sellout crowd at Reynolds Coliseum fell silent almost instantly. Thompson lay motionless, a pool of blood forming under his head.

The team physician, Dr. James Manley, ran onto the court and was among the first to reach the unconscious Thompson. Manley thought he saw blood coming from one of Thompson's ears, a sure sign of internal bleeding.

Wally Ausley, long-time radio voice of the Wolfpack, sat up in his booth wondering if Thompson was dead or alive. He wasn't alone.

Charlie Bryant, sitting in the stands, thought Thompson was seriously injured.

State's star player was out cold for four minutes. Gradually,

Manley turned the player over and examined the back of his head. He revealed a gash that appeared to be the cause of all the bleeding. He fixed Thompson's head with a makeshift bandage, placed him on a stretcher, and hustled him off to Rex Hospital in Raleigh to make certain there wasn't any more damage the physician did not see. The crowd prayed silently as they awaited word from the hospital.

Thompson remembers waking up and seeing his mother, but for a long time after the incident, could not remember anything about the game itself. He took fifteen stitches in the head before returning to Reynolds Coliseum, where Sloan had told the team at halftime that they had to win the game for Thompson. Monte Towe and others were openly crying. Towe played much of the remainder of the game in tears.

When the bandaged Thompson walked back into the arena with 6:51 remaining and the Wolfpack ahead by 20 points, it created a scene no one in attendance would ever forget. The game stopped. Teammates ran over to hug him. The crowd roared and stood in unison to offer the best college basketball player they had ever seen a standing ovation. Even the Pittsburgh players came over to Thompson on the Wolfpack bench to tell him they were glad he was okay.

"The response was overwhelming," Thompson said. "Just the show of affection from my teammates and the fans—it was probably the greatest feeling I've ever had in my life. I can't really describe it. It showed love by the people. That moment is what made everything in my whole career seem worthwhile. I could see and feel that these people were concerned about me as a person, and not just as a basketball player. It was a moment when they seemed to be express- ing pure love. It was special, and something I'm sure I'll never, ever forget."

The rest of the game was anticlimactic as State rolled, 100–72, sending the Pittsburgh team home and the Wolfpack to Greensboro Coliseum—barely an hour's drive from Raleigh—for a Final Four encounter with UCLA, the seven-time defending national champion. The Bruins, led again by Bill Walton, were 25-3, and they wanted the Wolfpack to remember their earlier meeting. Coach John Wooden of UCLA thought the earlier rout, when the Bruins had beaten State by 18 points even though a foul-plagued Walton played only half the game, gave his team a decided psychological advantage going in.

State had a different view of their previous game against UCLA. Thompson hadn't played anywhere near his best that day. Neither had Burleson. The way they looked at it, this was a whole new ballgame, *and* it was being played in their own backyard. The crowd was sure to give them a home court advantage. The team's practices in Greensboro prior to the game were raucous affairs attended by more than five thousand fans. Thompson thrilled them by hitting a shot from beyond half-court to end the final practice before the UCLA game.

"That was a good way to close it down," he said.

Prior to that final practice, Sloan and everyone else had serious concerns about Thompson's health. Was he really okay? Was it possible that all he needed were those fifteen stitches? Or was it possible that something more serious was wrong but that it just hadn't reared its ugly head yet?

Thompson heard the whispers and thought he knew how to silence them. In the locker room before practice, he sensed that everyone was tense. So he decided to loosen the team up by toying with their minds. The hot movie of the day was *The Exorcist.* Thompson tried to re-create the scene where the girl in the movie, possessed by the devil, spins her head around and rolls her eyes back into her head.

"Coach Sloan almost had a heart attack," Thompson said. "Everyone ran back there to where I was sitting and going nuts. They all were having heart attacks. Then I just straightened up and started laughing. Soon everyone else was breaking up about it.

"It broke the ice and let everyone know I was fine. That and the way I hit the shot to end practice did as much as anything to loosen everybody up and get us ready to play UCLA."

The UCLA game was not easy. Twice it appeared that the Wolfpack were defeated. But with Thompson leading the way with 28 points and 10 rebounds, they rallied from 11 points down in the second half to tie the game at 65 and force overtime. Neither team could take charge in the first overtime, so it went to a second where the Bruins surged ahead 74–67 with 3:27 left.

Then Towe made two free throws and drew a charging foul against UCLA's Tommy Curtis to begin yet another N.C. State rally. Thompson finished it by hitting a twelve-footer and two free throws to clinch a 78–75 victory and a spot in the NCAA championship game against Marquette. UCLA's incredible streak of seven titles in a row and thirty-eight straight NCAA Tournament victories ended in the loss.

Most folks assumed North Carolina State had just won the

national championship. Sloan warned that one game remained against a capable Marquette team coached by Al McGuire.

"Some people felt that the Marquette game would be automatic, but I think Coach Sloan was more worried about that one than the UCLA game," Thompson said.

The coach worried needlessly. State clearly had the better team, beating Marquette, 76–64.

After all the difficulties involved in his recruiting and the year of probation that followed, Thompson had at last guided his school to its first national championship. Over two seasons, they had won 57 of 58 games, gone a combined 24-0 during the ACC regular season, and swept two ACC Tournament titles. The 1974 North Carolina State Wolfpack had earned a place in history as one of college basketball's greatest teams, and Thompson had carved his place as one of college basketball's greatest players.

True to his word, Maryland coach Lefty Driesell hopped onto the State team bus, congratulated them, and accompanied the team back to its hotel.

Thompson surprised many people by announcing almost immediately that he would return for his senior season, saying he wanted to win another national title. But without Burleson (who went to the NBA), the Wolfpack were only a second-place team. They went 22-6, including 8-4 in the ACC, and lost to North Carolina in the finals of the ACC Tournament. The players voted not to accept a bid to the NIT, calling it "a losers' tournament."

Thompson added: "After winning it all the year before, going from winning the NCAA championship to the NIT didn't make sense to any of us."

Thompson's career was over. He had set school records for points in a game (57 against Buffalo State in December 1974), points in a season (838), points in a career (2,309), career scoring average (26.8), and consecutive free throws (31 over five games in 1972–73). He was named ACC Player of the Year three times and national Player of the Year twice. He was, in a word, special.

Sloan later told Douglas Herakovich, author of *Pack Pride:* "David was the only player I ever coached that I never had to talk to about working on one specific area. He was a player who always had an agenda to work on something that he felt was a weakness in his own game. He always felt he was less than he really was. Most athletes believe they're better than they really are. David always had something he was working on."

Many called Thompson the greatest college basketball player of all time.

"David wasn't the greatest player," Billy Packer said in 1998, nearly a quarter-century after Thompson completed his career at State. "To me, Kareem Abdul-Jabbar [then Lew Alcindor with UCLA] was the greatest college player. But David, for the ACC, given the flare that he played with and his ability to control a game at his size, he was the best.

"Everybody talks about Michael Jordan. Well, we never saw Michael in college the way we see him today. David was in college what Michael is now with the Chicago Bulls in the NBA."

Thompson's appeal reached well beyond Raleigh. He made so many spectacular plays for the United States at the 1973 World University Games in Moscow that Russians eventually began chanting "Thomp-son! Thomp-son!" And this was during the championship game against Russia at the height of the Cold War.

The next great player to lead a Big Four school to a national championship would be similar in the kind of grace and style that transcends politics and makes all nations cheer. And he would do it while sticking his tongue out at the rest of the ACC schools and any other opponents who stood in his school's way.

11

MICHAEL'S TIME

Dᴀᴠɪᴅ Tʜᴏᴍᴘsᴏɴ was the best highlight for the ACC in the early 1970s, but far from the only one. The decade also marked the beginning of the Big Four Tournament. North Carolina, North Carolina State, Duke, and Wake Forest would play against each other for bragging rights and money in Greensboro Coliseum. When Thompson came along in 1974, his play prompted the first in what would be a string of uninterrupted sellout crowds until the tournament was dropped eleven years later.

Fans loved the Big Four Tournament. The coaches, except for State's Norm Sloan, hated it. Carolina's Dean Smith, Duke's Bill Foster, and Wake's Carl Tacy (who had replaced McCloskey in 1973 to start an exceptional twelve-year run) figured they already faced their Big Four foes twice in the regular season. Why beat each other up on another occasion when it wasn't necessary?

Tacy didn't particularly like the tournament even though Wake, historically the weak link in the Big Four, won it four times—more than any other participant. Duke didn't win it until 1978; then they won it again in 1979 in Bill Foster's last season as coach. State won it the two years Thompson played and then failed to win it again until 1980 during Jim Valvano's first year as coach. Carolina won it just twice—in 1971–72 when the Tar Heels went on to lose to Florida State in the Final Four semifinals and again in '77–78 when point guard Phil Ford was in the process of capturing national Player of the Year honors and UNC's all-time scoring (2,290 points) and assists (753, a record later broken by Kenny Smith) titles.

Ford was a treat to watch. He was the next great Big Four player after Thompson, and he ran Smith's dreaded Four Corners offense with such ball-handling brilliance that Smith later told Ron Morris in *ACC Basketball: An Illustrated History,* "I admit, it was with Ford unfair."

The Four Corners was basically a stall offense Carolina routinely went into late in a game, when Smith figured all the Tar Heels had to do was run time off the clock. It was called "Four Corners" because the point guard took the ball and held it or handled it, depending on how the defense reacted, while the other four players retired to the four corners of the half-court—taking only occasional passes from the point guard and then usually returning the ball to him. If any of the Carolina players got into trouble, he knew where to find an open man against a defense that in theory was always spread too thin. If any one of the Carolina players was double-teamed, one of the others had to be open. It was a win-win situation as far as Smith was concerned.

Opposing coaches hated it, particularly when Ford was running the offense. Smith didn't care about opposing coaches or scoring unnecessary points; all he wanted to do was win. Since there was no shot clock, Carolina could hold on to the ball and then take a layup when the opportunity presented itself, with either the point guard driving in for a layup himself or dishing off to one of the other players, who would suddenly break for the basket out of one of the four corners. Smith had been running versions of the offense since early in his reign as head coach. He even opened the 1968 national championship game against UCLA and Lew Alcindor in the Four Corners because he figured his team might be outmanned, drawing much criticism for it.

But Smith was an expert at shrugging off criticism. He kind of enjoyed irritating a few opposing coaches along the way—and their fans along with it. This led to the beginning of the ABC gang—which stood for "Anybody But Carolina." The ABC club would grow rapidly in numbers with each passing year and its fan base came directly from the other three Big Four schools.

But the emergence of the ABC gang wasn't the only new thing to hit the Big Four scene. In 1975 the NCAA Tournament field was expanded from twenty-five to thirty-two teams. Two teams from a single conference could now be invited to the tourney. The ACC seemed a lock to send two every year. Maryland's Lefty Driesell finally got to go after winning 10 of 12 regular-season games to capture the ACC regular season title, but Thompson and State derailed his team in the ACC Tournament by beating them in the semifinals. The Terrapins were ranked number two in the nation at the time.

In 1976, after several requests from Dreisell, the ACC Tournament was played outside of the state of North Carolina for the first time. Despite the "home-court advantange" of playing at the nearby Capital Centre in Landover, Maryland, Lefty's squad fell again in the semifinals, this time to Virginia. The Cavaliers went on to upset Carolina, ranked number four in the nation with a 25-2 record, in the championship game.

In 1977, Duke finally emerged as Big Four threat again, posting their first winning season since 1972 in Foster's third season. The dunk returned to college basketball and Dean Smith was ejected from a game for only the second time in his career, getting two technical fouls and an automatic ejection from new ACC referee Jack Manton at Greensboro Coliseum in a game against Memphis State.

Smith and Norm Sloan had by the mid-1970s become notorious throughout the nation for baiting referees, and both coaches accused the other of having certain ACC refs in their pockets. One rookie ACC official recalled working his first game. The game was at Reynolds Coliseum and it featured Sloan and Smith in an early-season ACC matchup.

As he walked past the rookie official on his way to the Carolina bench before the game, Smith nodded toward the new guy and said, "Watch Norman. He's going to try to intimidate you and get this crowd going against you. Don't worry about it. Don't listen to him. Just remember—you've got to be fair to us, too. Don't let him get to you, or you'll end up giving us a raw deal."

A moment later, Sloan passed by as he made his way to the State bench. He stopped to shake the new official's hand.

"Keep an eye on Dean over there. He's a complainer. He's going to try to intimidate you. Just remember to try and be fair. The rules are the same for us as they are for Carolina, no matter what he or anyone else might think. He's going to try to get to you to the point that you end up screwing us. Don't let that happen."

The game itself was a typical Big Four matchup, with the lead going back and forth between the teams. In the final minute, two players from each of the teams collided. What was the call? Was it a charge? Or a blocking foul? It was the rookie official's call to make.

With the fate of game hanging in the balance, he made the call in favor of Carolina. The Tar Heels went on to win as Sloan cursed the ref from the bench.

As he tried to make his way off the court through an angry mob at the game's conclusion, a fellow official approached. The rookie felt relieved.

But instead of backing the rookie's call, the other ref said, "I can't believe you screwed ol' Norman like that—and in his own building, too!"

Sloan wasn't the only person who had problems with Smith. The Carolina coach was roundly criticized when, as coach of the 1976 U.S. Olympic team, he chose four North Carolina players and seven players overall from the ACC for the Olympic roster. In addition to taking Tar Heels Walter Davis, Mitch Kupchak, Tom LaGarde, and Phil Ford, he also took Kenny Carr of N.C. State, Tate Armstrong of Duke, and Steve Sheppard of Maryland. Half the Olympic team that year was comprised of players from the Big Four schools. Smith also caught heat from forward Wally Walker of Virginia and guard Jerry Schellenberg of Wake Forest because they were passed over for the team. Schellenberg went public with his complaint after Wake won yet another Big Four Tournament championship in 1977, beating Carolina in the finals. Wake then went on to the NCAA tournament (as the league's second representative) and lost in the Midwest Regional to Marquette. Marquette would go on to the finals to face Carolina.

It was about this time that Wake Forest also began accusing Smith of turning up the thermostat in old Carmichael Auditorium before Carolina home games. Since Carolina usually had more depth than anyone else, the Heels could withstand the heat better than their visiting opponents. It was the same charge that later would be leveled at Mike Krzyzewski, Smith's rival from Duke.

The Carolina crowds at Carmichael Auditorium were cozy and loud, and seemed to be rowdier than the "wine and cheese" crowds that inhabited the much larger, more spacious Dean E. Smith Center where Carolina moved to in 1986.

No matter how rowdy that old Carolina crowd was, they still weren't like Duke or N.C. State, or even the Wake crowds that used to pack old Gore Gymnasium. Carolina was different. Always had been. The fans and students who attend the school like it that way and pride themselves on the fact that their basketball team is always the one the others want to beat. The fans and students of the other schools construe that as arrogance, and take the Carolina folks to task for it whenever they can.

One of the popular sayings of UNC students is, "If God is not a Tar Heel, then why is the sky Tar Heel blue?"

In-state tuition is reasonable enough that Carolina always draws the largest portion of their students from within the state of North Carolina. That makes it easy for them to poke fun at Duke, whose students often hail from New York or New Jersey and seem, to the Carolina people, to simply be renting nearby land and space while they make their way through college.

By the mid-1990s, enrollment at North Carolina would soar to nearly 25,000 students compared to barely 11,000 at Duke (nearly half of whom were graduate students). North Carolina State's enrollment was roughly 16,500, and Wake's was around 6,000. Carolina took only 39 percent of its applicants, and Duke took only 27 percent. North Carolina State took 66 percent, and Wake, by far the smallest of the Big Four schools, accepted 44 percent of its applicants.

Tuition for the four schools has much to do with the makeup of their student bodies. In 1997, tuition was less than $1,500 for in-state students at both Carolina and N.C. State (less than $9,000 for out-of-state applicants); it was $18,590 at Duke for both in-state and out-of-state students, and $13,850 for both in-state and out-of-state students at Wake.

The bottom line is: Carolina is made up mostly of Carolinians who feel, rightly or wrongly, that they are the cream of their state's crop. They think Duke students are Yankees from the north; State students are inferior to them; and Wake students are just an afterthought.

But Carolina didn't always like the public's perception that Duke and State fans, in particular, were rowdier than them in a basketball arena. Many Carolina students actually took pleasure in the fact that their own state's long-time U.S. senator, Jesse Helms, once complained that they were too wild in Chapel Hill.

When a site for a state zoo was being chosen, Helms remarked: "They ought to just fence in Chapel Hill."

THE 1977 NCAA FINALS pitted North Carolina against Marquette. The Tar Heels had rallied from 14 points down to beat Notre Dame in a second-round game, and in the East Regional championship, they defeated Kentucky.

By this time, North Carolina was hobbling. During the Notre

Dame game, Ford injured his elbow. Walter Davis, the All-ACC forward and one of the greatest shooters in conference history, had broken the index finger on his shooting hand. Tom LaGarde, a member of the '76 Olympic team, had injured his knee during a practice prior to the ACC Tournament and then reinjured it again—ending his college career for good—just prior to the East Regional championship game against Kentucky.

The situation looked bleak heading into the Final Four semifinal against the explosive Nevada-Las Vegas Runnin' Rebels. But at least North Carolina was back for its fifth Final Four appearance under Smith—their first since 1972. Freshman Mike O'Koren scored 31, and the Heels, operating out of the Four Corners for the last fifteen minutes of the contest, held on for an 84–83 win over UNLV. Marquette beat UNCC, 51–49 in the other semifinal.

Smith and the Tar Heels were back in the NCAA title game against one of the game's true free spirits, Marquette coach Al McGuire. Smith opened himself up for criticism once again when, after rallying from a 12-point halftime deficit, he elected to go to the Four Corners. The Heels held the ball for three full minutes as Marquette refused to come out of their 2-3 zone. Carolina lost all momentum in the process.

While the Heels held the ball, O'Koren sat at the scorer's table, unable to report in. By the time he got back in, Marquette had come up with a key block, taking control of the game. The Warriors went on to win the game and the NCAA championship, 67–59.

Again, Smith had failed to capture The Big One.

After the season, Smith approached Ford and suggested that his brilliant guard consider turning pro. Ford was surprised at first, but in retrospect realized he shouldn't have been. Smith was unlike most other college coaches in this respect. Since the early 1970s when he encouraged Bob McAdoo to pursue the NBA after only one season at Carolina, Smith always took a hard look at three things when evaluating a player's future career: the player's current academic standing and his chances of graduating at a later date if he turned pro early; the player's projected status in terms of where he might be drafted and how much money he might make because of that; and the player's personal and home life. If those factors added up to what Smith figured was a common-sense decision that would better the life of the player and his family while still giving the player a chance to graduate at a later date, Smith often told the surprised player "Go pro."

Ford listened to Smith, but decided against leaving school. He told Smith he wanted to stay for his senior season.

"First of all," said Ford years later, "no one was going to tell my mom that I was going to go pro. She didn't want to hear anything about that. But you're also talking about 1977. The money wasn't as astronomical then as it is now, and I enjoyed college. I enjoyed my four years here at Chapel Hill. They were the best four years of my life—and I never entertained the idea of leaving. Coach Smith recommended that I go, but I never really gave it serious consideration.

"It was never discussed with my family, because when he brought it up I just told him I wasn't interested. He recommended that I go, and that wasn't uncommon for him. I don't know about other coaches, but that wasn't uncommon for Coach Smith."

In retrospect, perhaps Ford should have considered taking Smith's advice.

In 1978, the Duke-Carolina rivalry was reborn in all its glory. Most of the glory, however, belonged to Duke. Even though Ford put on a clinic in his final game at Carmichael Auditorium—playing all forty minutes in an 87–83 victory over Duke, registering a career-high 34 points, five assists, two steals, and just three turnovers—it would be the last game the Heels won with Ford in the lineup. In the first round of the ACC Tournament, they lost to Wake Forest, and in the first round of the NCAAs, they lost to San Francisco.

Ford was so distraught he didn't remove the athletic tape from his ankles until two weeks after the San Francisco loss.

By then Duke was just getting started. The Blue Devils, led by freshmen Gene Banks and Kenny Dennard, sophomores Mike Gminski and Bob Bender (a transfer from Indiana who had made the Final Four with the Hoosiers in 1976), and spectacular junior Jim Spanarkel, won their first ACC championship since 1966 by beating Wake Forest in the tournament final.

The Blue Devils kept winning and they advanced to the NCAA championship game against Kentucky after beating Notre Dame in the semifinals.

Duke, unranked when the season began, regularly put three players on the court who were under twenty years old. Kentucky, ranked number one in the nation throughout the season, started four seniors.

The age and experience edge was too much. Kentucky won handily.

But the point had been made: Duke was back.

Gminski, a center who measured 6 feet, 11 inches, finished his career as the school's all-time leading scorer (2,323 points) and rebounder (1,242). Although his scoring record later was surpassed by two players—Johnny Dawkins and Christian Laettner—his marks for career rebounds and blocks (345) remain the best in Duke history.

Banks would prove to be one of the most popular players in Duke history, and an example that illustrated the unfairness of the old 800 rule that once had kept African American players from playing in the ACC. Despite failing to score even a 700 on the Scholastic Aptitude Test in high school, he graduated from Duke with a degree in history and delivered the commencement address to the class of 1981. Before his final home game at Cameron Indoor Stadium (Duke Indoor Stadium was eventually renamed to honor long-time athletics director Eddie Cameron), Banks tossed red roses into the crowd. Then he helped beat North Carolina, first by forcing overtime with an improbable eighteen-foot turnaround jump shot and then by clinching victory with a rebound basket with only twelve seconds left on the clock. The Cameron Crazies grabbed him and lifted him to their shoulders afterward. He then grabbed a public-address announcer's microphone and called for his mother to join him on the floor.

But that scene and the circumstances surrounding it were no less captivating or emotional than the ones involving the coaches at Duke and North Carolina State the year before. After the 1979–80 season, Foster at Duke and Sloan at State, two coaches who brought success to their schools, announced they were leaving. Sloan departed for Florida; Foster left for South Carolina.

THE COACH AT DUKE for Banks's senior season was one Mike Krzyzewski, who was coming off a 9-17 season as head coach of Army. He beat out two other head coaches for the job—Bob Weltlich of Mississippi and Paul Webb of Old Dominion—and Bob Wenzel, an assistant at Duke under Foster. State's new coach was Jim Valvano. He was chosen after Morgan Wooten, the legendary coach at De-Matha High School in Washington D.C. turned down an offer for the job. Krzyzewski was thirty-three, Valvano thirty-four.

Krzyzewski had been recommended to Duke by Bob Knight, the fiery and controversial coach of Indiana. Krzyzewski had played under Knight at Army and coached under him as an assistant at Indiana.

"He has all of my good qualities and none of my bad ones," Knight insisted.

He would need more than just "good qualities" to battle Dean Smith and other ACC foes over the coming years. Valvano would need more of the same. During one of Valvano's very first encounters with the media after taking the N.C. State job, a reporter asked State's new coach a very important question.

"How do you expect to beat the Dean?"

"I don't expect to beat him. But I expect to outlive him," Valvano joked.

Valvano later admitted he thought he knew what to expect when he took his new job, but he quickly discovered he really didn't have a clue. When Wake Forest beat the Wolfpack by 30 before fifteen thousand screaming fans at Greensboro Coliseum in an early-season Big Four tournament encounter, fans screamed, "Welcome to the ACC, Valvano!"

Krzyzewski experienced similar setbacks before settling into his new digs at Duke.

"There's no way you can be prepared for it," Krzyzewski said of coaching in the Big Four environment. "You've got to experience it to begin to understand it. You can never be ready for it completely and the fact is that in this area you're always going to be a minority. There are going to be many more North Carolina fans. Then there will be more State fans. Duke and Wake Forest are in a minority."

Before Krzyzewski and Valvano could completely get their programs in order and start making national names for themselves, it was the Dean's turn to shine again on the Big Four stage. Thanks to a talented young guard named Michael Jordan, the Tar Heels would gain national recognition.

After losing to Marquette in the NCAA championship game in 1977, three straight first-round exits followed for the Tar Heels in the NCAA Tournament. Then, something started to click during the 1980–81 season, the year before Jordan arrived. After finishing second in the ACC regular season to a Virginia team led by Ralph Sampson, the Heels ripped off seven wins in a row to win the ACC Tournament and advance to the Final Four for the sixth time under Smith.

Carolina's Final Four opponent was Virginia, a team that had beaten the Heels twice during the regular season. It was only the second time in the history of the tournament that two teams from the same conference advanced to the Final Four—the other coming in 1976 when Indiana beat fellow Big Ten member Michigan to complete a perfect season and win the title. But the Cavaliers couldn't make it three in a row against the Tar Heels, losing 74–58. Virginia lost because they could not find a way to stop Al Wood. During one stretch Wood outscored the entire Virginia team, 22–21, as Carolina expanded a 2-point lead to a 16 point advantage.

Wood, a smooth, sharp-shooting senior forward who could get on serious rolls, ended up setting a national semifinal scoring record with 39 points—one more than West Virginia's Jerry West had scored in 1959. He made 14 of 19 shots from the field and 11 of 13 free throws. He also grabbed 10 rebounds. Virginia's star center Ralph Sampson, hounded relentlessly by the defense of Sam Perkins, struggled to score only 11 points.

This time the opponent in the title game was Indiana, coached by Bobby Knight and led by guard Isiah Thomas. Playing great man-to-man defense on Wood and everyone else, Indiana eventually pulled away for a 63–50 victory, leaving Smith 0-for-3 in championship games.

"We lost, but I think we set the table for the 1982 team," Wood said years later.

Even though Wood departed for a checkered NBA career, James Worthy, Sam Perkins, Matt Doherty, and Jimmy Black, returned the following season. Michael Jordan was a freshman on that team. Although Jordan would, over time, go on to become a household name, in 1980, he was nobody. After being cut from his junior-high team and failing to make the varsity squad as a sophomore at Laney High School in Wilmington, North Carolina, his dream of playing in the ACC for North Carolina *State*—yes, State, not North Carolina—seemed nothing more than just that, an impossible dream.

Even as he began to emerge as a player his junior year at Laney, most of the big-time college recruiters stayed away. All except one. Smith sent long-time assistant coach Bill Guthridge to take a look. Apparently, Jordan fell under "the Cedric Maxwell rule." That rule states that every kid from the state of North Carolina who might possibly have a chance to play for UNC deserved a look.

"We missed on Maxwell. Make sure we don't miss on another kid like that from our own state," Smith told Guthridge.

Cedric Maxwell hailed from Kinston, North Carolina, but had been ignored several years earlier by Smith and other ACC coaches. Maxwell attended UNC-Charlotte instead and promptly helped that team, coached then by Lee Rose, to the Final Four in 1977. Only a close loss to Marquette in the semifinals had kept Maxwell and UNCC from a showdown against Carolina.

Guthridge was the only ACC coach to scout Jordan as a junior. Some of the other coaches came down later, but the recruitment of Jordan was nothing at all like the feeding frenzy that had taken place when David Thompson was preparing to enter college nearly a decade earlier. Ironically, Thompson was the player Jordan had admired most growing up. He was the main reason Jordan grew up a fan of N.C. State.

Many of Jordan's first scholarship offers came from smaller schools like UNC-Wilmington or Appalachian State. His high-school principal encouraged the bright student to attend the Air Force Academy.

"He wanted me to go to the Air Force Academy so I would have a job after I got out," Jordan said.

Soon enough, though, other schools caught on. It started to change when he excelled in a summer basketball camp between his junior and senior years. He still wasn't being recruited as hard as Thompson was or even several other players in the state at the time. Buzz Peterson, who later went on to become Jordan's roommate and today is head coach at Appalachian State, was as heavily recruited as Jordan out of high school.

"I thought he had a chance to be pretty good," Guthridge said years later of his first impression of Jordan. "But it wasn't like the first time I saw him I said, 'This is going to be the greatest player ever.' "

Guthridge reported back to Smith.

"He's somebody we should recruit because he's an ACC-type player," Guthridge told his boss. "But I'm not sure how good he will be."

At the time, Jordan wasn't so sure he wanted to go to North Carolina. "I knew the Big Four schools—and the team I hated most was North Carolina," Jordan said. "I never thought they played basketball. I thought they stalled the game with the Four Corners and stole games that way. That drove me nuts. I loved N.C. State. That was my team.

"All four schools recruited me, but I just visited N.C. State and North Carolina. At that time I had no interest whatsoever in Duke or Wake Forest."

The other Division I schools he eventually visited were Clemson, South Carolina (then coached by Bill Foster), and Maryland.

"I went to State first, then Maryland, and then I went to South Carolina—and at that point I was leaning toward South Carolina. They were going to let me play baseball, they took me to the Governor's house . . . they just treated me so well. And I loved Bill Foster. He was an easy guy to get along with and I could see playing for him," Jordan said.

"But then I went to North Carolina and that was it."

The visit to Chapel Hill's scenic campus was pivotal.

"I went to North Carolina and I wanted to commit before I even left," Jordan said. "I liked the campus, the coaching staff, I liked the opportunity to play with guys like James Worthy and all that. I liked everything about it. But my [high-school] coach [Pop Herring of Laney] wouldn't let me do it right then."

Herring made the visit along with Jordan and Jordan's parents, James and Deloris.

"Just wait a couple days and see if that feeling wears off. You want to be sure," Herring told Michael.

It didn't. And once Smith made his customary visit to the Jordan family home, the decision was made. Like others recruited by Carolina before and since, Jordan expected Smith to tell him how great he was and how he might fit in at North Carolina in terms of his basketball future. Smith did nothing of the sort. He talked about what a good education Michael would receive and pointed out all the former players who had their degrees and held good jobs as lawyers, doctors, coaches, and successful businessmen.

Jordan was holding a basketball when the conversation with Smith began, fondling it nervously. Finally, he put it down and listened to the nonbasketball lures of North Carolina that Smith was talking about. It wasn't until late in the visit when Smith finally started talking about the game that Jordan picked up the ball again.

When he signed with the school, Herring told reporters: "Dean Smith will win his first national championship during Michael's four years."

When he arrived at Carolina, Jordan certainly wasn't thinking along those lines. He wasn't sure if he would fit in or how he would do it. He only wanted to come off the bench and contribute a few minutes as a freshman, or at least that was his initial goal. But when Smith walked to the chalkboard in the Charlotte Coliseum prior to the season-opener against Kansas to write the starting lineup, he surprised Jordan by including his name. It was a high honor. Only three other freshmen had ever started their first varsity game for the Tar Heels—Phil Ford, Mike O'Koren, and James Worthy, who was then a sophomore.

"When he named me a starter at the beginning of my freshman

season, it was kind of a shock," Jordan said. "We had a junior, Jimmy Braddock, who could have played the position and knew the system better than I did. I was more talented from a skill standpoint, but he was far more experienced. I thought he would be the starter and I would come off the bench."

At first Jordan was not the great player he later would come to be. As a freshman, he measured only 6 feet, 4 inches and weighed barely 180 pounds. It wasn't until his sophomore season, after he had grown to 6-6 and gained sixteen pounds, that Smith was ready to concede he had something special on his hands. Regardless, Jordan first had to learn how to fit into the team's scheme. Everyone who played for Smith at Carolina had to do that, and Jordan was more than willing to take his time and grow into whatever role Smith had carved out for him.

Not only was Jordan starting, but he was also starting for the number-one team in the nation. The Tar Heels solidified that ranking by whipping number-two Kentucky, 82–69, on a neutral court in East Rutherford, New Jersey, in the sixth game of the season. But with Perkins sidelined because of a virus, the Demon Deacons wrecked Carolina's perfect record and number-one ranking by beating them 55–48 in Carmichael Auditorium in late January. It was a defeat Jordan could not—would not—forget.

"At that time, we considered State our biggest rival—and Virginia second-biggest because they were so good," Jordan said. "Wake Forest was the forgotten rivalry. But then they beat us and instantly they became a major rival again. We played a poor game, a really poor game, and they dominated us."

The loss motivated the Tar Heels, who would lose only one more game the entire year—at Virginia two weeks later. That loss was avenged in the championship game of the ACC Tournament, when Smith got under the skin of Virginia coach Terry Holland (who once named his dog "Dean" because it whined so much) by suddenly playing stall ball with a 44–43 lead and seven and a half minutes remaining. Holland would not come out of a zone that had the 7-foot-4 Sampson planted underneath the basket, and six minutes ran off the clock before Virginia finally started to chase and to foul. The Cavaliers committed five fouls in less than a minute to put the Tar Heels in the bonus and on the foul line—and with twenty-eight seconds remaining, Doherty made one of two free throws to give the Heels a 45–43 lead.

As boring as Smith's strategy may have seemed initially, it was, in the final analysis, nothing short of brilliant. Doherty hit two more free throws with three seconds left to seal the victory for Carolina.

With the NCAA Tournament now expanded to forty-eight teams, the ACC placed not only Carolina and Virginia but also Wake Forest and State in the field. After surviving a first-round scare against James Madison at Charlotte Coliseum—when Worthy was responsible for a three-point play, drawing a charge, and making two key free throws in the final minute of a 52–50 victory—Carolina's next two games in the East Regional were at Reynolds Coliseum in Raleigh. Alabama and Villanova fell to them there, putting the Heels in the Final Four for the second year in a row.

Cynics were beginning to wonder if Smith would ever win a national championship. Dean, who had in the previous sixteen seasons been to the Sweet Sixteen eight times, the Final Four six times, and the national championship game three times, had never won the coveted title.

Jimmy Black and Worthy called their teammates together on the eve of the Final Four semifinal against Houston.

"Let's do this for Coach," they said.

Jordan and the others nodded.

"I was just following whatever leadership they were offering," Jordan said later.

Houston had Larry Micheaux, Michael Young, Clyde Drexler, Akeem Olajuwon, and a guard Jordan called "Rob something, who was supposed to be a big factor." "Rob something" was really Rob Williams, and he was a nonfactor. Williams, guarded mostly by Black, missed all 8 shots he attempted and Carolina won 68–63.

"That wasn't really a game," Jordan said. "Akeem wasn't a factor. He came off the bench, and he couldn't walk and chew gum at the same time. Yeah, they had Larry Michaeux and Michael Young and Clyde Drexler. But we had some great players, too, and we were on a roll. Akeem didn't even know how to play the game at the time. So it was a game, but it wasn't a game, if you know what I mean. I felt like we kind of handled them."

Black, the team leader, reminded the players again that they were on the threshold of doing something great—not only for themselves and the University of North Carolina, but also for Coach Smith. Interestingly, four years earlier Black had been headed to Iona to play for Jim Valvano when Guthridge convinced Smith that Black was the "motor" needed to replace the departing Phil Ford as Carolina's playmaker.

The title game was against the Georgetown Hoyas, who had handled Louisville in the other semifinal.

While riding on the bus on the way to the game that evening, Jordan envisioned himself making the shot to win the national championship.

"Let's get this monkey off Coach's back," Black told his team-mates one more time before taking the court of the packed Louisiana Superdome. Again, Jordan and the others nodded in agreement.

Smith seemed loose and confident. Though the fifty-one-year-old coach was a heavy cigarette smoker whose idea of physical exer-cise was to play a round of golf in a cart, he made a surprising promise to his players: "If you win this game, I'll run wind sprints after our first practice next fall," Smith said.

In the other locker room, Georgetown coach John Thompson was busy telling his star center, Patrick Ewing, to block everything in sight even if he thought goal-tending might be called. His plan was to intimidate the Tar Heels immediately.

"They thought they had the intimidation factor going in their favor," Jordan said. "Patrick goal-tended our first five shots. But the thing was—they were all against James Worthy—and James didn't get intimidated by it. He just kept going to the hoop."

The intense, tight game went back and forth until North Caro-lina—trailing 62–61—called time-out with thirty-two seconds left to set up the final play.

Smith grabbed his clipboard and diagrammed a play "with a lot of options," Jordan said.

"First we look inside for James or Sam," Smith told his players. "But I anticipate them doubling down on James, so then we'll swing it around and Michael will have an easy shot. They won't figure he'll take it. He's the youngest guy on the floor and they don't think he'll take it."

Then Smith turned to Jordan.

"Don't be afraid to take the shot," Smith said, looking into his prized freshman's eyes.

Jordan's eyes locked on his coach's. He didn't have to say it. They both knew he wouldn't be afraid to take the shot.

As they broke from the huddle and Jordan started back toward the court, Smith's eyes caught his again.

"Knock it in, Michael," the coach added.

It was all Jordan needed to hear.

"As soon as he said that, any tension I had went out the win-dow," Jordan remembered years later. "He was giving me the go-ahead to take the shot. So when the ball hit my hands, there was no hesitation. I didn't even know where the defense was. I knew he knew I would be wide open. I just threw it up in rhythm and made the shot.

"Once he said I would have a shot in that huddle, it stopped there for me. I started focusing on taking the shot. I didn't even know what he said to do if I didn't have the shot. He may have said it, but I didn't hear it. When I took the shot, I felt real good about it. It left my hand and I was in rhythm. It was all positive thoughts from my end."

In the stands, Jordan's mother couldn't watch. She covered her eyes.

The roar of the crowd told her Michael had made it.

"Holy shit! He made it! He made it!" she shouted to Michael's father, James.

The eighteen-footer from just in front of Smith and the Carolina bench gave the Tar Heels a 63–62 lead with seventeen seconds left. But the game was far from over. Georgetown still had plenty of time to set up a play and spoil Smith's championship party.

Guard Fred Brown brought the ball up the court as Carolina scrambled to set its defense.

"I knew he was confused," Jordan said. "James [Worthy] jumped in the passing lane first, then I jumped in the passing lane—and he must have thought I was James coming back. He threw it right to James."

Inexplicably, Brown threw a perfect pass right to a very surprised, but appreciative, Worthy.

"I was pretty surprised because it hit me right in the chest," said Worthy, who scored a game-high 28 points and was named the Final Four MVP.

Worthy tried to dribble out the clock, but was fouled. He missed the ensuing two free throws, but it didn't matter. Georgetown could only get off a fifty-foot desperation heave by Floyd at the buzzer. It wasn't close. Smith finally had his first national championship, in his seventh Final Four and his fourth championship game.

Leonard Laye, covering the game for the *Charlotte Observer*, tracked down James Jordan in the locker room to ask him about his son's game-winning shot. James Jordan related the story about how his wife had covered her eyes and shouted, 'Holy shit! He made it!' "

Laughing loudly, James Jordan yelled: "I don't know how you're going to put that in your newspaper, but that's what she said. That was her reaction—and mine!"

Laye laughed at the memory years later.

"I wanted so badly to use that story, but I couldn't use it," Laye said.

Smith and his Tar Heel followers were more than relieved with the victory—they were ecstatic.

The ABC bunch said it was about time. A real coach would have won it three or four times by then, they crowed.

As reporters waited outside the Carolina locker room immediately following the game, James Jordan was spotted pretending to kick an imaginary object down the hallway. He obviously was enjoying himself.

"What are you doing?" one of the reporters asked.

"It's the monkey off Coach Smith's back. I'm kicking it outta here," he said, grinning.

12

JIMMY V

A FEW YEARS PRIOR to becoming coach at North Carolina State, Jim Valvano became acquainted with Lou Bello, the long-time ACC referee who later went into radio and hosted his own popular talk show in Raleigh. One night the two were having several drinks together. Bello told Valvano, then the coach at Iona College in New York State, that if he ever was in the Raleigh area recruiting and needed a place to stay on a moment's notice to go ahead and stop by.

"I'll take care of you," Bello said. "No problem."

Bello made the offer. He even gave Valvano directions to his house. But deep down, Bello surely thought Valvano would never take him up on his offer.

One night, though, Valvano and Tom Abatemarco, his assistant at Iona who would follow him to State, were driving through Raleigh on a recruiting trip. They were thinking about getting a hotel when Valvano remembered Bello's offer.

"Let's take Lou up on that," Valvano said.

To the surprise of Abatemarco, Valvano even remembered the directions to Bello's house. Or at least Valvano thought he did. After circling a certain neighborhood for some time, Valvano pulled up to what he thought was Bello's house. By then it was getting late in the evening.

As Valvano pulled in, a door to the house opened and a woman came out. Valvano opened his door and leaned out, shouting: "Excuse me, ma'am. Is this Lou Bello's house?"

212

"Yeah, yeah, yeah. Just toss him out on the driveway. He can crawl up from there," said the woman, turning to go back inside.

A few years later, in 1980, Jimmy V arrived in Raleigh like a breath of, well, hot air. He was a fast-talking, native New Yorker of Italian descent who seemed instantly out of place in the slow-moving environment where natives talk with dreamy Southern drawls. He took the job at State at the age of thirty-four, a little naive about what was going to be expected of him.

Valvano came from Iona, a small Catholic school located in New Rochelle, New York. He used to joke that he would greet potential recruits by saying, "Hi, I'm Jim Valvano, Iona College."

The universal response, according to Valvano was, "Holy God, man. You're what, thirty years old? And you already own your own school?"

At Iona, Valvano coached in conference play against good coaches: Mike Krzyzewski at Army, Tom Penders at Fordham, and P. J. Carlesimo at Wagner. But Jimmy V's teams were usually the best. His star player was Jeff Ruland, who briefly went on to gain NBA fame and today coaches Iona himself.

Valvano, a man with a considerable ego, later said of his time in New Rochelle: "I figured it was just a matter of time before somebody found Iona and V."

He didn't know who that somebody would be. He just knew it would be a much bigger school than Iona. It turned out to be N.C. State.

Willis Casey, who had known Everett Case, was the athletics director at State who handled the negotiations to bring Valvano to the Wolfpack after DeMatha High's Morgan Wooten turned them down. Casey began his first meeting with Valvano by asking him why he wanted the job.

"Because I want to win the national championship," Valvano replied.

"Do you think you can do that here?" Casey asked.

"You guys have done it before," Valvano said. "I would think you can do it again."

Later, another administrator asked him: "What do you need to win?"

Valvano's reply was simple, and true.

"I need players," he said.

Eventually, Valvano got them. It was, after all, his area of responsibility once the job was his. And he was a natural at recruiting. But first he had to learn a few essentials about coaching in the ACC.

Valvano had taken the job at State so quickly that he couldn't even inform his Iona players that he was leaving until after the fact. Ruland was so peeved at him for this that he refused to speak to Valvano for nearly ten years. The rupture of his relationship with Ruland and others from Iona bothered him, but only a little and not for long. Jimmy V had bigger things to be concerned about. He had his dream job, and he intended to do whatever it took to make State a success.

He was walking into a place that took its basketball seriously. It was, after all, the place where Everett Case put Big Four basketball on the map in the 1950s, fueling the rivalries with North Carolina, Duke, and Wake Forest that now consumed fans from every part of the state. David Thompson and Norm Sloan took State a step further by capturing the 1974 NCAA championship.

Nonetheless, Valvano got off to an inauspicious start. Wearing a bright red sports jacket and loud, red-checked pants, he attended some league meetings in Myrtle Beach, North Carolina, and then hopped a plane to Greenville to speak at his first Wolfpack Club meeting. During the flight, Valvano was asked by the woman sitting next to him if he was the new basketball coach at N.C. State.

"Yes, I am. Are you a State fan?" Valvano replied.

"No, I'm not," she said with a hint of disdain.

"I'll make you one," Valvano pressed.

"No, you won't," she shot back.

A similar scene took place with a man at the luggage carousel. Valvano began to wonder why he was in such hostile territory. He was still wondering about this an hour later, while he was waiting for his ride that hadn't shown up. A few moments later, he heard his name being paged. It was Charlie Bryant, director of the Wolfpack Club.

"What the hell are you doing there?" Bryant demanded.

"What do you mean? I'm in Greenville, waiting on my ride to the meeting," Valvano said.

"You're in Greenville, South Carolina. You're supposed to be in Greenville, North Carolina. You're in the wrong state," Bryant said.

In a book he later wrote with Curry Kirkpatrick of *Sports Illustrated*, Valvano recalled of the incident: "[It was a] nice start to a new career. For the most important speech of my life I had dressed up like Bozo the Clown and flown to the wrong state."

When he returned to the ticket counter to find his way to the right Greenville, the man behind the counter told him: "Coach, you're getting into a tough enough league as it is. If you don't know what state you're in, ol' Dean is gonna beat yo' ass regular."

After going 14-13 his first season, Valvano received further indication that he had much to learn about the fans of both Carolinas when the hate mail started pouring in. One letter read:

> "Coach V,
> "You don't seem to get the hang of this thing down here. First, you fly to the wrong state. Okay, we can tolerate that. But then you lose to those blue bellies in Chapel Hill and you come back to Raleigh and lose to them again. That's twice in the same season by a few points. We can't tolerate that. I'm telling you I know where you live and I'm coming to Raleigh to shoot your dog."

What really shocked Valvano was that this wasn't just an anonymous letter. Its author had listed a business address and references, even a picture of himself, on the back. Valvano said he wrote the guy back, telling him that he didn't like to lose to North Carolina either, and that he didn't plan to make it a habit. He added that State didn't need fans like him, that State needed fans who were going to support the team whether it won or lost, and that if he didn't like that maybe he should start rooting for someone else.

Then, feeling quite proud of himself, Valvano added this note to the bottom of the letter: "P.S. I hate to spoil your day, but the Valvano family doesn't even have a dog."

Two weeks later a UPS truck rolled up to the Valvano home and delivered a package to the front door. Inside, Valvano claimed, was a little puppy with a note around its neck. The note, according to Valvano, read: "Coach, don't get too attached."

Was the story true? Or just another story Valvano concocted to get a few laughs on the after-dinner speaking circuit? It didn't matter, with Valvano nothing was ever entirely certain.

The coach had a way with words. Everyone knew that. He could charm administrators. He could woo players. And he loved to yuk it up with the media—most of the time. But there were other times when he seemed, as one reporter put it years later, "just crude and inconsiderate. It was like you couldn't believe this was the guy who had this great image and was in charge of this basketball program. There were plenty of times when you couldn't believe the junk that was coming out of his mouth, and it made you uncomfortable to be around him. Those were the times when he came off like a bad used-car salesman."

One administrator told a reporter that there were "six sides to Valvano," and that no one could be certain which side would surface at any given moment on any given day. Bryant, who grew to be one of Valvano's closest friends, insists that he only knew one Jim Valvano. And he was proud to know him. He said that some folks simply misunderstood Valvano, or they placed an unfair label on him.

One night Bryant and Valvano were in Greenville (North Carolina, that is) for a Wolfpack meeting. As Valvano put the wraps on what Bryant described as "a beautiful speech in front of a packed house, some fellow in the back who had been into the juice a little too much stood up and said something about graduation rates." Everyone knew the graduation rates of State's players under Valvano were not the best.

"Obviously, that's important to you," Valvano said to the man.

Bryant, sensing discomfort on all sides, grabbed his briefcase and motioned to Valvano to let it go, that it was time to leave anyway and start heading back to Raleigh. Instead, Valvano proceeded to talk for another fifteen minutes, quoting educators, philosophers, even Shakespeare.

"Education is not a race," he said. "You start the day you are born and you continue until the day you die. A lot of people get degrees and don't get an education—and a lot of people get an education, but don't get degrees. Let's not forget that."

When they piled back into their car to drive back to Raleigh, Bryant turned to Valvano.

"My God, Jim, that was deep," Bryant said.

"I just wanted that son of a bitch to know that everybody in athletics is not a dumb jock like some people think," Valvano said.

Years later, Bryant said of the incident: "Of course he made that guy look about an inch tall when he got through. Jim could embarrass you and then turn around and apologize and make you feel like he was your long-lost brother. He was the best at that."

□

WHILE NORTH CAROLINA was winning their first national championship under Dean Smith in 1982, State was returning to respectability under Valvano. The Wolfpack went 22-10 overall, including 7-7 in the ACC, and was one of four conference schools invited to participate in the NCAA Tournament. Although State lost in the first round to Tennessee-Chattanooga, the immediate future looked bright.

But not as bright as the future of their neighbor to the Northwest.

Michael Jordan was returning to North Carolina for his sophomore season. So was Sam Perkins. They also had a sixteen-year-old, 7-foot freshman with a big body and a soft shooting touch from Black Mountain, North Carolina, named Brad Daugherty.

Daugherty grew up a fan of college sports and had always kept a close eye on the ACC.

"Growing up in the area that I did, there were no professional teams," Daugherty said. "So our identity through sports came through the college teams. Everybody in the state of North Carolina pulls for one of the college teams. I don't care if you're a transplant or not.

"North Carolina, obviously, was God's country. But everybody basically either loved North Carolina or despised them. There was no middle of the road with North Carolina."

Surprisingly, Daugherty actually grew up a fan of the Clemson Tigers. He regularly made the trek to Death Valley to watch Clemson play football, and to Littlejohn Coliseum to watch the Tigers play basketball. But very early on in Daugherty's life, Dean Smith made a positive impression on him.

"Just the legacy of Dean Smith, ever since I was a kid, has always been one of great stature," Daugherty said. "Whenever anyone talked about basketball in the state of North Carolina, you had to mention his name. What I saw as I grew on and on was that even fans who liked other teams—and I'm talking about friends of mine —they would compare what kind of season their teams had based on what they did against North Carolina. That left an indelible impression on my mind."

So did the recruiting process that led him to the Tar Heels. By the time he was a junior in high school, all the big-time schools were after him. One day he was late for a Spanish class that was being taught by a woman who had already scolded him for tardiness.

"I had done something to piss her off," Daugherty said. "I think it might have had something to do with the fact that I always did well on the tests, but I never did my homework or anything like that. She would always try to catch me off-guard, but couldn't. So one day she told me that she had had it with me and she wasn't going to put up with any more from me."

The next day, Daugherty was late for her class again.

"I was just standing out in the yard bullshitting with some guys or something, but I was late," he said. "The bell rings. I'm already late, and I'm running to try to get to class. I'm going down the hall and I drop my books, and papers are flying everywhere."

Daugherty frantically gathered up all his books and papers and ran around the corner to his classroom door.

It was blocked by Jim Valvano.

"Wow, it's Jim Valvano," said Daugherty, who then started to chuckle.

"You don't know me right now, Brad," Valvano said. "Or maybe you do. But you need to get used to looking at this ugly mug, because you're going to be seeing it for four years when you come to North Carolina State."

Years later, Daugherty still had a vivid memory of the moment.

"I can still remember him standing there, pointing at his chin and saying that," Daugherty said. "I knew it was a violation of NCAA rules for him to just be there, talking to me. So I didn't really say anything at first. I just started laughing."

Finally, Daugherty said half in jest: "Okay, I'll see you when I get to Raleigh."

Valvano knew Daugherty wasn't taking him seriously. He grabbed the boy's arm and gripped it firmly.

"No, I'm serious," he said.

"Okay, I understand. But I'm late for class," said Daugherty, trying to break free.

Valvano held on to Daugherty's arm, intent on making his pitch.

"Listen, I really gotta go," Daugherty pleaded. "I'm late for class and this teacher can't stand me. I really gotta go."

"Okay, okay. But just remember this face. You're going to be seeing a lot of it," said Valvano, finally releasing his hold on Daugherty's arm.

Daugherty later added: "He wasn't supposed to even be near

me. That was a direct violation of NCAA rules. But you know, that kind of thing happened a lot."

Other coaches took different approaches. Lefty Driesell of Maryland tried to get to Brad through his mother.

"He was calling my mama all the time," Daugherty said. "My mom loved Lefty Driesell. She thought he hung the moon. He sweet-talked my mama every night of the week. She was just so set on me going to Maryland because she thought Lefty was so nice.

"We used to play pickup basketball games every day after school. For about three weeks straight, every day I went into the gym, Lefty was sitting there to watch me play pickup. He wouldn't say anything to me. He'd just sit there and watch me play pickup. Then he'd get up and go call my mom."

Driesell did a good enough job winning over Daugherty's mother to at least secure an official visit from her son. When Brad visited Maryland, Lefty told him to bring along one of his high-school teammates and his old coach. Daugherty was screwing around in Driesell's office, sitting in Lefty's chair and "just looking around and taking it all in" when Lefty walked in from another appointment.

Daugherty, slightly embarrassed, jumped up from the coach's seat.

"Aw, sit right down, son. That's all right. I don't care if you sit in my chair, as long as you come to Maryland to play basketball," Lefty said. "And you know what? If you come to Maryland, there might even be a scholarship in it for your buddy to come here and play, too."

Daugherty was stunned. His friend was thrilled.

"I mean, the guy was nowhere near that type of talent," Daugherty said. "But this guy's head swelled up so damn big. We went back home and he was going around telling everyone that he was going to Maryland, that they had offered him a scholarship to come there and play ball. I mean, he had averaged maybe 10 points a game and a couple of rebounds a game in high school."

One day Daugherty finally pulled his friend aside.

"Look, you're not going anywhere to play ball. You need to open up your eyes and look around, look what the guy is doing," he said.

"What do you mean?" his buddy asked.

"I mean that the only reason Lefty even said that was to try to get me to commit to Maryland. He doesn't care about you. He's not going to give you a scholarship—especially not if I don't go there."

That wasn't even the worst of the recruiting violations. Knowing his earlier ties to Clemson, the Tigers pushed hard to get Daugherty to go there. One night the phone rang in the Daugherty home. On the other end was Danny Ford, coach of the Clemson football team that had just won the national championship.

"I'm just calling to put in a good word for our basketball program. Bill Foster sure is a fine coach to play for," Ford said.

So Daugherty agreed to an official visit, and had dinner at coach Foster's house. A year earlier, another one of Daugherty's former high-school teammates and friends, Kevin Logan, had unexpectedly received a partial scholarship to Clemson.

"This guy was no rocket scientist," Daugherty said. "I mean, he's a good buddy of mine and all that. But one time for six weeks in Spanish class, I think his average was twenty. But he got this near-full ride to Clemson—not for academics or to play basketball, but for basketball team manager."

Shortly after Logan enrolled at Clemson, Daugherty's phone started ringing off the hook.

"What are you gonna do, man? Where are you gonna go to college?" Logan would ask his friend.

Daugherty had narrowed his potential choices to Georgetown, North Carolina, Clemson, and maybe Maryland. But he didn't want to tell anyone outside of his family that—not even Logan.

"I don't know yet. I've got some time," he said.

Clemson's coaches, meanwhile, started "showing up everywhere, out of the blue." They encouraged him to visit Clemson again and see his friend, which Daugherty did.

"I go down to visit my buddy at Clemson and we have a great time. I mean, he's a Big Man On Campus," Daugherty said. "They're treating him like a king. He was a scratch golfer at the time and even plays some on the Nike Tour today. And so they start talking about how they might just have a spot for him on the golf team, too."

One of the basketball coaches nodded at Logan and said: "Kevin's doing such a great job as basketball manager. We think we're going to add to his scholarship next year and get him on the golf team. It will be a full ride."

Daugherty and Logan thought this sounded great.

Signing day for Daugherty was November 10. On November 9, Logan called Daugherty in a panic.

"Rumors down here have it that you may be going to North Carolina," Logan said.

"Well, maybe. I still haven't made my mind up," Daugherty said. "I've got twenty-four hours left to think about it. What's going on down there with you?"

"I don't know, man. The last week or so, they've been treating me like shit. I had a Watts line [to make free long-distance phone calls] and they cut that off. I've just had a lot of problems all of a sudden."

"Well, don't worry. It'll all shake out," Daugherty said.

"I sure hope so," Logan said. "I just can't figure it out."

The next day, Daugherty announced he was going to North Carolina. The day after that, Logan called him again.

"Man, they told me to get all my shit and clean out my locker. My scholarship has been revoked," he said.

"On what grounds?" Daugherty asked.

"Man, they made up all kinds of stuff," Logan said.

"You know what this is all about, don't you? They created that scholarship for you to try to get me to come there."

"Well, I didn't understand that in the beginning. Then I kind of realized what was going on—but I wanted to think it was all going to work out."

Daugherty still shakes his head today thinking about what happened.

"That's unbelievable, isn't it? But it happened as plain as the nose on your face," he said.

Before he settled on North Carolina, Daugherty also gave Duke some consideration. He came away impressed with their coach.

"I went to Duke and met Coach Krzyzewski. I have a lot of respect for him," Daugherty said. "I really liked him right away. At the time, their program was really, really young. But I gave them a lot of consideration because I thought I would enjoy the academic side of Duke. The basketball program, I thought, was going to go a long way. I thought it would take a while, but I thought it was going to go a long way because of Mike Krzyzewski. I thought he was a stand-up guy."

Daugherty's visit to Chapel Hill, however, firmly made up his mind.

"My visit to North Carolina was unlike any other," he said.

He got out of the car he was riding in at The Carolina Inn, and one of the team's assistant coaches grabbed Daugherty's luggage and carried it in. Before Daugherty could let himself be impressed too much by this small but seemingly thoughtful touch of hospitality, Coach Dean Smith intervened.

"I'm going to tell you right now. If you come to North Carolina, that will be the only time we carry your bags. From now on, you'll have to carry your own bags," Smith said.

Daugherty nodded.

As they talked later in the day, Daugherty became more impressed by what Coach Smith didn't say than by what he did.

"Coach Smith didn't promise me anything except that I would receive an excellent education," Daugherty said. "That was it. He didn't say I was going to play a lot; he didn't say I was going to start; he didn't say I was going to get a car. He didn't say anything like that. And I can't say that for everyone else who tried to recruit me."

Smith knew that other schools sometimes dangled illegal deals in front of recruits. But he didn't say anything bad about any other schools, either. He only talked about what he was certain North Carolina had to offer Daugherty. None of the other coaches who had pursued Daugherty spent so little time talking basketball, and so much time talking about the other benefits of receiving a scholarship.

"You will receive an excellent education. I can guarantee that," Smith repeated again and again.

Eventually, he talked about basketball with Daugherty. But he talked more about life—and how an excellent education can prepare you for anything in life. He talked more about all the doctors and lawyers, coaches and successful businessmen his program had produced than he did about the professional basketball players that had passed through. Daugherty was bright for his age, but he was only sixteen, having graduated from high school early on an accelerated academics program. What Smith was saying struck a nerve. And it made most of the others who had been recruiting him suddenly seem more superficial than ever.

"Even at that young age, it stuck in my mind what he kept saying about getting an education," Daugherty said. "So many people have passed through this program. It's been stellar since Moses parted the waters of the Red Sea. It would have been easy to take the money and go to some other institution. It would have been nice to have a little pocket money and a nice car while I was playing a little basketball.

"But to me, that was a road to nowhere. I have to give credit to my parents for making me realize the importance of making a good decision at that time. I was obviously going to have a free education wherever I went. So the financial end of it, to me, was not that important because I knew I was going to be able to get a scholarship no matter where I went. I wanted to get a good education, too, and set myself up for a good future."

What clinched it for Daugherty was Smith's one visit to his home in Black Mountain. As the coach sat down with the young man and Daugherty's parents, he produced a Carolina media guide.

"I thought he was going to show me his coaching statistics or something like that," Daugherty said. "But he turned to the back of the media program, where it listed what the former basketball players are doing today. And if you look at that, there are literally hundreds of players in there . . . there's a doctor, a lawyer, a mayor, a corporate engineer, so on and so forth. There are not just a bunch of guys playing pro basketball. And his graduation rate is something like ninety percent. It's phenomenal.

"All of that really meant something to me. I grew up in a small town. I didn't want to be a farmer for the rest of my life. I didn't want to work in the blanket mill. God bless those people who do that; I have a lot of admiration for them. But I didn't want to do that. I wanted to achieve something more than that, either professionally through sports or professionally through business. So I just thought North Carolina offered me—a home-grown product—a wonderful opportunity to do that. To have something like that available to me in my home state, I felt like I had to take advantage of that."

WHEN WOLFPACK POINT GUARD SIDNEY LOWE first heard Norm Sloan was leaving North Carolina State to become the coach at Florida, he became so upset that he stormed into Sloan's office at Reynolds Coliseum and began screaming at the departing coach.

"I came here because you told me you were going to be here my whole four years, and now here you are telling me you're leaving after I've only been here one," Lowe said. "I feel betrayed. I'm crushed."

As the words gushed from Lowe's mouth, tears began to stream from his eyes. Lowe openly wept. Sloan tried to choke back tears himself as he explained that he had to do what was best for himself and his family, that Lowe would be fine and so would the basketball program at North Carolina State.

"I feel like it's best for me to move on," Sloan said.

"Then I'll come with you. I'll transfer to Florida and come with you," Lowe pleaded.

"No," said Sloan, leaving no room for argument. "I told you when I recruited you that N.C. State was the best place for you, and I still believe that. Based on all the things you were looking for—like staying close to home, so your family can see you play—this is still the best place for you. Believe me, you will get over my leaving."

Lowe wasn't so sure. He had long ago fallen in love with the school and the coach. He had played high school ball for the legendary Morgan Wooten at DeMatha High, and a couple of former DeMatha players—Olympian Kenny Carr and Hawkeye Whitney, to name two—had gone on to play for Sloan at State. Lowe used to watch those alumni play on television. Lowe thought State was the place to go.

"I liked Coach Sloan. I thought he looked like a fun guy to play for. I used to get a kick out of the checkered sports coats he would wear," Lowe said.

Lowe, a stocky point guard who was listed at 6 feet, 195 pounds, arrived in Raleigh as a freshman for what would be Sloan's last year at the school. Clyde Austin was the senior point guard then, and Lowe figured he could study and learn under Austin before he took over as the starting point guard.

Then Sloan left unexpectedly. Many thought it was because of Austin, who had come under scrutiny when the *News & Observer* of Raleigh reported that he had two cars—a brand-new 1980 Cadillac sedan and a 1976 MG sports car—registered in his name. Austin and Sloan insisted there was nothing to the report, even though Austin did admit to having the cars. He said his fiancée was making payments on the Cadillac and that a buddy of his from his hometown of Richmond, Virginia, was making payments on the MG. Austin eventually was cleared of wrongdoing, but the entire incident raised suspicion about how Sloan was operating his program.

Lowe thought Sloan left because he was frustrated on two fronts: no matter what he did he always felt overshadowed by North Carolina and Dean Smith; and he didn't feel State was appreciative enough of all that he had done for the school.

Nonetheless, Sloan left after the 1979–80 season and was succeeded by Jimmy Valvano. Shortly after accepting the job, Valvano met with Lowe and the other players.

"I didn't recruit any of you, so I don't owe any of you anything," Valvano began. "Let's be clear on that. I don't owe any of you anything. Let's get that straight right off the bat."

Lowe and the others were taken aback. They weren't sure what to think of this fast-talking coach from New York.

"I'm here to teach you about basketball and help you grow as individuals," Valvano continued. "But I just wanted to be clear on that first point—that I don't owe you any favors. You will have to compete for playing time and positions on this team. I don't care what you've done in the past or been told in the past by the previous coaching staff. None of that matters now.

"You have to earn my trust and respect now. That's how you will earn your playing time and positions on this team from this day forward."

Valvano knew he would have to earn respect, too.

The first time he got his hair cut in Raleigh after taking the position, the barber mused, "So you're the new coach at State, eh?"

"Yes, I am," Valvano stated proudly.

"Well, I sure hope you do better than the last guy," the barber cracked.

Valvano later told friends that he thought to himself: "Now wait a minute. Didn't the last guy go undefeated one year, win 57 of 58 games over one two-year stretch, and win a national championship? What's wrong with that? What have I gotten myself into here?"

All of the State players figured it would only be a matter of time until Valvano replaced them with his own recruits, guys he felt more loyalty to, guys he owed something. But Valvano promised them a chance to compete on the court to earn their standing on the team—and that, in the end, is all they wanted.

"I wasn't concerned about the competing part," Lowe said. "That never bothered me because I loved to compete. I figured I could beat out anybody he brought in. What I was worried about was the new coach bringing in one of his own guys and playing favorites, not giving me a fair chance to compete."

To Lowe's relief, that wasn't the case. Valvano was fair to the returning players. After struggling to a 14-13 record his first season and improving to 22-10 with an NCAA appearance in 1982, the Wolfpack entered Lowe's senior season, 1982–83, full of confidence.

They won 7 of their first 8 games, with the only loss coming at Louisville by a mere 5 points. In 3 of those victories, the offense clicked to score over 100 points. No team seemed better prepared to take advantage of experimental rules adopted by the ACC: a thirty-second shot clock and a 3-point basket from the seemingly short distance of nineteen feet. Valvano, now in his third season and becoming increasingly popular with both his own players and the alumni, was even rewarded with a ten-year contract early in the season.

Despite their quick start, the Wolfpack were not the favorites to win the ACC. Virginia had center Ralph Sampson back for his senior season. North Carolina had Sam Perkins, Matt Doherty, Brad Daugherty, and a much-improved Michael Jordan. North Carolina State figured to win their share of games, but no one expected them to beat Virginia or North Carolina.

One week before an early season loss to North Carolina, the Wolfpack took a serious blow when Dereck Whittenburg, a valuable team leader, broke his foot against Virginia. But later that season, with Whittenburg still out, State avenged that loss by posting a 70–63 upset victory against North Carolina that set off a wild celebration in Reynolds Coliseum. Whittenburg returned for the final three regular-season contests, including a most impressive win against Wake Forest, 130–89, at Reynolds in the season finale.

Sitting in the stands watching that day, Charlie Bryant told some companions: "This [State] is a good basketball team. Good teams can run, handle the ball, and shoot. All great teams have two outstanding guards—and with Whittenburg back, we have two of the best guards in the country."

The rout over Wake improved State's record to 17-10 and put the Pack in position to make the NCAA Tournament again if it could win a game or two in the ACC Tournament.

"That was something all of us seniors wanted," Lowe said. "We didn't want to go out not having gotten to the NCAAs in our final season."

Lowe said he and his teammates talked about how they needed to win the ACC Tournament to assure it happening. They didn't want to win only one or two games and then be left sitting on the bubble when the NCAA selection committee started calling out at-large bids.

"I didn't even want to think that way," Lowe said. "I thought we would have to win the ACC Tournament, or we would end up in the NIT. That was not what we wanted."

Their first-round opponent in the ACC Tournament was Wake Forest. This time, the Deacons were determined to put up a better fight. It wasn't until Lowe stole a pass and made a nice feed to Lorenzo Charles—who drew a foul and made a free throw with three seconds left—that State escaped with a 71–70 victory to set up another rematch against North Carolina.

The Tar Heels thought they had the Wolfpack beaten, but State battled back. After trailing by 6 points early in overtime, they nipped the Heels again, 91–84. State fans began calling their team "the Cardiac Pack," because of all their last-minute heroics. To this day, Michael Jordan remains perplexed by the loss.

"We knew we were the dominant team, and they would have to play a perfect game to beat us every time we met. But they did it twice—and it hurt," Jordan said.

North Carolina State clearly was on a roll. But Virginia and Ralph Sampson still stood in the way of an ACC championship. The Cavaliers were on a roll of their own: they beat Duke 109–66 for the most lopsided defeat in Blue Devil and ACC Tournament history, and then pounded Georgia Tech 96–67 in the semifinals.

But while Virgina had Sampson and a fine supporting cast, State had developed a perfect inside-outside scoring balance that could not be matched. Lowe scored 18, Whittenburg 15, and Terry Gannon 12 on four 3-pointers to make the Pack impossible to defend on the perimeter while Thurl Bailey (24 points) and Charles (12 rebounds) dominated inside. State won, 81–78.

Bryant was on the floor during the State celebration when a large black man surprised him by putting his arm around him from behind. Bryant turned and heard the man say, "Charlie, we had a great ride last year. But I'm going to be pulling for you this year. You guys are going to win it all."

The man was James Worthy, Sr.

At the press conference the day before State was to play Pepperdine in the opening round in Corvallis, Oregon, Jim Harrick, then the coach at Pepperdine, suggested to the media that as good as State's backcourt was with Lowe and Whittenburg and the sharpshooting Gannon, his was better.

"He said something in that press conference, implying that their backcourt was better than our backcourt," Lowe said. "We wanted to prove him wrong."

Lowe may have tried too hard. He fouled out with several minutes left to play, and watched from the bench, horrified, as Dave Suttle, one of Harrick's sure-shooting guards, lined up for a one-and-one chance with Pepperdine leading by 6 points with one minute left in the first overtime. Suttle ranked third in the nation in free-throw percentage.

"I can't believe I'm going to end my career here this way, fouling out in a losing ball game," Lowe thought to himself.

In the stands, Bryant muttered: "I can't believe we came all the way to Corvallis, Oregon, to see this."

But Suttle, a 90-percent free-throw shooter, missed. State grabbed the rebound and went down to score before fouling Suttle yet again. It still looked bleak, but at least there was some hope.

Lowe looked up from the bench and thought, "He's a great free-throw shooter. There's no way he's going to miss again.

But Suttle missed again and State pulled out a remarkable 69–67 win in double overtime.

Afterward in the State locker room, Valvano told his players: "Hey, we may be destined to win this thing."

Lowe said he didn't really begin believing until after the next game, a 71–70 win over powerful Nevada–Las Vegas. State had trailed by 12 points in the second half and again benefited from some poor free-throw shooting by their opponent down the stretch.

Then State crushed Utah in the third round, shooting 79 percent from the field in the second half to turn a 32–30 deficit into a 75–56 victory. The Wolfpack's opponent in the West Regional final was Virginia.

This was Sampson's final shot at redemption in a college career that had been undeniably great, but had lacked any championships. After beating the Wolfpack twice during the ACC regular season, the Cavaliers had suffered the indignity of losing in the ACC Tournament championship game 81–78. This was a chance to avenge that loss. Virginia soared ahead by 10 points in the first half and led by 7 with seven minutes, thirty seconds to go. But that meant nothing to the Cardiac Pack. They were used to working from behind.

Whittenburg hit 11 of 16 shots for 24 points and Charles nailed 2 free throws with twenty-three seconds left to put State ahead 63–62. Virginia tried to get the ball in to Sampson for the final play, but couldn't. Virginia's Tim Mullen missed an eighteen-foot jumper and Othell Wilson missed a six-footer as time expired. Sampson's career ended with 112 victories and only 23 losses, but no ACC championships and no NCAA title.

For State, it was on to the Final Four in Albuquerque, New Mexico, and a date with Georgia—the team that had eliminated North Carolina in the East Regional. State built an 18-point lead and held on to win, 67–60, setting up a championship game against number-one-ranked Houston, which featured Clyde Drexler and a much-improved Akeem Olajuwon. The Cougars loved to run and dunk and they called themselves the fraternity of Phi Slamma Jamma.

As State was finishing up its shootaround the day before the game, Houston arrived for their prechampionship game tuneup.

"The Houston team walked in, wearing sunglasses, listening to their Walkmans, and with their slippers on—like they were going to the beach or something," Lowe said. "Me and Dereck were there looking at each other and getting kind of angry about it. Us and Terry Gannon, who at five-ten would fight anybody or anything at the drop of a hat if he felt like he needed to. We all got fired up about that thing. We felt right then and there that we could beat them if we played our game.

"When Dereck and I watched them beat Louisville in the semis, we had some doubts ourselves. . . . But that was the day before they came strolling into the shootaround with their slippers on. It was clear to us that they felt they had already won the national title. They weren't even thinking about us. No one had to say a word to us. Dereck and I were fired up just looking over there at them. Here we were, dripping with sweat because we had just finished up a pretty good workout. And then these guys come in like they don't have any work to do. It just pissed us off."

No one outside of the Wolfpack den felt State had a chance. Columnist Dave Kindred of the *Washington Post* wrote: "Trees will tap dance, elephants will ride in the Indianapolis 500, and Orson Welles will skip breakfast, lunch, and dinner before State finds a way to beat Houston."

Charlie Smith of the *Tulsa World* wrote: "North Carolina State's best chance is a bus wreck."

And on the day of the big game came these disturbing words from Joe Henderson of the *Tampa Tribune:*

Blindfold? Cigarette? Last words?
Sayanora, N.C. State.
State will probably be escorted by armed guards and priests mumbling the 23rd Psalm as it comes out for tonight's national championship game against the Houston High Phis. There'll be no reprieve. The noose drops at 9:12 P.M.

Valvano and his North Carolina State players duly noted all the disrespect, perceived or otherwise, and filed it away to use as motivation. Then the Cardiac Pack came out and played what Valvano would later call a "perfect" first half, controlling the tempo and moving out to a surprising 33–25 lead. But Houston went on a 17–2 run at the beginning of the second half to move in front, 42–35, with ten minutes left.

Then Houston coach Guy Lewis made the mistake of trying to take some time off the clock instead of building on the momentum his players had gained. North Carolina State began fouling the Cougars, and Houston struggled to hit their free throws. With one minute, five seconds remaining, State tied the score at 52 before fouling Houston guard Alvin Franklin.

Franklin missed the front end of the one-and-one and State called a time-out with forty-four seconds left to set up the final play. Valvano, who was a master in this situation, told Lowe to let the clock run down to about six or seven seconds and then try to penetrate. When the defense collapsed on him, all Lowe had to do was find the open man. Valvano figured either Gannon, Whittenburg, or Bailey would be left free, and each had the ability to knock down an open jumper. Lorenzo Charles would remain underneath the basket to take a stab at grabbing the rebound and putting it in if one of the others misfired. By making his move with six or seven seconds left, there would be time for a tip-in or a quick shot off a rebound—but not enough time for Houston to get a shot off at the other end if the Cougars rebounded instead.

Lowe was calm in the huddle. It sounded good. The plan should work, he thought. He was confident as he began to make his move toward the basket with just under ten seconds remaining, a little earlier than Valvano had wanted.

"We came out in a semi-spread offense. They started out in a zone, but they started cheating out," Lowe said. "I actually went a little soon, which turned out to be good. I went when I did—with about eight or nine seconds left—because Thurl was in the corner, and that was his shot.

"So I made a move and—bang!—I hit Thurl down on the baseline."

Lowe thought the game was won. All Bailey had to do was shoot and hit his favorite shot from the corner.

"But he didn't shoot it!" exclaimed Lowe, still in disbelief fifteen years later. "He threw it back out to Dereck."

The rest is vintage college basketball history. The surprised Whittenburg, fired a thirty-foot shot off in a hurry.

"From my angle," said Lowe, "Dereck's shot didn't look bad.

My first reaction whenever Dereck shot the ball was: he's going to make it. He made so many big shots for us. So I thought it was going in. I couldn't tell it was so short."

It was really short. And off to the right. It wasn't even close to hitting the rim.

But Charles instinctively grabbed the ball and dunked it while Olajuwon and the rest of the Houston Cougars basically just stood by and watched.

The buzzer sounded.

State had pulled off the impossible. They won 54–52.

The Wolfpack were national champions.

"When Lorenzo got in there and grabbed it and dunked it, I immediately looked at the officials to see if they were going to call offensive goaltending," Lowe said. "When they didn't, that's when I knew we had won the game.

"Lorenzo wasn't sure what he had just done. He had no clue how big it was. Coach V came running out onto the court. We all started going nuts. My first reaction was to find my mother. I ran up into the stands and hugged her and Mrs. Bailey. Then I came back down and joined the celebration with everyone else."

Television cameras caught Valvano running all over the court, looking for someone to hug. The players were too busy hugging each other. Finally he found Willis Casey, the athletics director who had hired him three years earlier.

"He hugged me," Valvano later told reporters. "That wasn't so bad. But then he kissed me right on the lips, too. I could just see some guy out in Kansas watching this on television and saying, 'Martha, come here. You've got to see this.' "

During the jubilant celebration that followed, Coach Jimmy V smiled widely and joked: "My wife is going to be pregnant—she doesn't know this yet—and I'm going to name the kid Al B. Querque."

Lowe, who went on to play and coach in the NBA, said time has not diminished the accomplishment of the 1983 N.C. State team. When it was suggested that the team will go down as one of the greatest Cinderella stories in the history of college basketball, he said: "It really doesn't matter what they want to call it. It's the highlight of my basketball career. I don't know if it can ever be topped. It put a lot of people on the map, so to speak. No one gave us a chance to win it. The odds were totally against us. But we did it. And the way we did it, I don't think anything else could top that.

"When people think about Sid Lowe, everything goes back to

that NCAA title team. I was fortunate enough to be drafted into the NBA, and that was a big deal for me. I was fortunate enough to be a head coach in the NBA [of the Minnesota Timberwolves]. But I could be part of winning an NBA title, and people will still say, 'Ah, yeah, Sid Lowe. I remember him. He was an integral part of the Cardiac Pack.' And that's okay with me."

It was more than okay with Jim Valvano in 1983. It was an affirmation of everything he believed he could accomplish as a coach.

13

DUKE POWER

NOT EVERYONE in Big Four country was ecstatic about North Carolina State's incredible dash to the 1983 national title. Outsiders might theorize that when one school from the Big Four is eliminated from the NCAA Tournament, boosters of the ousted school then root for the teams from the area who remain in the hunt. That isn't the way it works in most cases in the Tarheel state.

The father of former North Carolina star James Worthy, James Sr., was the exception to the Big Four rule when he sneaked up behind Charlie Bryant and said he would be pulling for State to win in '83. Michael Jordan certainly didn't pull for State after Carolina got eliminated by Georgia.

"If there was anybody we wanted to win, it wasn't N.C. State," Jordan said. "They were too close, and we had won the national championship the year before. We didn't want them to have any comeback conversation for us."

Then again, North Carolina State fans weren't pulling for North Carolina during the Tar Heels' 1982 championship run either. In fact, State fans later broke into Carmichael Auditorium, stole the Heels' 1982 national championship banner, and hung it from an overpass on Interstate-40 adding the words "NEVER AGAIN" underneath "national champions." The Heels saw this as their team bus passed by on the way to a game against State that night.

Perhaps that explains why Jordan didn't really want to give the Wolfpack much credit for their 1983 national title even fifteen years later.

233

"We lost to Georgia in the NCAA Tournament in Syracuse. Then Georgia goes to the Final Four and loses to N.C. State. Certain things were meant to be and that was it," Jordan said. "We were the best team that year without a doubt. That is a prime example of the best team not winning."

But if you talked to some folks from North Carolina State, they would say that for once it was a year when their counterparts from North Carolina didn't receive all the lucky breaks. Leonard Laye and Ron Green, Sr., were covering the national championship game for the *Charlotte Observer*. They ran into Frank Weedon, State's long-time sports information director, on the court during the wild celebration after the Wolfpack's epic win over Houston. He did not look as pleased as they thought he would.

"Did you see how those ACC officials tried to screw us?" he demanded, complaining about some call made or not made during the game by the all-ACC crew of Joe Forte, Hank Nichols, and Paul Housman. Earlier, the appointment of the all-ACC crew had drawn criticism and considerable skepticism on the part of Houston and every other non-ACC school. But the NCAA wanted to get a crew that had worked together before and had developed some chemistry.

Standing near Weedon was Jim Pomerantz, who had gone to school at State and served as Weedon's assistant in the SID office.

"You know the greatest thing about this?" he asked Laye.

"What?"

"The ACC media guide cover won't be Carolina blue next year."

These were the thoughts running through State fans' minds just moments after their team had carved a place in college basketball history. Yeah, it was a great win, but the best thing about it was sticking it to Carolina.

"There does seem to be some rooting within the conference, but it's always excluding Carolina," Laye said. "That gets back to the ABC bunch."

The passion with which fans root for their teams in the Big Four is unmatched anywhere else in the United States.

No one came to know that more quickly than the coach who arrived on the Big Four scene on March 18, 1980.

Before Mike Krzyzewski took the Duke job, he found out as much information about the school as he possibly could. Vic Bubas's name kept popping up. One of the first things Krzyzewski did when he got hired was seek Bubas out for advice. It began a relationship they would continue for many years.

"One of the reasons his place in history is not as well-marked as maybe it should be is that he did it all in one decade and it happened to be the decade that UCLA stood in everyone's way, not just his," Krzyzewski said of Bubas. "He was unbelievable in the sixties, but it was really before the explosion in popularity that college basketball enjoyed later on a national level. He was appreciated in this region for what he did, but UCLA overshadowed him nationally—as UCLA did to everyone at that time.

"I respected his accomplishments. After meeting him, I saw right away that he had a great mind for sports and organization. I knew he was someone I should listen to for advice if he was willing to give it."

Bubas was willing.

"Just be yourself," the old Duke coach told Krzyzewski. "And don't get too caught up in the Carolina rivalry. If you do, it can eat you alive. Be close-minded to all that stuff and just worry about what you can do to get this program where you think it ought to be. If you do that and avoid getting consumed by comparisons to Carolina or even North Carolina State, you'll be fine and all the other stuff will take care of itself."

The early years were extremely hard for Krzyzewski, yet Tom Butters, the man who hired him, never left him with the impression that he was in danger of losing his job. For that, Coach K would be forever grateful. As he watched Valvano's stunning success twenty-odd miles to the north in Raleigh, and witnessed the magic Dean Smith was spinning just 10.6 miles down U.S. Highway 15-501, Krzyzewski longed to experience the same kind of euphoria.

It took time. In 1981–82, when Smith was winning his first national championship at Carolina, Krzyzewski struggled to a 10-17 finish. In 1982–83, when Valvano won his national title at State, Duke finished 11-17.

"Those were difficult times. I was really young," Krzyzewski said. "But I always felt we were going to be good. I did not sit down and see the success we would eventually have. But I felt we would be good. I felt good about the future.

"I did not pay that much attention to the fans. That may be because I was young and naive. It may have been because of my military background. At West Point, you always had someone in your face screaming at you. You learned to live with it. I really think my discipline in that regard helped."

Over time, Krzyzewski's players would learn to live with and understand the same type of discipline. Coach K could be profane and emphatic when he wanted to get a point across, much like his former coach, mentor, and friend, legendary Indiana coach Bob Knight. He preached aggressive play and favored hounding man-to-man defense over the gimmickry of zones. He told his players that if they played hard for forty minutes, they would have nothing to hang their heads about—win or lose. And he assured them that if they would only do that, they surely would win much more often than they would lose.

Danny Ferry, who ended up being one of Krzyzewski's early prize recruits, had trouble getting a feel for his coach at first. Yet he liked him immensely almost instantly.

"Going to Duke on a recruiting visit was kind of a home-style thing where we went over to Coach K's house with his family," Ferry said. "I was there the same weekend as Quin Snyder, and we ended up rooming together for four years. The way Coach K recruited you was different. He's funny, he's serious, he's intense, he's a very warm person. He's all of those things. It kind of catches you off-guard because all you knew about him before was: he's a Bobby Knight guy. So then you're thinking after you meet him, 'Maybe he's not a Bobby Knight guy.'

"He was a man's man. He was a good communicator who told you where you fit in. . . . Coach K is so good at helping you gain confidence in both yourself and the group you're playing with."

Krzyzewski's way of doing that would be to sidle up to a player and make quick, subtle comments, often laced with profanity for effect. When Ferry was a freshman, Krzyzewski watched him make a play during practice. The Coach then sauntered over to him and said, "Danny, that was a great play. You're really getting to be fucking good."

Krzyzewski's real talent though, was building his players up. He might tear them down little by little to rebuild them, but the process made them stronger as individuals and as a unit.

"Overall, he's a positive reinforcement type of guy," Ferry said. "He's not afraid to smack you on the butt to get you going, either. But he can really bring people together and make you feel good. His communication is so good."

Ferry didn't head to Duke to play basketball without first considering a number of other top-notch schools. Like Sidney Lowe and Dereck Whittenburg and others who had played for Morgan Wooten at DeMatha High, Ferry was heavily recruited.

As usual, Maryland coach Lefty Driesell was in the mix of things. So was Dean Smith. Ferry gave both schools strong consideration before settling on Duke.

"I like Lefty a lot," Ferry said. "He's a good guy and a good coach and the whole deal. But when I was choosing a school, I kind of wanted to go away. My high school is literally two miles from Maryland and Cole Field House. So that kind of ruled them out."

Driesell knew this, but made a run at Ferry anyway. He dispatched a limousine to pick up Ferry one day, and then had the limo take Ferry and assistant coach Ron Bradley to College Park Airport only a mile away. The two men then boarded a small airplane, which first flew over Ferry's nearby home before heading to Cole Field House.

As they flew over Cole Field House, Ferry blinked and rubbed his eyes. There in huge letters that stretched maybe forty feet across the top of the building was a sign that read: "DANNY'S HOUSE."

Ferry laughed.

"I tell you what, Lefty has style," he said.

But Ferry wanted to go away. He almost went to Carolina, but the clincher came one night when he was out having a few beers with Tar Heel star Joe Wolf in a Chapel Hill bar. Earlier he had done the same with some guys from a fraternity at Duke and really had hit it off with them. Suddenly, his Duke drinking buddies entered the same Chapel Hill bar where Ferry sat with Wolf. They started talking again. When he left the bar, it wasn't with Joe Wolf and the Chapel Hill crowd. He left with the Durham gang.

Krzyzewski, meanwhile, learned quickly that life as coach at Duke was a lot like life in a fishbowl—not only on his own campus and among his own alumni, but also throughout the state of North Carolina. Butters, whose strong belief in the coach had never wavered, gave Krzyzewski the time he needed to begin building a strong program.

The athletic director's faith in his coach soon paid off—thanks in large part to a high-scoring guard named Johnny Dawkins who, according to Krzyzewski, "committed to me before it was fashionable." Dawkins averaged 18.1 points, 4.9 assists, and 4.1 rebounds as a freshman, and went on to become the first player in school history to lead the team in scoring four straight years. He was joined by Mark Alarie, David Henderson, and Jay Bilas in what was rated the best recruiting class in the country by many publications. The four started together most of their freshman year and endured the hardships of that 11–17 finish, using it as motivational fodder to help the Blue Devils to records of 24-10 and 23-8 en route to NCAA Tournament bids each of the next two seasons.

Then came the breakthrough year of 1985–86. Duke opened with 16 straight wins, and were ranked number three in the national polls prior to a January showdown in Chapel Hill with top-ranked North Carolina. But this wasn't just any meeting between the two rivals. Michigan, ranked number two in the nation, had already lost earlier in the week—so the teams knew they were playing for the number-one ranking. Plus it was the first game ever in the Dean E. Smith Student Activities Center, a 21,444-seat arena named after the living legend himself.

Having an arena built and named in honor of a coach still active was highly unusual and Smith had not endorsed it at first. Not only was Smith reluctant to have a building named after him, but he also openly questioned whether the school needed to fork out $30 million to build it. In the end though, it was a magnificent structure—except for one oversight. No one had thought to put in a room where the media could work, giving some indication of Smith's opinion of the Fourth Estate. He put up with them, but did not consider them essential to the ultimate success or failure of his program. For opening night, the press had to work in a makeshift area in one of the hallways.

The game that night was well worth reporting.

"It was really kind of an exciting deal," said Ferry, who was then a freshman. "They were number one and we were trying to get there. The energy in the building that night was great."

The result, from Duke's standpoint, was not so great as Carolina won, 95–92. Following the narrow loss at the Smith Center—or the Dean Dome as it would come to be called—Duke stumbled again in its next game, losing at Georgia Tech. Tech entered the game 15-1 and ranked third in the nation—having come a long way from their early years in the ACC. After joining the conference in 1980, the school had won only 8 of its first 56 league games.

After the loss to Tech, however, Duke ran off 21 straight victories to advance all the way to the NCAA championship game. Along the way, the Devils finished first in the ACC regular season for the first time since 1966 and won the ACC Tournament for the first time since 1980. Dawkins clinched the 68–67 victory over Georgia Tech in the title game with a key late rebound and two free throws.

The magical season, however, ended with a narrow 72–69 loss to Louisville in the NCAA championship game. But it was the beginning of a new and wonderful era for Duke basketball. Dawkins finished his career as the school's all-time leading scorer with 2,566 points and was named the National Player of the Year after helping the Blue Devils to an NCAA-record 37 wins.

After Dawkins, Alarie, Henderson, and Bilas came Tommy Amaker, Billy King, Ferry, and Snyder; and after Ferry came Christian Laettner, Bobby Hurley, Grant Hill, and others. Suddenly Duke was on top again, making additional Final Four appearances in 1988, 1989, and 1990. People were talking about Krzyzewski's program and writing about it. The only things he had yet to prove in their eyes was that he could win The Big One. That would come soon enough.

WHILE KRZYZEWSKI was reestablishing Duke as a national power, Valvano was busy establishing himself as a national icon. Maybe too busy. His program at North Carolina State slipped a little on the court in the process. Off the court, his program slipped into trouble.

Following the national championship season, State stumbled to a 4-10 record in the ACC and failed to gain a return bid to the NCAA Tournament. Valvano won 20 or more games in each of the next five seasons—advancing to the Elite Eight in the NCAAs in both 1985 and 1986 and winning the 1987 ACC Tournament—but Valvano gained a reputation for being so intent on building himself up that he too often forgot he was supposed to be a builder of young men. Although he gained a reputation for being one of the best coaches in college basketball if you were talking about in-game strategy and adjustments in the heat of battle, he was one of the worst in terms of putting in the necessary time for pregame preparation. Oftentimes he left the running of practice to assistant coaches while he ran off to a speaking engagement or a television broadcasting commitment, telling his assistant coaches to inform anyone who asked that he was off visiting a sick aunt or uncle.

Within a few years of winning the national title, chinks were beginning to show in the North Carolina State basketball armor. One time Valvano was walking through an airport with Billy Packer and a reporter. Valvano was beginning to do some color analyst work on television even during his own season, and he was flying from Louisville, where State had lost a game that afternoon, to Illinois to do network analyst work on a Big Ten game the following day.

"Billy, give me some tips," Valvano said. "I'm doing this game tomorrow."

As always, Packer was blunt.

"Jim, the only tip I would give to you is to not go to Illinois and go back to Raleigh with your team," Packer said. "Your team just lost a lousy game by playing lousy. And now those kids are going to be back in Raleigh tomorrow afternoon watching you on television enjoying yourself? I don't think that's a good idea. If I'm going to give you any tip, it's to get on a plane and go back home with your team."

Valvano ignored the advice. He got a little peeved about it, in fact, especially when the reporter who had been walking with the two men through the airport reported what they had believed was a private conversation in the newspaper the next day.

Packer's phone rang shortly thereafter. It was Valvano's agent.

"You're jealous. You think he's going to take your job," he accused the television analyst.

"I don't give a shit about that," Packer insisted. "He asked for my opinion and I gave it to him."

Packer later thought about the incident. It made him think of his old coach at Wake Forest, Bones McKinney. Like Valvano, McKinney had been a great in-game strategist who cared little for pregame preparation. He also remembered how McKinney self-destructed and wondered if Valvano was coming closer to the edge himself.

"I think that Jimmy was probably one of the most talented business minds in the game," Packer said. "He also was like Bones in that he was a tremendous game strategist. But what happened to Jimmy was he lost sight of the picture of the coach. Because he was so talented like Bones McKinney, he got himself into too many things and spread himself too thin. But he was a guy of magnificent talent in a lot of areas. Unfortunately, I think he realized too late that he should have focused better on the things at hand."

But Valvano also had a softer side. Charlie Bryant's son, Gary, had been team manager for the Wolfpack prior to graduating. After home games, Valvano had the kid run off to the local convenience store to fetch a bottle of wine and a bag of Fritos. Then Coach V would sit in his office drinking the wine and munching on the Fritos long after everyone else had left the building.

When Gary Bryant got married in Atlanta a few years later, Valvano showed up at the church with a brown paper bag in his hand.

"What the hell is he doing with that paper bag? What's he got in there?" Charlie Bryant wondered aloud.

He soon found out. After the wedding ceremony, Valvano handed the bag to Gary Bryant.

"This is for all the times when you ran out and got me my postgame goodies," Valvano told him.

Inside was a bottle of wine and a bag of Fritos. When Charlie Bryant's mother celebrated her hundredth birthday a few years later, all she could talk about was how Valvano had "just added so much life to the wedding" when her grandson Gary had gotten married.

Valvano even had a soft spot in his heart for other coaches. When Carl Tacy suddenly retired at Wake Forest after thirteen seasons in 1985, Bob Staak replaced him. Staak not only found the cupboard bare when he arrived in Winston-Salem, he also had some bad luck when a number of his key players got injured. The Demon Deacons went 0-14 in the conference in 1985–86, Staak's first year as coach.

One of those losses came against State. Near the end of the game, Wake was flirting with pulling off an upset. Packer was announcing, and with about eight minutes left he suddenly found himself doing something he thought he had trained himself not to do. In his heart, he was pulling for one of the teams to win. He was pulling for Staak.

"I'm praying to let the guy win a game. I'm rooting so hard in my heart . . . not because it's Wake Forest, but because Bobby is working his ass off and every time he takes one step forward, he goes two steps back. Muggsy Bogues is on a team that otherwise is just a disaster," Packer said.

Alas, Wake lost in double-overtime. Afterward Packer ran into Valvano in the hallway outside the two teams' locker rooms.

"I want to tell you something," Packer said. "This was only the second time in my life I've ever rooted for someone to win a game I was broadcasting. I was rooting against you."

"Billy, let me tell *you* something," Valvano said. "I was sitting over there on our bench hoping he would figure out a way to win the game, too. It was really weird. I wasn't going to do anything to give it to him, but deep down I was hoping he would find a way to pull it out."

Valvano meant it. He had known Staak for years and figured the embattled Wake coach needed the victory a whole lot more than his own established program did.

"It wasn't a bullshit statement," Packer concluded.

Yet by 1989, Valvano (who was also the school's athletic director) had his own problems. Allegations of all kinds of abuses were leveled in a book written by Peter Golenbock entitled, *Personal Fouls: The Broken Promises and Shattered Dreams of Big Money Basketball at Jim Valvano's North Carolina State.* Word of the book's many allegations leaked prior to its publication, prompting some quick action by Charlie Bryant.

Bryant said allegations that grades were fixed and millions of dollars were funneled to players through alumni and other means were untrue and outrageous. He and other members of the Wolfpack Club helped convince one publishing house to cancel its plans to put out the book—but another publisher quickly came forward and printed many of what later were proven to be unsubstantiated charges. But the book also raised some legitimate questions that led to an investigation of the basketball program by the school itself and the NCAA.

One of the allegations raised by the book was that "millions of dollars raised annually by the private, 11,000-member Wolfpack Club were secretly distributed by Valvano and the Club." Bryant later joked that the Wolfpack Club "didn't even have thousands of dollars lying around anywhere to secretly distribute to anyone. The charge was ridiculous and totally irresponsible."

Nonetheless, a pattern had been set that indicated Valvano hadn't been paying close enough attention to his players or the inner workings of his own program. Evidence was traced back to the early days of the Jimmy V years, such as the time Lorenzo Charles assaulted a pizza-delivery man or Chris Washburn stole stereo equipment. These so-called "student-athletes" and others like them often were absent from class but somehow retained their eligibility year after year. Yet they rarely graduated.

Soon outsiders were making fun of the program. Pat Williams, then general manager of the Philadelphia 76ers joked that he heard Valvano had a huge scandal on his hands. "Three of his players were spotted heading to class," he told a reporter.

It didn't help when Charles Shackleford, a star center in the mid-1980s, described how he could shoot with either hand by saying, "Sure, I'm amphibious." Or when South Carolina native Cozell McQueen, another player under Valvano, told reporters he "came to N.C. State to get out of the South."

Again Bryant emerged as Valvano's staunchest defender.

"All this business about exploiting athletes and not caring about athletes, well, absolutely nothing could be further from the truth in talking about Jim Valvano," Bryant said. "If there was ever a coach that lived who cared about education, it was Jim Valvano. He would get on the team bus and start telling the players how to structure a sentence. I'm serious. On the way to Chapel Hill, he would be talking about sentence structure and how you could change a sentence. He was an English major and he enjoyed talking and educating people.

"I saw Jim many times from my office window go and pull kids out [of their dorm rooms or wherever they happened to be] and take them to class. You can take them to class, but you can't make them work. He tried the old adage, 'You can take a mule to water, but you can't make them drink.' What Jim tried to do was make them thirsty so they would want to drink. But it's still up to the individual."

Some of the individuals who attended N.C. State and played under Valvano ended up disliking him. But this happens with some players at virtually every single college and university across the country. Others who played under him absolutely adored the man.

"He was very easy to talk to," said Sidney Lowe. "As time went on, he proved to be just a treat to play for. He would always let you go out and just play your game. If you showed you could do something, he would just turn you loose and let you do it."

That same free-wheeling style caught up to him off the court, however. Even though Valvano cooperated with NCAA and N.C. State investigators along with Bruce Poulton, the school's chancellor, he could not survive the subsequent findings. Among them were two major violations: players had sold or traded basketball shoes and complimentary tickets. Other violations considered less serious by the NCAA involved a local jewelry store giving players special discounts, boosters feeding and boarding players without charge for short periods of time, and Wolfpack coaches taking a recruiting prospect to a local television station to meet with and tour the station with a former Wolfpack player.

The academic practices of the basketball program remained under scutiny by the UNC system, which eventually determined that "the system has been misused. The spirit, not the letter of the law, has been broken." It was enough to break the coaching career of Jimmy Valvano, the one-time boy-coach with the seemingly inexhaustible golden touch.

Dean Smith, whose player-graduation rate at North Carolina was superb and unmatched in college basketball, said grimly of Valvano's demise: "He was hired by [State athletics director] Willis Casey to win basketball games and he did that pretty well. They never said to graduate players."

The implication was clear. It wasn't the way Dean chose to do

things. It was faint, backhanded praise for Valvano at best; a truthful
and highly critical statement at its core.

Poulton resigned in August 1989, effective the next month.
Valvano tried to hang on even as the public criticism mounted
against him. He resigned as athletics director but continued coaching
through the 1989–90 season. One day he arrived at his office to find
a small crowd of television and newspaper reporters waiting for him.
He told them how he was receiving so much generous support from
fans and alumni, pointing out that his office was filled with flowers
sent by well-wishers.

"Yeah, well, they send flowers to funerals too, don't they?" one
television reporter snapped.

Valvano's coaching funeral, as unthinkable as it may have
seemed only a couple of years earlier, was inescapable. He resigned
under pressure on April 7, 1990.

Soon thereafter, Valvano collaborated with *Sports Illustrated*'s
Curry Kirkpatrick on a book of his own that was advertised as an
autobiography but was essentially a rebuttal to Golenbock's book.
The title: *Valvano: They Gave Me A Lifetime Contract, Then They
Declared Me Dead.*

WHILE VALVANO and the State program stumbled into the '90s,
Duke, under head coach Mike Krzyzewski, seemed ready to dominate. The 1991 and 1992 seasons began with high hopes, as usual,
for the Blue Devils. They had advanced to the Final Four in four
of the previous five years and they had played for the national
championship in 1986 and 1990, losing both times. Krzyzewski had
now been the coach at Duke for a full decade. Would the Blue Devils
ever get over the national championship hump? Or would Coach K
need two decades—just like Dean Smith—before proving he could
win the Big One?

The 1990 season had been an interesting one for Krzyzewski.
He thought he had a good team, maybe even a great one. Freshman
point guard Bobby Hurley arrived and quickly began piling up assists at an NCAA record pace. He would finish the season with a
school-record 288 after starting all 38 games. Christian Laettner was
a sophomore coming into his own, averaging 16.3 points. And Crazy
Phil Henderson, as some in the media called him, was the senior
who tried to hold everything together. He was called "Crazy Phil"
because it seemed he might at any moment do or say just about
anything.

But after getting off to a terrific start, winning 23 of their first 28 games, the Blue Devils dropped their last two regular-season ACC contests, including an 87–75 decision to North Carolina on Senior Day at Cameron Indoor Stadium.

The Devils stumbled again, this time in the semifinals of the ACC Tournament, losing 83–72 to Georgia Tech. That gave them three losses in four games and a record of 25-8 heading into the NCAAs. In the locker room afterward, Crazy Phil went off. He blasted his teammates to anyone who would listen.

"We're too soft. We've got a bunch of fuckin' babies on this team. We've got some guys who need to get tougher or we're not going anywhere this year," Henderson said. He went on and on, but that was the gist of his tirade. He thought some of his teammates whined and complained too much. He thought some of his teammates cared more about their own statistics than just about anything else. He didn't think some of his teammates had enough heart. It became pretty obvious after a while that he probably was talking about Hurley, Laettner, and senior center Alaa Abdelnaby.

Al Featherstone was covering the game for the *Durham Herald.* He listened to Henderson go off and then sought out Krzyzewski for his reaction to Crazy Phil's open criticism of his teammates. Coach K's reaction surprised Featherstone, leaving him and other reporters who were there with the impression that Kryzyzewski actually welcomed the outburst.

"Well, I'm glad Phil had the courage to say that. We'll have to address it," Kryzyzewski said.

It was a turning point.

Hurley and Laettner reacted to the criticism by trying to complain less and play through more. They did get tougher, and even better, almost immediately.

The Devils ripped off wins against Richmond, St. John's, and UCLA to set up a battle with Connecticut for the East Regional championship. The hard-fought game ended up going into overtime, but Duke won when Laettner hit an incredible shot from the wing with less than one second left for a 79–78 victory.

In the Final Four semifinals in Denver, Duke continued their run by beating Arkansas 97–83. Henderson poured in a game-high 28 points, Abdelnaby added 20, and Laettner 19. That set the stage for the national championship game against UNLV. The Blue Devils were embarrassed, 103–73. And though the 30-point loss stung, Krzyzewski realized what his team had accomplished simply by getting there. It had overcome a great deal and come together in the process, and the core of the team was set to return a year later.

As good as they were on the court, the 1990 team was not one of Krzyzewski's favorites. What embarrassed and angered him the most wasn't the loss to UNLV, but the fact that three of his seniors —Henderson, Abdelnaby, and Robert Brickey—weren't anywhere close to graduating. Krzyzewski refused to hang the Final Four banner in the rafters of Cameron as a result, saying he would not do so until all three had earned their undergraduate degrees. Abdelnaby returned and got his the following semester and Brickey followed suit several years later. But as of the summer of 1998, Henderson still had not received his degree (although he reportedly was working toward it). The 1990 Final Four banner is the only one missing from Duke's ever-growing collection.

The Final Four banners were nice, of course. But Krzyzewski and his returning players wanted something more in 1991. They wanted to win it all.

"We were a real young team," Krzyzewski said. "But we had excellent talent. I'm not sure that people realized how good we were because we started out so young and we had lost three starters from the team that lost the national championship the year before. I think people felt, 'Well, they will be good. But they're essentially in a rebuilding phase.' "

Not only were they young, but some folks questioned if some emotional scars from the battering absorbed in the championship game might not eventually come back to haunt the Blue Devils.

The talent, however, was in place and the Blue Devils seemed to mesh almost immediately.

Christian Laettner was back for his junior season and Bobby Hurley, who continued to pile up assists at a record pace, was back for his second year. That gave the Blue Devils an inside presence and a point guard who could run the show. The prized freshmen recruits were Grant Hill and Antonio Lang. The team also had the outside shooting of Billy McCaffrey and the physical toughness of gritty players like Brian Davis and Thomas Hill.

"All of a sudden, as we went through the year we started to gain momentum," Krzyzewski said. "And we didn't get hurt. We didn't have any serious injuries, and that was important. By late February we were really good. And we were fresh."

After a January 9 loss at Virginia, the Devils' only other ACC losses came at North Carolina State and at Wake Forest. They won the rest of their conference games to finish first at 11–3. Then came the ACC Tournament, and a championship showdown with Carolina. Duke entered the game with an overall record of 26-7. The Tar Heels, which had lost 83–77 to Duke at the Dean Dome in an embarrassing regular-season finale that had cost them the regular-season ACC championship, entered with a record of 22-5.

The game was a rout in Carolina's favor, 96–74, in front of a stunned crowd at the new Charlotte Coliseum. The result, however, was not quite as stunning as the proclamation Krzyzewski made to his players when he boarded the team bus immediately following the loss.

"We're going to win the national championship," he told them.

This was not what the players had expected to hear. They thought Coach K was going to blast them for playing so poorly.

He looked them in their eyes and said it again.

"We're going to win the national championship," he repeated.

Krzyzewski had decided to give his players something positive to think about. Plus he really did believe they could win it all.

Four straight tournament wins over Northeast Louisiana, Iowa, Connecticut, and St. John's by an average of nearly 19 points per game confirmed his belief and landed Duke a rematch with Nevada-Las Vegas in a Final Four semifinal in Indianapolis. This was the team that had pounded the Blue Devils by 30 a year earlier to deny their championship dream.

"As we got to the tournament we just kind of rolled," Krzyzewski said. "But I don't think anyone expected us to beat Las Vegas. We had a week to prepare for Las Vegas, and that helped. I don't know if we would have beaten them in another national championship game.

"The fact that they had beaten us by thirty in the championship game a year earlier probably gave us a psychological advantage. We prepared very well. No one believed we would win. But if you watched their kids walk out on the floor that night, you would have thought that they already had beaten us again. They were overconfident because of what happened the year before. I thought right then that we would beat them this time."

Still, the Runnin' Rebels had reason to be overconfident. They had won 45 straight games. They had Greg Anthony and Stacey Augmon and Larry Johnson. Their youngest player, Anderson Hunt, was one month older than Duke's most grizzled veteran, senior captain Greg Koubek. They had so demoralized Krzyzewski and his team a year earlier that the coach had refused to watch videotape of the rout for nearly a year. He probably never would have pulled it out if the rematch hadn't forced him to finally take a long hard look at it to help him prepare for the second go-round.

When he finally popped the tape in, he saw a tired Duke team with a sick point guard, Hurley, who had been battling the flu and diarrhea. He told his players that they had backed down against UNLV the year before, and challenged them to not let it happen again. Get them in a close game, he added, and they will not know how to react because they haven't been in many close games.

"Keep it close and at the end the advantage will swing into our favor," he added. "And don't back down. Play hard and play with your heads and your heart, and we can live with whatever happens after that."

Early in the game, Brian Davis drove toward the basket and appeared to have an easy layup. But when he was challenged by a UNLV defender, he changed his shot and missed.

"Dunk the son of a bitch next time!" Krzyzewski yelled.

Later Davis took a charge from Anthony, fouling out the Las Vegas point guard with 3:51 still left to play. Without Anthony and having little experience in close games to fall back on, the Rebels crumbled down the stretch and blew a 76–71 lead in the final two minutes, thirty seconds. Duke won, 79–77.

The other Final Four semifinal, played earlier, had pitted North Carolina against Kansas. It was Dean Smith against old friend Roy Williams, a former Tar Heel assistant. And it set up the possibility of a dream Duke–North Carolina championship final that many fans in the Tar Heel state had long dreamed of—and others feared.

But the Tar Heels lost 79–73. In the final few minutes of the game, Smith was ejected when he received a technical, his second of the game, for walking a substitute to the bench. Bill Guthridge, his loyal long-time assistant whom many wrongly assumed was a milquetoast who never got fired up, was furious with referee Pete Pavia for tossing Smith. As soon as the game ended, Guthridge sprinted after Pavia toward the tunnel leading to the locker room at the Hoosier Dome.

"That was bush league!" he said. "That was the worst bush-league thing I've ever seen!"

He tried to follow the ref into the tunnel, but didn't get far. A wall of security guards, failing to recognize who he was, threw him up against a wall and pinned him there. When several North Carolina players started running past and realized their beloved assistant coach was being held against his will, a riot almost ensued. Only then did security personnel finally release Guthridge and allow him to proceed on to a subdued Carolina locker room.

The Carolina loss set up a Duke-Kansas final. Krzyzewski, like other coaches in similar situations before him, worried that his players thought they already had won the national championship. His worries were confirmed the next day when the team boarded the bus to head to the Hoosier Dome for practice.

"All anyone wanted to talk about was the win over Vegas. You could tell that our kids were a little different," he said. "We were walking differently. A couple of them had hats on when they didn't normally wear those kinds of hats—Indiana Jones hats. They were just different.

"We got to the locker room and I could just tell we were still living in the past."

So he kicked everyone out of the room except his players.

"Look, why don't you guys just pack up and go back to the hotel? Go watch a tape of the Vegas game," he told them. "And then everybody will pat you on the back and tell you how great you are. Because there's no way you're going to beat Kansas. You don't want to play Kansas right now.

"I don't like the way you talk. I don't like the way you look. I don't like your attitude. Why don't you just get out of here? Go back to the hotel."

The players looked at one another. They didn't go back to the hotel. They walked out together to the practice court and talked a little amongst themselves about what Coach K had said.

When Krzyzewski confronted them again at midcourt on the Hoosier Dome floor five minutes later, he had another question for them.

"Okay, are we ready now to take the next step?" he asked.

They nodded. Very few words were spoken. But Krzyzewski thought their eyes spoke volumes when he looked into them.

"At that point, I knew we would win," he said. "From that point on, we could prepare and I just knew in my heart that we would win."

Everyone else in America seemed to realize it shortly into the game when Hurley lofted an errant alley-oop pass to Grant Hill. Just as the overthrown pass seemed headed into the seats, Hill somehow elevated to grab it and slam it down. Billy Packer, working as a color analyst for CBS, felt his jaw drop in amazement. The crowd of more than forty-seven thousand roared.

This was going to be a different Duke NCAA final. Hill's dunk made that much clear.

It was different, all right. Kansas was good, but Duke was better. The Blue Devils led the whole way and finally won their first national championship 72–65, after eight Final Four failures—four under Krzyzewski, three under Vic Bubas, and one under Bill Foster.

Jay Bilas, a graduate assistant on the 1991 team after playing on the first Final Four team under Krzyzewski in 1986, spotted Quin Snyder in the stands at the Hoosier Dome and signaled for him to come down to the floor and join the celebration. This was Snyder's victory, too. This was for all the former Duke players who had sweated in pursuit of this same goal in years past.

"We all felt like we were part of it," Snyder said. "I'll never forget Jay doing that."

Danny Ferry was playing in the NBA for the Cleveland Cavaliers at the time, but he felt the same way as Snyder.

"You do feel like you're a part of it," Ferry said. "Even after you leave the Duke program, you still feel like you're a part of what's happening there. That's one of the nice things about it."

Krzyzewski added: "When we won, it kind of validated all the other things we had done over the years. I really felt all the teams that represented Duke in all those Final Fours won that night."

It wouldn't be long before they experienced the feeling again.

WHEN THE DUKE TEAM met again shortly after returning to Durham following the 1991 championship, Krzyzewski surprised his players again. It was spring. They had just won it all. It seemed like it was time to celebrate. Instead, Krzyzewski challenged them to do it all over again. To commit themselves to becoming the first repeat national champions since UCLA had captured the last two of its seven titles in a row nearly twenty years earlier in 1972 and 1973.

"The NCAA hands you certain things for winning the national championship," Krzyzewski told them. "They give you a ring. Normally we would have made up a ring for you guys to signify our national championship. But you know what? We're not going to do that."

The players again looked at each other, not quite knowing what to think.

"Nope. We're going to wait until next year to give out rings because we're going to win our second national championship," Krzyzewski said. "And I never want to hear anyone say we're defending the national championship. The word *defend* is not going to be used. The word *pursue* is what we will use.

"To defend, in some ways, you protect. But when you pursue, you attack. There's no way we're going to win the whole thing again unless we attack."

So the Blue Devils attacked the 1991–92 season like a team hungry to do it all over again. Most of the players, with the exception of Billy McCaffrey, Greg Koubek, and Crawford Palmer, returned. McCaffrey, the team's second-leading scorer, had surprised Krzyzewski by transferring to Vanderbilt in search of more playing time and some experience at point guard. He knew he wasn't going to play point guard ahead of Hurley at Duke. Koubek, the hardworking senior captain on the '91 team, had graduated. And Palmer, a little-used big man, transferred to Dartmouth.

Like Michael Jordan before him, Grant Hill made a tremendous leap in improvement between his freshman and sophomore seasons. Laettner was primed for his senior season. Hurley was continuing his march toward what would be an all-time NCAA record for assists. In some ways, Krzyzewski found that losing McCaffrey and Koubek from the rotation actually helped his 1992 team improve.

"We needed the players that were really good playing more. We were a great team," he said.

Duke spent the entire season ranked number one in the nation. After opening the season with 17 victories in a row, the Devils suffered a 75–73 loss to North Carolina in Chapel Hill on February 5. Worse yet, Hurley broke his foot in the first half of that game— even though he played the entire second half on it and didn't discover it was broken until later.

"Wow. A broken foot. That could really hurt us," Krzyzewski thought to himself.

Hurley, a quick healer, returned in a mere three and a half weeks. Then Grant Hill got hurt.

Along the way, the Blue Devils suffered one more close defeat —72–68 at Wake Forest on February 23. But that was it.

They stormed through the ACC regular season with a 14-2 record and laid claim to first place. They avenged the earlier loss to North Carolina by beating the tar out of the Heels in the ACC championship game, 94–74. Then they easily handled Campbell,

Iowa, and Seton Hall in the NCAA Tournament, setting up a show-down with powerful Kentucky in the East Regional Final in Philadelphia.

It was a game that would not be forgotten. Duke took control early, as Laettner hit every shot in sight.

"We had just played a very emotional game to beat Seton Hall," Krzyzewski said years later. "That was a game where brother played against brother, with Bobby and Danny Hurley playing against each other. And I was going against one of my close friends in coaching, P. J. Carlesimo. We knew we were going to have a very difficult game against Kentucky.

"But we played very well. We were always in the lead. Midway through the second half we got a double-digit lead and it looked like we were going to move on. Then all of a sudden Kentucky came on and [Jamal] Mashburn hit two three-pointers. From that point on, it was remarkable. Both teams hit shot after shot."

Along the way, Laettner stirred controversy by doing something utterly stupid. After Kentucky freshman Aminu Timberlake fouled Laettner and fell to the floor beneath him, Laettner lost his balance. As he regained it, he intentionally tapped Timberlake on the chest with his foot. Officials immediately called him for a technical foul and Krzyzewski immediately called his star to the bench to admonish him.

"That was really a dumb thing to do! We have the game in hand and you do something like that. What in the hell are you thinking about out there?" Krzyzewski said.

Laettner did not say a word back to his coach. He knew Coach K was right. Later, Laettner would downplay all the criticism by offering the press a lame excuse: "Hey, if I had really wanted to stomp the guy, I could have," he said.

The score was 73–68 in Duke's favor when the incident occurred. It was 81–72 when Kentucky scored 9 in a row to forge the first tie in the game since the two were locked at 20–20. The score was still tied at 93 when regulation ended.

But when Kentucky senior Sean Woods banked in a shot for a 103–102 lead with just 2.1 seconds left in overtime, it seemed as if Duke's reign as national champion was over.

In the subsequent huddle, Krzyzewski insisted that it wasn't.

"We're still going to win!" he yelled. Then he designed a play that would make it possible.

He asked Grant Hill if he could make a three-quarter court pass to Laettner at the top of the key. Hill said he could. He asked Laettner, who surely would be double-teamed, if he could catch such a pass after flashing to the top of the key from the left corner.

"Yeah, coach. I can do it," Laettner nodded.

Of course, he would have to not only catch it but shoot it as well.

The pass from Hill was perfect. Laettner, guarded by Kentucky's John Pelphrey and Deron Feldhaus, faked to his right with his back to the basket, taking one dribble. Then he pivoted to his left and shot the ball over the 6-6 Feldhaus from about seventeen feet.

"I knew it was in as soon as he shot it," Krzyzewski said. "I had seen him take that same shot so many times in practice, I knew it was in."

Duke won 104–103. The much-maligned Laettner, a moody but obviously talented young man who sometimes annoyed even his own teammates, had played a game for the ages: 10 for 10 from the field, and 10 for 10 from the free-throw line. Bill Lyon, a columnist for the *Philadelphia Inquirer*, wrote what many agreed was the perfect description of the contest in six simple words.

"The best basketball game ever played," he wrote.

Krzyzewski added: "You had two teams with huge hearts and very talented players. And it wasn't just one player playing well; everybody was hitting shots. Their kid hits a shot with a few seconds to go, and we had to go to a time-out and create a mindset of being very positive. That's not easy.

"Then Grant makes an amazing pass to Christian, who knows he has time and makes a little move before making the shot. I don't think a lot of people realize in that game that Christian Laettner was twenty for twenty, or what that means. It was truly one of the most remarkable performances by an athlete in a big game. Because it was his shot that won the game, we tend to look only at that shot, which was remarkable in itself. But his game—ten for ten and ten for ten—is what's really remarkable. We weren't beating some no-name team by thirty points. Every shot was pressure-packed."

Next it was Hurley's turn to excel in a narrow 81–78 victory over Indiana in the Final Four semifinal. Laettner, appearing on the verge of physical and mental exhaustion after the huge performance against Kentucky, scored just 8 points and missed 6 of the 8 shots he took. Hurley scored 26 points on 7-of-12 shooting to pick up the slack, and also added 4 assists and 2 steals.

That left only Michigan and its Fab Five freshmen standing in the way of another national championship for Duke. Krzyzewski knew Laettner's tank was running on empty.

"Against Michigan, Laettner played the worst half he's ever played at Duke," Krzyzewski said. "He looked like he was completely worn out."

Hurley implored Laettner to lay it all on the line at halftime, and with eight minutes to go—with the game still close—he finally did.

During a time-out, Krzyzewski grabbed the board he used to diagram plays and wrote 'G' for Grant Hill on the side where the ball would be inbounded. Then he looked at Laettner.

"Do you feel it?" he asked.

"Yeah," replied Laettner, too tired to say much more.

Krzyzewski erased Hill's initial and scribbled in Laettner's. He knew Laettner would not be played closely after throwing the ball inbounds. The idea was to have the ball thrown right back to Laettner, who would be open for a 3-point shot.

"I'm going to do it," Laettner mumbled as he left the huddle.

But when Laettner received the return pass after throwing it inbounds, he fumbled it. Instead of forcing up a 3-point shot, he started driving the baseline. Chris Webber, Juwan Howard, and Eric Riley—three future NBA players—were waiting to block his shot.

"It looks bad for us," Krzyzewski admitted. "He makes one of the worst moves ever in college basketball and it looks like he's going to get his shot blocked. But somehow, he doesn't. He makes the bucket."

Duke scored on eleven of their next twelve possessions and ended up burying Michigan, 71–51.

"There aren't many kids who ever played the game who were as tough as Christian Laettner," Krzyzewski said. "I just thought Christian at that moment—it was so appropriate, being that he had led us throughout the whole year. And no one will ever think that was a great play. But they don't know what made it. To me, that was as big of a play as the one he made against Kentucky. If we don't make that play, there is a good chance we lose."

They didn't lose. The Blue Devils finished 34-2 and went down in history as one of only a handful of teams to win back-to-back NCAA championships—even if they didn't win back-to-back ACC championships in those same years.

Looking back years later, Krzyzewski chuckled as he reflected.

"People say, 'What was your best win? The Kentucky win in ninety-two or the Vegas win in ninety-one?' And I always say, 'No, the best win we ever had was the ninety-one win against Kansas because it came after one of the great games in the history of college basketball—and it ended the frustration of excellence for us. How many times had Duke gone to the Final Four and not won?

"It was like a unifying experience. There was a feeling that not just the nineteen ninety-one team had won, but they all had won. It was a game for the whole history of the basketball program."

And after that, Krzyzewski only kept building on it. He even felt good enough to finally hand out some NCAA championship rings.

14

DEAN TRIUMPHS . . .
AND EXITS

B‍Y THE BEGINNING of the 1992–93 season, Duke and Krzyzewski had two national championships, and Dean Smith sat in his office a mere eight miles away with only one national championship to show for more than three decades of coaching at North Carolina. Suddenly the program that represented hoops excellence throughout the region and perhaps even the nation wasn't seeming so superior after all.

Sure, the Tar Heels were a factor every year in the ACC. They were always ranked highly and usually they made noise in the NCAAs. But the numbers didn't lie. Despite twelve straight Sweet Sixteen appearances, only once in thirty-one seasons under Smith had they won it all. When Duke beat Kansas in the 1991 championship game, many Duke fans in attendance rejoiced by chanting, "Go to Hell, Carolina! Go to Hell!"

Despite starting out the 1992 season 18-3, including an upset of number-one-ranked Duke, Carolina faltered, suffering through a stretch of 5 losses in 6 games toward the end of the season. The Heels eventually recovered enough to at least make it to the Sweet Sixteen in the NCAA Tournament, but there the season ended with an 80–73 loss to Ohio State. They finished the season 23-10. It was the second time in three years North Carolina had reached double-digits in losses (the Heels went 21-13 in 1989–90)—something that hadn't happened even once in the previous twenty-three seasons.

Prior to practice opening the next fall, Smith had an idea. He dispatched assistant coach Dave Hanners to find a photo of the Louisiana Superdome scoreboard after Carolina's 1982 national championship triumph over Georgetown. The photo Smith had in mind read: "1982 NCAA CHAMPIONS NORTH CAROLINA."

"See if you can doctor the photo. I want it to read '1993 NCAA CHAMPIONS NORTH CAROLINA,' " Smith told Hanners. "Then place a copy of the doctored photo in each of the player's lockers."

The 1993 Final Four, like the 1982 Final Four, would be played in New Orleans at the Louisiana Superdome. Smith wanted his players to be focused the entire season on getting there. He also wanted them focused on winning it.

The players—an experienced crew led by Eric Montross, Donald Williams, George Lynch, Pat Sullivan, Derrick Phelps, and Brian Reese—fed off their desire to fulfill the coach's goal all season. This wasn't like past North Carolina teams fueled by the great play of fantastic individual talents like Lennie Rosenbluth, Larry Miller, Charlie Scott, Phil Ford, Walter Davis, Mitch Kupchak, Michael Jordan, James Worthy, Sam Perkins, Kenny Smith, or Brad Daugherty. This team was made up of guys who were much better collectively than they could ever hope to be individually, and they played like they were well aware of this fact.

The team won 17 of its first 18 games, losing only to Michigan by a single point, 79–78, in the Rainbow Classic in Hawaii. That was no disgrace. Michigan had lost to Duke in the NCAA championship game the previous year and was still led by the Fab Five—Chris Webber, Juwan Howard, Ray Jackson, Jalen Rose, and Jimmy King.

In improving to 17-1, the Tar Heels proved they might be a team of destiny by rallying from a 21-point, second-half deficit to beat Florida State at the Smith Center on January 27, 1993. Lynch keyed the comeback, hitting a 3-pointer to begin the long road back from what was still a 19-point deficit with nine minutes left. He later stole a cross-court pass and dunked to give Carolina a 78–77 lead with 1:41 remaining—its first lead since the opening minutes. The Tar Heels eventually won 82–77, and the hard-working Lynch finished with 14 points, 10 rebounds, and 7 steals.

Their only two ACC regular-season losses immediately followed when they got beaten 88–62 at Wake Forest and 81–67 at Duke. But those defeats were followed by nine consecutive wins to close the regular season, including an 83–69 revenge victory over Duke at the Smith Center in the finale.

With the ACC Tournament at hand, Carolina was the top seed

with a 25-3 record. Smith's Superdome vision of another national title seemed within his grasp.

BROADCASTING THE DUKE-CAROLINA GAME for ABC Sports at the end of the 1992–93 ACC regular season was one Jim Valvano, who had exchanged his coach's seat for one in the broadcast booth shortly after resigning from North Carolina State. But this was a different Valvano than the guy who previously had wowed the public at every turn with his charm and energy and self-effacing humor. Valvano had been humbled—floored, even—when he had been diagnosed with cancer on June 12, 1992.

Doctors gave him, at best, one year to live.

Suddenly basketball didn't seem quite as important to him anymore, although it remained at the center of his life until the very end.

As Valvano came to grips with his disease, he thought about some of the mistakes he might have made. He realized perhaps he should have spent a little more time at home with his wife, Pam, and their three daughters, Jamie, Nichole, and LeeAnn. He talked about those things in a moving article for *Sports Illustrated*, and mentioned some of them again when he spoke in public prior to the North Carolina State–Duke game at Reynolds Coliseum on February 21, 1993.

In the *SI* article, a somber Valvano admitted to writer Gary Smith that he wished he had been around more for his wife and kids. He admitted he spread himself too thin toward the end of his tenure at State, leaving too little time for his second family—the North Carolina State basketball players.

"I was an absolute maniac, a terrible husband and father," he told Smith. "Everybody in the stands went, 'Awwwww, isn't that cute?' when my little girl ran across the court in a cheerleader's outfit and hugged me before every home game, but for twenty-three years, I wasn't home."

As he rambled on in the long piece, Valvano still admitted— despite some regrets—that he had been blessed during the ten magical years he coached at N.C. State and the ones before them as a coach at Johns Hopkins, Bucknell, and Iona.

"I can't sit here and swear I'd do everything differently. I wouldn't trade those years," he said. "Nobody had more fun than me. How many people do you know who've had their dream come true? You're looking at one. That was my creative period, my run, my burst of energy."

By February 21, 1993, Valvano had very little energy left. He tried his best to hide this fact, but it was true.

It was the first time Valvano had stepped foot in Reynolds Coliseum since his resignation nearly three years earlier. He did so as a very sick man. He carried a little hand-held pump with him that would shoot morphine into his cancer-ravaged body whenever the pain got too bad. He gobbled up to twenty-four tablets of Advil a day, and for a long while had walked around clutching a black leather bag that perhaps contained the miracle cure—holy water from Lourdes. He didn't walk so much as he shuffled, often stopping every few steps to make the sign of the cross and splash some of the treasured holy water onto his back, his hips, his knees, his aching hands and feet. Every word he uttered required effort.

But you wouldn't have known it that night.

"Jim grabbed that microphone and started walking around the court just like the Jim of old," Charlie Bryant remembered.

"Cancer has taken away a lot of my physical ability—but what cancer cannot touch is my mind, my heart, and my soul. Those three things will carry on forever," Valvano told the crowd, using words he would repeat a couple of weeks later when he was presented with the Arthur Ashe Award on ESPN.

It was then that Valvano delivered these lines, which would become his mantra: "There are three things we all should do every day, every day, of our lives. Number one is laugh. You should laugh every day. Number two is think. Spend some time in thought. And number three, you should have your emotions moved to tears. It could be happiness or joy. But think about it: If you laugh, if you think, and if you cry, that's a full day. That's a heck of a day. You do that seven days a week, and you're going to have something special."

Less than one month later, prior to the Duke-Carolina game Valvano broadcast in Chapel Hill, Valvano talked with Charles Chandler of the *Charlotte Observer*. It was the last interview Valvano would ever do.

With former player Terry Gannon, a member of the 1983 national championship team, sitting nearby, Valvano told Chandler that he appreciated life more than ever now that the end was near. He said he thanked God every morning for letting him get out of bed for another day. And he talked about what his family and friends meant to him.

"I cry when I look at friends, when I look at people who were in my world and important in my world," Valvano said. "I can't ever look at my kids and my wife without getting all choked up."

Still, when he was in public, Valvano mobilized every ounce of energy he could to mask the pain in an attempt to make people feel comfortable around him. The cancer by now had progressed to the point where it wasn't just in his spine—where it first had started eating away at his body—but it was in his back, legs, and hips as well. His hands and feet hurt so much that an hour after he finished broadcasting Carolina's 82–77 victory over Duke, he couldn't accept a pen from a teenager who asked for an autograph.

Valvano refused the boy's pen, but not his request for an autograph. Instead Valvano removed an oversized felt-tip marker from his sports jacket and used that to grant the request, later explaining that he had learned to carry the larger marker with him because it was the only thing he could write with anymore.

"I can't write," he admitted to Chandler after the autograph seeker had left the small office in the Smith Center where they sat. "I have no feeling in my hands and feet at all. All they do is hurt.

"I can't button my shirt. I can't tie my shoes. I can't tap-dance on a bar at midnight. It's really frustrating when people come up [and ask for autographs]. It's hard for me. It hurts my hands, but how do you tell them that? If I don't have this kind of pen, I can't do it. But what do you say to somebody?"

Valvano knew one thing. He wasn't going to say no. He always did have a hard time saying that.

So he took the special marker with him wherever he went.

One of the places he went to receive chemotherapy and other treatments was the Duke Comprehensive Cancer Center in Durham. It wasn't a happy place.

"We're down in the basement," a somber Valvano explained to Chandler. "There are no cameras. There are no newspaper articles. Everybody is battling a disease that can take their life. It's a very lonely place.

"But it's also uplifting because everybody cares so much for everybody else. There's no selfishness down there."

Valvano talked about one time when he was waiting for a treatment, and he was approached by a frail man in a wheelchair. Valvano looked him over. The man was a shell. Valvano estimated he must have weighed about ninety pounds.

The two men started talking.

"I used to weigh about one hundred and eighty pounds, but now I've got stomach cancer and I can't eat," the man explained.

Valvano nodded.

"I read the article in *Sports Illustrated*. It gave me inspiration to go on," the man said. "I'm not going to quit. You'd better not go quittin' either."

"Now you've given me inspiration," Valvano said. "Don't worry. I won't quit."

After he told this story to Chandler, Valvano looked at the writer to make sure he understood its implication. This was why Valvano still made the effort to go out in public and smile. This was why he took his special marker with him and signed everything he could.

He admitted there were many times when he was approached at the hospital and didn't feel like talking or signing anything. But he always did it anyway.

"Sometimes it's burdensome. Sometimes I don't feel that good," Valvano said. "But I always feel afterward that it's a special role I've been given. It's for all the people who are struggling, dying, fighting it, and trying to have a miracle happen.

"You fight with the mind and the will. You give up, you've got no shot. I'm not giving up."

Then, at the ESPN Arthur Ashe award ceremony, Valvano uttered the memorable lines: "Don't give up. Don't *ever* give up." It was these two lines that provided endless inspiration for him and many others time and time again.

Among those who grew closer to Valvano during his illness was Mike Krzyzewski, the Duke coach. Krzyzewski often visited Valvano in the hospital and talked long into the night with him about life, about basketball, about just about anything.

"We knew each other since our playing days and our early coaching days, when I was at Army. We weren't close friends then, but we knew each other. I don't know if you can become that close when you're competing against each other. But I always respected him and he always respected me," Krzyzewski said.

"We came down here at the same time. Our ethnic backgrounds and the roads we traveled were all the same. Our styles were somewhat different, although not as much as some people think. I got to know Jimmy really well while he coached at State and even better when he left and got into broadcasting. I think our relationship grew closer after that. Then when he was diagnosed with cancer, we had a special relationship.

"He was a remarkable guy. When you were with him, you were

never bored. . . . You knew what you were getting with Jimmy. He had a lot to give. He gave a lot and had a lot more to give."

Krzyzewski insisted years later that Valvano received a bum deal at North Carolina State.

"He was a northern Italian and very outgoing, and in our area there are some people who did not want to embrace that," Krzyzewski said. "I think that with some things he was not given the support that he needed. We all at times need somebody to stand up and support us. In that moment when he needed that the most, the right people didn't stand up and do it. That's a shame."

Sidney Lowe, the former Wolfpack player, said virtually the same thing at a gathering to celebrate the ten-year anniversary of the 1983 national championship team coached by Valvano.

"Coach V always preached that we were a family, that we needed to stick together and stand up for one another," Lowe said. "Yet when it came time to do that for him, it didn't happen. That's sad."

Valvano never gave up, but there was no miracle. He passed away quietly on the morning of April 28, 1993—almost three years to the day after he resigned as coach of the North Carolina State Wolfpack. At his side when he died were his wife, their three children, and his mother, Angela.

Charlie Bryant still mourns the loss of Valvano.

"Not a day goes by that I don't think about him," said Bryant, looking around his old office on the North Carolina State campus. "Jim loved this place. He loved it until the day he died."

Valvano never announced another game after doing the Duke-Carolina game in Chapel Hill. He became too weak. But before he left the building that day, he made a prediction.

"North Carolina," said Valvano, "will win the national championship this year."

It was a reminder that life in the basketball-crazy state would go on—with him or without him.

NORTH CAROLINA'S MARCH to the 1993 Final Four did not go on uninterrupted. After beating Maryland and Virginia in the first two rounds of the ACC Tournament to run the their winning streak to eleven games, Carolina was upset by Georgia Tech 77–75 in the championship final. The Yellow Jackets had finished the regular season just 8-8 in the ACC and North Carolina had beaten them twice during the season.

The Heels were stunned. All year long they had won virtually all the games they were supposed to. But they failed to win the ACC championship.

As disapppointing as the loss in the ACC championship game was, maybe it was precisely the wake-up call the Tar Heels needed. They responded by beating East Carolina, 85–65, and Rhode Island, 112–67, in the first two rounds of the NCAA Tournament, and then held off Arkansas 80–74 to advance to the East Regional final against Cincinnati. The Bearcats gave Carolina all they could handle, but the Tar Heels still prevailed 75–68 in an overtime victory.

That victory set up a rematch of the 1991 Final Four semifinal against Kansas and former Tar Heel assistant coach Roy Williams, who had helped recruit many of the North Carolina seniors who stood between him and a national championship. George Lynch thought the 1991 team had been a little too friendly about the whole encounter with the Jayhawks. He reminded the current Tar Heels that they owed Coach Williams nothing; but they did owe Coach Smith the satisfaction of seeing his doctored photo become a reality.

Bill Guthridge, Smith's long-time assistant who was very close to Roy Williams, agreed with Lynch. In 1991 he went running with Coach Williams in Indianapolis prior to their Final Four encounter. The group jog was just a little too cozy for Guthridge's blood this time. Williams called Guthridge the night before the game to see if he wanted to run together again on the morning of the game, and Guthridge politely declined.

"No, thanks," Guthridge said. "We ran with you in Indianapolis and you beat us."

The next morning Guthridge ran along the waterfront near the team hotel with Scott Montross, Eric's father. They saw Coach Williams and Oregon coach Jerry Green, a former Kansas assistant, jogging toward them from the other direction. Guthridge quickly sprinted across the street to avoid any contact or conversation, and kept right on running past them.

The tone of the game was set.

Led again by Donald Williams, who scored 25 points, Carolina avenged their 1991 loss. Roy Williams met with reporters and admitted, "Come Monday night, I'll be pulling hard for North Carolina. If you don't understand that, you don't know anything about Roy Williams."

The opponent on Monday night was Michigan—the same Michigan team that had lost to Duke in the NCAA championship game the previous year. They had also defeated North Carolina in Hawaii earlier in the 1992–93 season. Smith and Guthridge told their players that the earlier loss to Michigan meant nothing. At the pregame meal at 4:00 P.M. Monday, Guthridge produced a pair of gold-plated scissors that had been sent to him by a fan.

Inscribed on the scissors was the following: "North Carolina, 1993 NCAA champions."

"Here are the scissors we're going to use to cut down the nets after we win tonight," Guthridge told the players. "The opportunity is right there in front of us."

The players nodded.

In the huddle before the tip-off that night, Lynch looked around at his teammates and echoed a thought that was uttered by Jimmy Black and James Worthy in the same building eleven years earlier.

"Let's win this one for Coach Smith!" he shouted above the din.

It wasn't easy. Michigan led much of the game. When Jalen Rose hit a 3-pointer from the top of the key for a 65–61 lead, even Smith started to think the game was getting away. But the Tar Heels pulled to within one and then scored 9 unanswered points to gain the lead 72–67. Suddenly it was Michigan who looked finished.

The Wolverines refused to give up and pulled to within 2 with only one minute remaining. Then Chris Webber made a play that would haunt him forever. After he rebounded Pat Sullivan's missed free throw, he looked toward official Jim Stupin and started to call time-out—a time-out the Wolverines did not have.

Stupin looked away. He knew Michigan had no time-outs left and later told reporters he "wanted to give the kid a break." He didn't want the national championship decided on some kid's stupid mistake. But when he looked away, Stupin inadvertently allowed Webber two more mistakes. The Michigan star took two awkward steps, clearly dragging his foot. The Carolina bench went wild, thinking he would be whistled for the obvious travel violation—but Stupin didn't see it.

Webber darted downcourt, where Derrick Phelps and George Lynch double-teamed him in the right corner. Confused, Webber turned to another official, Tom Harrington, and with eleven seconds left in the game, signaled for a time-out. Michigan had used its last time-out thirty-five seconds earlier, and Coach Steve Fisher of the Wolverines had told his players then that they had no more remaining.

Webber either didn't hear Fisher or forgot what his coach said in the huddle. Harrington hit him with a technical foul and Williams, who led all scorers with 25 points and would be named Final Four MVP, hit four subsequent free throws to seal a 77–71 victory and Smith's second national championship.

The photo of the 1993 North Carolina national champions, with the Louisiana Superdome as its backdrop, was now a reality.

"I'm not sure we were the best team in the country that year," Guthridge said. "But we won it, and it was great."

Smith tired quickly of questions in the postgame press conference that referred to the on-court gaffe by Webber that had sealed his national championship. His critics were quick to point out that he got lucky; his supporters were quick to point out that the Tar Heels would have won regardless. It was a debate that would rage on for years.

Smith didn't want to hear it that night in New Orleans.

"Okay, call us lucky if you want. But also call us national champions," he told reporters.

Jim Valvano's last prediction had been right on the money.

CHANGES WERE COMING FAST in the Big Four. Wake Forest—under Coach Dave Odom, who had replaced Bob Staak prior to the 1989–90 season—turned its program around and began a string of seven straight NCAA Tournament appearances in 1991. Odom successfully recruited a little-known center named Tim Duncan from St. Croix in the Virgin Islands in 1994, and behind Duncan became the first team to win back-to-back ACC Tournament championships in fourteen years.

When Odom first recruited Duncan, he had some difficulty explaining to the lanky center what playing in the ACC was all about. Duncan had his choices narrowed down to Wake Forest, Providence, and tiny Delaware State.

Duncan visited Providence.

"I knew he wouldn't go there," Odom said. "I think he liked the Providence people. He liked their school okay. But I knew he wasn't going there because of the weather. He visited in the dead of winter."

Odom called him up.

"Well, you've visited us and Providence. Don't you want to go ahead and make your decision?" he asked.

"No, I promised Delaware State I would visit there, too," Duncan replied.

Odom wanted to tell Duncan that he didn't understand. Delaware State might be a nice place to play and all that, but it was a far cry from the ACC. He decided to wait it out and let Duncan see for himself. The tall center finally figured it out: Wake was the place for him. But even after committing to the school, it took time for Duncan to understand just what ACC ball was all about.

"I didn't realize the rivalries that were going on," Duncan said. "But you learn about that real quickly when you step into opposing gymnasiums. You see how the teams and the fans are going at it, and it hits you real quick."

It didn't take long for Odom to realize he had landed something special in Duncan, who really emerged as a player his sophomore year, averaging 16.8 points and 12.5 rebounds. He and Randolph Childress, then a senior, helped Wake win the ACC Tournament in 1995, when the Deacons staged an epic battle with North Carolina in the championship game.

Childress was fantastic in the tournament, pouring in a career-high 40 points as Wake beat Duke in the opening round and scoring another 30 in the semifinal win over Virginia. He had 35 when he took the ball and sliced into the lane for a floating twelve-footer that gave Wake an 82–80 lead over Carolina with four seconds left in overtime in the championship game. When Jerry Stackhouse missed a 3-pointer and Pearce Landry couldn't get a desperation tip at the buzzer to go for Carolina, the Deacons had won their first ACC title in more than three decades.

Childress's three-game point total stood at 107, his last basket breaking the 38-year-old tournament scoring record of Carolina's Lennie Rosenbluth by one point.

"From start to finish, that was one of the greatest individual performances I've ever seen in an ACC Tournament," said Billy Packer.

When Childress moved on the following year, the onus was on Duncan to step up. He was ready.

"When I recruited Tim, I thought he was a good player who would develop," Odom said. "But he came in [as a freshman] in my mind, and certainly in the minds of the recruiting gurus who analyze all that stuff every year, as being the dot at the end of the exclamation point. We had [Ricardo] Peral and [Mahktar] Ndiaye. Duncan was the third guy behind them. He was the add-on. He was the extra. Well, he turned out to be a lot more than just the extra.

"When did we realize we had a much better player on our hands than we had bargained for? By the end of his freshman year. When did we realize he was a special player? By the middle of his sophomore year."

By his junior year, the 7-foot center was downright dominant. Wake finished second by a game to Georgia Tech in the regular season, but went on to win the ACC Tournament anyway. Duncan put together a monster game that included 27 points, 22 rebounds, 6 assists, and 4 blocks in the championship game against Tech, which rallied from an 11-point deficit with two minutes, twenty-three seconds left only to lose 75–74. After going thirty-three years between ACC titles, Wake Forest became the first team in fourteen years to win the tournament back-to-back.

The win over Tech did not come without a price; guard Tony Rutland injured his knee while driving to the basket with fourteen minutes remaining and the Deacons leading by 18 points. Rusty LaRue, a shooting guard, was forced to play point guard pretty much the rest of the way and Rutland's injury hampered Wake during the subsequent NCAA Tournament. Nonetheless, Duncan's late 3-point play gave the Deacons a dramatic 60–59 victory over Louisville—after earlier victories over Northeast Louisiana and Texas—advancing Wake, whose record was a lofty 26-5, to the Elite Eight.

That meant a matchup with Kentucky, coached by Rick Pitino. Odom had known Pitino for years and the two considered each other close friends.

"Wake Forest is an unusual team," Pitino told reporters. "They remind me of a college version of the Houston Rockets when the Rockets were playing great.

"They shoot more threes than free throws. They shoot an incredible percentage from the three-point line. They feed off the three and they have the equivalent of Hakeem Olajuwon at the college level in Tim Duncan."

Odom said Pitino was just being nice. But Pitino had great respect for Odom's program and meant every word. Pitino had once asked Odom to join his coaching staff when Pitino was coaching the NBA's New York Knicks. Even though Odom had politely declined, Pitino continued to be a big fan of the Wake coach. Perhaps the greatest endorsement of Odom and his revived program was the fact that Pitino had chosen to send three of his sons to Odom's Wake Forest basketball camp.

The only reason Odom declined the invitation to become Pitino's assistant with the Knicks was because he would have had to move to New York. Pitino wasn't surprised. He understood that Odom was more comfortable right where he remained—not far from where he grew up in rural North Carolina.

"Dave Odom has one of the best minds in the game," Pitino said. "There's nothing complicated about Dave. . . . But him being in Manhattan really wasn't the best fit."

Kentucky won the showdown, 83–68, and went on to win the national championship. Duncan, a lock to be the number-one overall selection in the NBA draft, chose to return for his senior season. His reason was simple: he wanted to win a national championship.

Even though the Demon Deacons began the 1996–97 season ranked as high as second in the nation in many polls, the national championship never materialized. Inconsistent and faulty guard play was the team's downfall. Duncan did all he could do; he even led the team in assists with 98 for the year. But his best wasn't enough. The Deacons fell 86–73 to North Carolina in the semifinals of the ACC Tournament and then won only one game in the NCAA Tournament before falling in the second round to Stanford, 72–66. Duncan's career ended despite 18 points and 20 rebounds in the loss. Wake's record his senior season was 24-7.

For the second season in a row, Duncan was named the national Player of the Year. He finished his career as one of only ten players in NCAA history to record more than 2,000 points and 1,500 rebounds, and his 481 career blocks ranks second in the NCAA record book. Odom said he had no doubt that Duncan was one of the greatest college players of all time.

"People wanted to say throughout his career, 'How good is he? How does he rank in the annals of ACC basketball?' And I would always say, 'Let's let him finish up. Let's find out statistically where he ranks, and every other way how he ranks.'

"But now I think we can say it. He was one of the two best centers to ever play in this league. I don't think there is any question about it, by every measuring rod. You've got to put him in the top five, six, seven, or eight all-time in this league, and only he and Ralph Sampson—a three-time Player of the Year [at Virginia] rank at the top among centers. There have been other great ones. But those two, by far, outdistance all the others."

Duncan went on to become the number-one selection in the 1998 NBA draft; he finished his first season with the San Antonio Spurs in impressive fashion. He was named Rookie of the Year. Yet playing in the pros, he insisted, wasn't as intense as playing in the center of the college basketball world.

"I don't think you'll find as big of rivalries in the pros as you do here," he said. "I think there are rivalries present in the NBA, but nothing like it's built up to be in college around here. Every year Carolina is good, Duke's good, and Wake is getting where they're good every year. N.C. State is always a challenge and they have great tradition. I think rivalries change every year in the NBA, depending on who's good. But they always stay the same around here."

WHILE THREE of the Big four schools were thriving in the first half of the decade, North Carolina State struggled. Valvano's replacement, Les Robinson, tried unsuccessfully to find a way to improve the academic standards of his players while still producing enough wins to keep anxious alumni happy. A former State player under Everett Case, Robinson ultimately improved on the former but didn't do enough of the latter to prevent his ouster in 1996. But in a rather bizarre twist of fate, the friendly and well-respected Robinson ended up the school's athletic director. He hired a promising young coach named Herb Sendek as his own replacement.

At Duke, Mike Krzyzewski sent another team to the Final Four in 1994, making it a remarkable run of seven Final Four appearances in nine years. But Coach K ultimately paid a personal price. Much like many of the Big Four coaches before him, the incredible success of his program brought more speaking engagements, more coaching clinics, more pressure to continue winning. It all caught up with him in 1995, when he had to step aside in the middle of the season to undergo back surgery. Without Coach K leading the team, the Blue Devils floundered under the interim guidance of long-time assistant coach Pete Gaudet. The Blue Devils were 9-3 overall and 1-1 in the ACC when Krzyzewski went out for the year; they promptly lost 5 straight, 9 of their next 10, and won only 4 of their last 19 games overall. Their record ended up 13-18 overall, 2-14 in the ACC.

Suddenly there were whispers that Krzyzewski might be finished—that the mighty Duke program he built might be in jeopardy of collapsing. But Krzyzewski returned to the bench the next season and by 1996–97 had the overachieving Blue Devils on top again in the ACC with a 12-4 mark.

At North Carolina, Dean Smith marched toward a record once thought unassailable: Adolph Rupp's all-time record for collegiate coaching victories. He led the Tar Heels to Final Four berths in both 1995 and 1997, losing to Arkansas in the '95 semifinal and Arizona in '97. Before losing to Arizona, however, Smith tied Rupp with victory number 876 when his Tar Heels outlasted a fiesty Fairfield team, 82–74, in a first-round NCAA Tournament game. The record-breaker came against Colorado two days later on March 15, 1997.

As the record fell, the accolades rained down on the man who once was hung in effigy by an angry mob of students at Chapel Hill. Stories were told about his photographic memory, his kindness, and his ability to adapt to the changing attitudes of many of today's players.

Smith deflected all the attention and praise and got his team ready for the next game. The '97 Heels had begun the season with an unthinkable string of three straight losses to open the ACC sched-ule—losing to Wake Forest, Maryland, and Virginia. The ABC gang had a field day. The game had passed ol' Dean by, they said. It was obvious. The guy couldn't coach anymore.

Carolina's struggles and the accompanying snickers lasted only a few more weeks. Then the Heels ripped off 16 wins in a row to get to the Final Four against Arizona. Though the heels lost the game, the team finished 28-7. It was Smith's twenty-seventh consecutive season with 20 or more victories. He made eleven trips to the Final Four. Only UCLA legend John Wooden, with twelve, made more. His teams played in twenty-three straight NCAA Tournaments. For one thirteen-year stretch—from 1981 through the 1993 national championship season—the Heels, under Smith, reached the Sweet Sixteen round every time in the NCAAs.

After the loss to Arizona, Smith would not coach again. For years, probably at least a decade, he had been telling Guthridge to get ready because he was worn out.

"I'm telling you, Bill, you might have to take over," Smith repeatedly told Guthridge. "You'd better be ready. I'm tired and I don't think I have the energy to pour it all into another year."

This usually would last until sometime in August. Then Smith would start thinking about fall practice. By the time September rolled around he usually was finished moaning to Guthridge about possibly quitting.

Then Smith would say: "I'll know it's time to quit when I'm not ready to start practice on October fifteenth."

The summer of 1997 was a little different though. August came and went, and Guthridge noticed once it was into September that Dean was still hedging about coming back for another season. September spilled over into October, and still there was no official word from Dean about coming back. Finally, around October 8, word began leaking out of Chapel Hill that Smith was going to retire. He did just that the very next day, holding a news conference that was attended by a throng of former and current players and coaches, plus a full house of media.

The entire nation watched as this humble man kept lowering his head and swallowing, biting back tears and avoiding eye contact with the television cameras as he tried to explain why he was quitting. It was difficult, but not as difficult as what he had gone through the previous evening when he called his current group of players together—Antawn Jamison, Vince Carter, Ed Cota, Shammond Williams, and Ademola Okulaja among them—to inform them of the news.

"I looked in their faces, and I just couldn't handle that," Smith said.

Smith's peers in the ACC paid him tribute in the wake of his retirement announcement.

"People have often asked me, 'How long is Dean Smith going to coach?' " Wake's Odom said. "And I always answered, 'Forever.' How can there be college basketball and you not have Dean Smith? He's always been around. He's always been there. I just always thought he was going to coach forever."

Krzyzewski, Smith's fiercest rival, added: "It's a big loss for college basketball and coaching. We competed very hard against one another, but I think that's good. That's one of those things that makes college basketball as great as it is. I'll miss coaching against him even if he beats me twenty more times."

Wooden himself may have paid Smith the ultimate compliment when asked to comment on the breaking of Rupp's record.

"What's more impressive to me about Dean than the record is how good he is as a teacher of basketball," Wooden said. "I've always said he's a better teacher of basketball than anyone else. I couldn't begin to teach players the things Dean has taught them. I've admired him because there's more to him than just wins."

At the end of his retirement press conference, Smith promised he would keep in touch. As if anyone thought he wouldn't. Smith's reputation for staying in touch with players and even former team managers was legendary.

Phil Ford, the former player who became an assistant coach in 1990, remembered one time when he was walking with Smith at the Erwin Special Events Center in Austin, Texas, where the Tar Heels had just pulled off an upset over highly ranked Oklahoma to advance to the Sweet Sixteen. As they were leaving the arena together, some-one in the stands called Coach Smith's name and caught his atten-tion.

Smith stopped, smiled, and took the time to shake the man's hand. Then he politely and patiently asked about the man's wife and kids, referring to each by name.

As he said his good-byes, Smith turned to Ford and shook his head.

"Gosh, I haven't seen that guy in twenty years," Smith said.

"Amazing," thought Ford, shaking his head.

On this day, Smith talked about what he believed a coach should be. He talked about owing each and every recruit an honest approach, a plan to build a productive life beyond college whether it be in basketball or some other profession. He talked about how a coach should be prepared to give all that he could, or he should get out of the business. And that's why he was getting out.

"My only guilt, if there is such a word, is that some team some day would be my last team," Smith said. "But I still believe this is what's best for these players unless I could give them what I want. I owe them. Any player that's played for me, I owe them. My dad felt that way coaching high-school football, basketball, and track. I've always felt that way, and always will, so they haven't seen the last of me."

It was, however, unquestionably the end of a most remark-able era.

15

ANOTHER DANCE

MIKE KRZYZEWSKI sat at a table located in a room in the bowels of Cameron Indoor Stadium, smiling and talking about an unprecedented event that would take place in just a few hours. Midnight Madness. It was a first for Duke, and Krzyzewski was fired up about it.

"It's a unique day," he said. "Since I've started coaching here, I've always known that I coached not just at a great school, but a special arena. Cameron is one of the best in all of sports. To me, it's one of those buildings that has a soul."

It's also one of those building that's filled with rowdy fans.

On one occasion, the Crazies absolutely infuriated former State coach Norm Sloan when one of them jumped from the stands dressed as a rather large older woman and began crooning the national anthem. It was a parody of Sloan's wife, who used to sing the national anthem at Reynolds Coliseum prior to State home games.

The Crazies camped out for tickets not just hours but days—sometimes even weeks—in a not-so-small tent city called Krzyzewskiville that sprouted up just outside Cameron fifteen times or so a year. There they would sit and talk and plot, anticipating the next chance to rush the arena for the best seats while setting detailed plans for another run at rattling a visiting team. One time years earlier, Maryland's Herman Veal visited shortly after he had been accused of sexual misconduct. He was greeted by all kinds of crude chants, not to mention the panties and condoms and so on that were thrown onto the floor. Despite this, Veal somehow went on to have a pretty good game.

Afterward a reporter approached Veal and asked him how he could concentrate despite all the distractions.

"I knew the Crazies would be on me bad—but I figured I would be okay as long as none of them were packing guns. I figured I could handle anything else," Veal said.

The Crazies weren't that crazy. But they were creative.

Once, they caught the ire of Dean Smith when he spotted a sign that questioned Carolina player J. R. Reid's academic abilities. The sign read: "J.R. CAN'T READ." Smith got so mad that he told reporters they might want to go back and compare the SAT scores of Reid and teammate Scott Williams to the likes of Duke's Danny Ferry and Christian Laettner. The implication was clear: he felt the attack on Reid was racially motivated. But he wanted to make certain the world knew his two black players had scored higher on the SAT than two of Duke's white stars. SAT scores were supposed to be kept private, and there was some question as to whether Smith was in violation of the law by making such a statement. But again, it was another case of Smith trying to do what he thought was right.

In 1984, when Duke was just beginning to become good again under Krzyzewski, the upstart Blue Devils, led by Tommy Amaker, Johnny Dawkins, and David Henderson, were giving a previously unbeaten Carolina team all they could handle. It was the first game in Cameron after the Veal incident, and Duke officials were under pressure to clean up the Crazies' act.

So the Crazies arrived with makeshift halos on their heads and they politely welcomed Carolina to the building during pregame introductions.

"It was kind of funny," said Al Featherstone, who covered the game for the *Durham Herald*. "It was good, clean fun—until the game started. Then it got ugly because it was a brutal game."

With five minutes left, David Henderson hit a jumper to put Duke ahead 67–64. Twenty-three seconds later, Sam Perkins of Carolina was whistled for his third personal foul. Smith jumped off the bench. He thought maybe the foul had been assessed to the wrong player. He wanted to confer with the officials over it, but the crowd was loud and officials Mike Moser and John Moreau didn't notice him right away. It was not a shooting foul, so they gave the ball to Duke out of bounds and play resumed.

Smith went ballistic. He started banging on the scorer's table, still demanding his conference with officials. He implored Tommy Hunt, the scoreboard operator, to blow the horn and stop play. Hunt refused.

Then Smith really lost it. He tried to punch the buzzer button on the scoreboard himself.

He hit the wrong button.

Smith inadvertently gave his own team 20 more points on the scoreboard, which suddenly read: Carolina 84, Duke 67.

"The crowd went bonkers," Featherstone said. "At that point, the whole place was bonkers."

The Crazies screamed at the officials, imploring them to give Smith a technical foul. Smith kept pleading that he only wanted to dispute the specifics of the earlier foul call. Krzyzewski was yelling at the officials, telling them to keep Smith in line.

Yet Hunt quickly corrected the scoreboard and the game went on. Carolina ended up winning, 77–73, after Michael Jordan hit three straight jump shots down the stretch.

Krzyzewski was fuming. He opened up his postgame press conference by saying, "I want to tell you something. When you come in here and start talking about how Duke has no class, you'd better start getting your stories straight—because our students had class and our team had class. There was not a person on our bench who was pointing a finger at the officials or banging on the scorer's table. . . . So let's get some things straight around here, and quit the double-standard that exists in this league. All right?"

Three days later, Butters rewarded Krzyzewski, who had a 52-51 record at Duke up to that point, with a five-year contract. Certainly the negotiations had begun prior to that, but Butters was not displeased that his young coach chose to stand up to the Dean of the ACC.

Krzyzewski and Smith feuded off and on until the day Dean retired. But they pretended not to.

Asked about it once, Krzyzewski said: "We respect and like each other, but it's not like we're going to go out and smoke a pack of cigarettes together."

It was the kind of snide remark Smith had come to be known for; yet Krzyzewski was pretty good at it, too. One reporter remarked that the older Coach K got, the more he acted like Dean. They were different in many ways: Smith smoked, Krzyzewski didn't; Smith loved golf, Krzyzewski played tennis; Smith never swore, Krzyzewski used language that would make a sailor blush.

But probably the two did grow to be more alike than either would care to admit.

When he was recruiting Christian Laettner, Smith was riding up an elevator one time with the prospect and Laettner's mother.

"What about this rivalry with Duke?" Mrs. Laettner asked Coach Smith.

"Ahhh, there's not much to it, really. They're just one of the teams in our league. Mike and I get along, the players all see each other out all the time and they get along. It's not that big a deal," Smith said.

Then the elevator doors opened. Located directly across the hall from the elevator was J. R. Reid's room. Plastered all over the door were signs that read, "Duke sucks! Fuck Duke!"

BILL GUTHRIDGE'S first season as head coach of the North Carolina Tar Heels had gone quite well. Five days prior to their annual show-down with Duke in Chapel Hill, the Heels were in Winston-Salem for a January Saturday afternoon date with Wake Forest. With Dun-can gone, the Demon Deacons were only a shell of the team that had only two years earlier advanced to the Elite Eight in the NCAA Tournament. But it was a Big Four matchup, and that meant any-thing could happen.

Actually, as far as Dave Odom was concerned, just about any-thing that could happen to his team had already transpired. The Demon Deacons would be playing 21-1 North Carolina, whose only loss came in overtime at Maryland two weeks earlier, without sopho-more center Loren Woods. Once considered the heir apparent to Duncan, the stick-thin Woods had a psyche as fragile as his phy-sique. Odom had suspended him "indefinitely" for taking the game too seriously—yes, too seriously—after Woods's latest funk had led to a fight during practice with swingman Joseph Amonett.

Woods's absence put four freshmen in the Wake starting lineup along with senior guard Tony Rutland. The best of the freshmen was without a doubt Robert O'Kelley, a tough muscle-bound guard listed at 6-1 but seemingly an inch or two shorter. It seemed this group didn't have a chance against a North Carolina squad featuring Guthridge's "starting six." But the Deacons made it clear very early on that they intended to give the Heels everything they could han-dle. With O'Kelley hitting 6 of 8 from 3-point range in the first half, the Deacons surged to a 17-point lead and still led by 12 at the end of the first half. Wake was so hot that even Jerry Braswell, a forgotten senior guard, hit a 3-pointer—his first basket in the 1998 calendar year.

It was just a mirage. With Carter moving out to the wing to disrupt the Wake shooters in the second half, the game quickly turned. Carolina won 79–73.

Afterward, as was his custom, the gracious Odom sat in a tiny corner of the Wake Forest locker room long after his postgame news conference was over and chatted with a small group of writers. In this setting, Odom always seemed more relaxed and open—even after a difficult loss like this one.

"It's fun to watch your team execute at the highest level," he said. "Even in the second half when it got away from us, we were executing. The shots were there; they just didn't go in."

About this time, Carolina's Makhtar Ndiaye strolled into the Wake locker room wearing a spiffy brown suit. "Coach, coach!" Ndiaye yelled out, smiling and extending a hand. "I just came in to say hi and look for my picture on the wall."

Odom returned the smile and shook Ndiaye's hand. To outsiders, this might have seemed strange. But Odom held no hard feelings over an incident that might have changed Wake's basketball history just a bit. Four years earlier, in the fall of 1993, Ndiaye committed to and practiced with Wake Forest. But because of a recruiting violation the native of Dakar, Senegal, was never permitted to play for the school. (Ndiaye's interpreter, appointed by Odom, gave Ndiaye some things the NCAA did not approve of. The violation was minor, so Ndiaye was allowed to transfer.) Odom had envisioned Ndiaye as a power forward or backup center—just the kind of rugged player who might have complemented Duncan inside.

He transfered to Michigan, where he played two seasons before transferring again to North Carolina. The second transfer came despite Ndiaye's claims that he would never play for another ACC school other than Wake.

"I couldn't do that to Coach Odom," Ndiaye said at the time through an interpreter.

It was suggested that the whole Ndiaye recruiting fiasco might never had occurred if Ndiaye had had a better interpreter—or Odom had spoken Senegalese. Nonetheless, here was Ndiaye four years later, in Odom's locker room. After the two shook hands, the coach pointed to a wall on the locker room where Ndiaye was pictured in the 1993–94 team photo, even though he never played a single minute for the school.

"Not bad. I look pretty good," Ndiaye said, still smiling.

"Yeah, well, you didn't have as nice a suit when you were here," said Odom, looking Ndiaye over. "Things got better for you after you left here."

Odom wished Ndiaye luck and mentioned the upcoming game against Duke.

"It's going to be a rumble in the jungle," Ndiaye offered.

Five days later at the Smith Center in Chapel Hill, number-one Duke tipped it off against number-two North Carolina. It was only the second time in the storied basketball histories of the two schools that one of their meetings represented the top-ranked team in the country versus number two. Scott Fowler of the *Charlotte Observer* previewed the showdown by visiting with some folks along U.S. Route 15-501, including one of the managers of a Bob Evans restaurant that sits precisely halfway between the office doors of both Mike Krzyzewski and Bill Guthridge.

"Usually the first thing we ask people is, 'Smoking or non?' " Mike Gaddy told Fowler. "For the rest of this week, we're thinking about saying, 'Duke or UNC?' I think that'll be the best way to keep the peace."

"I've always said that the center of the college basketball universe seems to float somewhere along 15-501," Al Featherstone of the *Durham Herald* later said. "When Carolina wins, the center moves a little more toward the Blue Cross-Blue Shield building, which is closer to Chapel Hill. When Duke wins, it shifts more toward Darryl's [Restaurant], which is closer to Duke's campus."

The game was obviously the biggest of the young head-coaching career of the oldest rookie head coach in college basketball history, sixty-year-old Bill Guthridge. The rivalry had survived the sudden retirement of Smith, and Guthridge was now the man in charge for the Heels.

Guthridge had been Smith's assistant for thirty years. Smith admired him for his organizational skills, among other things. Without a doubt, Guthridge was more organized than Smith, whose office once was described by writer Tim Peeler of the *Durham Sun* as "one broken-down recliner away from being classified as a landfill." Guthridge's, on the other hand, was always neat and free of clutter.

Both men were math majors in college and seemed inseparable. But they had their differences, too.

"The biggest difference," Guthridge noted, "may have been that he's a night person and I'm a morning person. So when we were together we pretty much had the clock covered."

To outsiders, Guthridge seemed like a low-key yes-man of sorts. But Smith valued his input in virtually all phases of the game—from Xs and Os to discipline matters and recruiting. Guthridge was, after all, the man who rode point on the recruitment of Michael Jordan years earlier.

"He did quite a job for us," Guthridge said in his typical matter-of-fact style. "But it wasn't like the first time I saw him I said, 'This is going to be the greatest player ever.' In fact, when he left Carolina I wasn't even saying he would be the greatest player ever. I think anybody who says that is not telling the truth. When we got him, we knew he was good. And when he left us, we knew he would be a very good pro. But there was no way anybody at that point could have imagined how good he would become."

Years later, Guthridge would have some fun with Jordan when Michael returned to Chapel Hill for a visit. Guthridge deadpanned: "Hey Michael, it's good to see you. What have you been doing since you left Chapel Hill?"

At one point during Guthridge's first season as head coach, Jordan asked, "What have you been doing with yourself in the last year, Coach? Anything new?"

Guthridge appreciated a dry sense of humor. When his players greeted him with the popular phrase, "Hi, Coach," his typical response was, "Hi, player."

But he didn't like excuses. For years he had kept a container on his desk with a cork lid that was labeled, "Excuses." Whenever a player missed a class or was late to a team meeting or function, whatever the reason, Coach Guthridge had them write out their excuse and place it in the container. After the first time or two, his players got the message.

His inaugural season as head coach hadn't all gone smoothly. There was the game at Virginia in February, when Shammond Williams, fresh off a rousing 42-point performance at Georgia Tech, had gotten angry because he didn't start (it was his turn to sit in the alphabetical starting rotation) and he didn't think he was playing enough. Guthridge and Williams exchanged angry words and Williams left the bench in the middle of the game. Williams was spotted outside the arena, still in his uniform, walking around and crying.

Guthridge defused the incident and took Williams back in without suspending him, prompting criticism that he wasn't tough enough. Guthridge shrugged it off and kept on coaching. He had, after all, endured years of criticism pointed toward Smith (and his staff) and had learned to ignore it.

Guthridge had proven unfailingly loyal to Smith and the North Carolina program through the years. When he arrived from Kansas State in 1968 after serving as Tex Winter's assistant there, Guthridge thought long and hard before deciding to replace the departed Larry Brown on Smith's staff. Winter more or less had to talk him into it. Once he took the job, Guthridge told himself that the next step would be to become a head coach.

It wasn't until he was pursued by Penn State in 1978 that Guthridge realized his personal goals had changed. After verbally accepting the head coach position there, Guthridge left Phoenix after the Tar Heels' first-round NCAA Tournament loss and started to fly to State College, Pennsylvania, where he was to be introduced as the new coach of the Nittany Lions. Guthridge had found himself overcome with emotion when he told the Tar Heel players he was leaving.

"I'm having some doubts about this," Guthridge told Smith. "I'll check my bags only as far as Chicago, where I have a layover. I'll make up my mind about it for good on the way there."

When he got to Chicago, Guthridge called his wife, Leesie, back in Chapel Hill.

"I'm coming home," he said.

Then he called Penn State and told them he was sorry, but he wasn't going to be taking the job after all. Among the men who expressed disappointment was Joe Paterno, the long-time football coach who would also go on to become Penn State's athletics director. He had spent many hours with Guthridge trying to convince him to come to State College.

"I had spent a lot of time with him on my visits up there," Guthridge said. "I was really impressed with him. I felt bad about that part of it. But I felt that it was the best decision and I'm glad I made it. It certainly proved to be the right one. I never looked back.

"I finally decided that I had the best job in the country as an assistant coach at North Carolina and that I would stay that way forever. And after that I never interviewed for another head-coaching job. I just wasn't interested."

But it didn't stay that way forever. Twenty years later he was named head coach at North Carolina without even having to go through the interview process.

Luckily for Guthridge, the rumble in the jungle quickly turned into a rout. Carolina students, who were wearing "DOOK SUCKS" T-shirts were ecstatic.

After the game, Duke's guard Steve Wojciechowski tried to run off the court with the game ball in a final act of defiance, protecting it like a fullback holding a football. But the North Carolina team managers converged on Wojo and wrestled the ball away from him as the crowd chanted the obvious: "We're number one! We're number one!"

One week before their next meeting with Duke, Carolina played North Carolina State in Chapel Hill. The Wolfpack—with a record of 14-11 overall but just 4-9 in the ACC—were struggling under young coach Herb Sendek. The Tar Heels were by then 26-1 overall, 12-1 in the ACC, and still ranked number one in the nation.

But rankings mean nothing in the ACC. Wolfpack swingman C. C. Harrison hit 7 3-pointers in the game's first sixteen minutes to lead State to an upset.

Among the fans in attendance was former Wolfpack great David Thompson, who was visiting the Smith Center for the first time in his life.

"I picked a good one to come to," Thompson beamed.

Sean Miller, an assistant coach at State who is regarded as one of the best point guards in Big East history, marveled about the coaching environment in the ACC.

"This is an incredible thing to be a part of," Miller said. "I thought the Big East was a great conference, and maybe it is. But it's nothing like this in terms of the rivalries and the degree to which the fans get fired up and all that. I mean, when we get back home—after a thirty-minute bus ride—there will be five thousand fans waiting to greet us outside Reynolds Coliseum. That's awesome."

THREE DAYS after Duke's loss at North Carolina, the Blue Devils played North Carolina State and romped to a 65–49 victory at Reynolds Coliseum—never an easy venue for a visiting team. "They eat their young at that place," was the way columnist Lenox Rawlings of the *Winston-Salem Journal* described it.

Fans at Reynolds didn't quite have the reputation of the Crazies at Duke, but they weren't too far behind. During this particular game against the Blue Devils, fans were all over Duke freshman Chris Burgess, who had made only 20 of 57 foul shots coming into the game.

"Hey Chris, why don't you shoot a couple of free throws for us?" a fan shouted. "After all, we are in a brick building."

A few seconds later, Burgess was fouled and went to the line.

His first attempt was short. The second was wide right and long, banking off of the glass backboard.

"That second one would've killed you if it hit you in the head," someone noted. "It wasn't a brick. It was a cement block."

Krzyzewski wisely pulled Burgess from the game.

Six days later, Duke was preparing to play another Big Four opponent, Wake Forest, at Cameron Indoor Stadium. Wake's Loren Woods was back from his suspension and Odom was worried about the kind of reception his sensitive center would receive from the Crazies. So was Krzyzewski. The Duke coach went out before the game and instructed the Crazies to take it easy on Woods, who had received counseling to deal with his emotional problems—which Odom believed stemmed mostly from the young center being too tough on himself and expecting too much from himself as he followed in Tim Duncan's footsteps.

The Crazies took it easy on Woods. But the Duke basketball team didn't. They rolled to a 78–47 victory.

Eight days later, the Crazies weren't prepared to cut anyone any slack. UCLA was in town for a nationally televised game that represented an unusual break right in the middle of Duke's ACC schedule. This was serious stuff. Following State's upset of Carolina one day earlier in Chapel Hill, the Blue Devils knew they now were playing for a number-one ranking.

As the Bruins trotted onto the court, the Crazies chanted: "Road kill! Road kill!"

As the introductions were made, they were even louder than usual, greeting each opposing player with a chant that went something like this:

Public-address announcer: "At guard for the Bruins, Toby Bailey."

Crazies: "Hi Toby! You suck!"

It was 21–8 in favor of the Blue Devils before the Bruins knew what hit them.

Krzyzewski kept going to his bench, and eventually, UCLA wore down.

Bucky Waters, the former Duke coach who is now in broadcasting, was sitting courtside. He shook his head in amazement and admiration.

"I can't remember any team in the ACC having this kind of depth—quality depth," said Waters, who had been around the league since playing for Everett Case at North Carolina State in the 1950s.

The UCLA mascot made the trip along with four or five bright-eyed Bruin cheerleaders, who sat along the baseline on the opposite side of the court from the Duke bench. At one point the Bruin bear attempted to do a little jig with the Blue Devil mascot during a time-out. The Blue Devil threw him down.

"That's wrong. That's just wrong," complained one of the UCLA cheerleaders.

Another cheerleader said: "These people are just so rude. Do these people even go to college?"

The Bruin mascot left the floor a few minutes later after some of the Crazies near courtside kept playing drums on his head.

With Duke leading 71–42, the Crazies kept it up.

"Show no mercy! Show no mercy!"

They didn't with J. R. Henderson, who had been suspended from the team earlier in the season along with Jelani McCoy for smoking marijuana. McCoy was subsequently kicked off the team by Coach Steve Lavin, but Henderson returned. Whenever Henderson touched the ball or went to the free-throw line, the Crazies waved fake marijuana leaves that had been distributed prior to the game and chanted: "Where's Je-lani? Where's Je-lani?" Then they answered themselves in unison with: "Smok-ing pot! Smok-ing pot!"

Once when Henderson was at the free-throw line they chanted: "Got the munch-ies! Got the munch-ies!"

Another Bruin, point guard Baron Davis, had gotten into some trouble over an automobile allegedly loaned to him by a UCLA booster. Every time he came to the free-throw line, the Crazies would rattle their car keys.

With three minutes, fifty-six seconds left in the game and the score 106–74, it seemed to hit them all at once; Duke would soon be the number-one basketball team in the nation once again. The chanting picked up, louder than ever.

"We're number one! We're number one!"

Followed by . . . "Go to Hell Carolina! Go to Hell!"

IT WOULD BE EASY to say it was predictable that North Carolina and Duke would meet again in the ACC Tournament championship finals after Duke avenged their loss in Chapel Hill by rallying from a 17-point deficit to win at Cameron Indoor Arena. But the paths taken to that seemingly inevitable meeting in 1998 were hardly routine. North Carolina nearly lost to Maryland in the semifinals, beating them 83–73 in overtime only after Maryland guard Laron

Profit inexplicably ran over Carolina's Shammond Williams as Williams attempted a 3-pointer with four seconds left in regulation. Williams then made two of three free-throw attempts to tie the score at 66 and force overtime. Duke nearly lost to Clemson in the semis, winning 66–64 only after freshman point guard William Avery, Wojciechowski's apprentice, drove the length of the court, missed, and tipped in his own rebound with 0.3 seconds left.

So it wasn't easy, but it was as it should be in a year when the two schools separated by such a small stretch of U.S. 15-501 had spent most of the season jockeying with each other for the top spot among the national polls.

Krzyzewski talked to his players about how much this trip to the ACC championship final meant to his team—especially the seniors who had, as freshmen, suffered through a 13-18 season.

"Soak this up because you're not going to have that many chances to explore this atmosphere," Krzyzewski said. "It's special."

The coach spoke with the media about how his team took some time to recover mentally from the hangover of the previous Saturday's showdown with Carolina at Cameron. He worried that some negative aftereffects might still be lingering. That's why Krzyzewski didn't plan much in terms of extra preparation for meeting number three of the season against the Tar Heels. They had played each other twice already. They had just played only a week earlier. What more was there to know?

Guthridge praised Maryland for playing a fine game against the Tar Heels in the other semifinal, and said his team was looking forward to the chance to atone for losing in the regular-season finale at Cameron. That loss kept North Carolina from sharing the ACC regular-season title, and gave the Blue Devils a record 15 regular-season wins in the league.

"We feel very fortunate to be here," Guthridge said. "I'm not sure how we did it. Just by playing with a lot of heart, I think."

It was meeting No. 201 between the two teams, dating back to 1920, when the series between the schools began. North Carolina held a 120-80 edge, being the only school in the ACC to own any advantage at all in its series with the Blue Devils.

As North Carolina was finishing off Maryland in overtime in the semis, the stage was being set by fans from both schools who taunted each other from opposite sides of Greensboro Coliseum.

"We want Duke!" went up the chant from the North Carolina side.

"Go to Hell, Carolina! Go to Hell!" was the predictable response from the Duke side.

In the Clemson section, where fans had stood en masse to sell their seats for the championship final within moments of the Tigers' loss to Duke a day earlier, someone waved a sign that summed up the strong ABC contingent in the building. The sign read: "Anybody But Carolina—Even Duke!"

The entire weekend, former State great David Thompson sat with Sandy Koufax, the Hall of Fame baseball pitcher, and watched from the stands. Both were pursued by autograph seekers.

The first half of meeting number 201 did not disappoint anyone, except maybe Krzyzewski. His team played well and led most of the way, but surrendered 12 unanswered points toward the end of the half to go down by four heading into the second half.

The second half was tight for awhile, the score last being tied at 57 with eleven minutes, thirty-eight seconds left. Then North Carolina took control. The Heels scored the game's next 13 points to go up 70–57, with only 5:11 remaining on the clock. The game was virtually over.

When it finally ended, the scoreboard read North Carolina 83, Duke 68.

Vince Carter and Shammond Williams jumped up onto the press table in front of the Carolina pep band and led a chorus of the school's fight song. Makhtar Ndiaye first jumped on the scorer's table in front of the Duke section, and provoked them by making some hand gestures that would be debated by the media for weeks and even months to come. Then Ndiaye jumped down and ran over to join Carter and Williams.

A North Carolina fan held up a sign that read:

> DEFEATED
> OUTPLAYED
> OUTCLASSED
> KRZYZEWSKI

Krzyzewski admitted that the loss hurt, but stressed the importance of forgetting it to prepare for the NCAA Tournament.

"We lost in the championship game in this tournament," he said. "But that's an ending. Now we've got to look at a new beginning."

Someone asked if he would like to meet North Carolina again

in the national title game. It looked as if both schools had a very legitimate chance to get there.

"I'm not caught up with Carolina. I'm caught up with Duke," Krzyzewski replied. "Vic Bubas told me a long time ago to approach this job that way, and I took it to heart."

It sounded good. Krzyzewski surely meant it. But no one really believed him. You couldn't coach at Duke and not be swept away at least a little by this rivalry. It was impossible.

In the Duke locker room, reporters were chatting with players when suddenly someone cried out for medical assistance. Wojcie-chowski, depleted by the flu and suffering from dehydration and exhaustion, had collapsed in the shower. He would be okay—just another casualty in this heated series.

Guthridge talked about his special first year as Carolina's head coach. He could not stop smiling.

"I remember the feeling I had when we beat N.C. State to win this tournament after I first came here as Dean's assistant for the 1967–68 season," Guthridge said. "That was thirty years ago. I was thrilled then and I'm thrilled today.

"This is still Dean's team. He recruited them all and taught them all how to play basketball as a team. It's his system. These guys were terrific from the start with the transition to a new coach. . . . It really could have been tough if the players weren't receptive to what we wanted to do. But it's been easy."

Antawn Jamison, who would go on to earn national Player of the Year honors, had been listed as questionable for the champion-ship game because of a groin injury. He played and was a major factor with 22 points and 18 rebounds in thirty-six minutes.

"This team is ready to get back to the Final Four," Jamison predicted.

Ed Cota gestured toward Guthridge.

"We know this is Coach Gut's team," Cota said. "He doesn't want to take any of the credit, but this is his team."

The Tar Heels were back on top in the state where they and three other schools only a stone's throw away had begun making basketball history forty-five years earlier.

ANTAWN JAMISON was right. North Carolina did make a return trip to the Final Four. But there the Cinderella first season of Coach Bill Guthridge ended with a semifinal loss to Utah. His first-year record: 34-4. That wasn't bad for a guy who had last coached a varsity team in 1962, when his Scott City High club in Kansas finished 10-14.

Mike Krzyzewski's new beginning in the 1998 NCAAs was promising until the Blue Devils ran up against eventual champion Kentucky in the South Regional final. There Duke fell 86–84 in a rematch of the game six years earlier when Christian Laettner's remarkable last-second shot kept the Blue Devils marching toward their second straight NCAA title. But this time, Duke blew a 17-point lead in the final nine and a half minutes to finish their season 32-4.

Wake Forest and N.C. State played well enough to earn invitations to the NIT. Although these two schools were both overshadowed by the Duke-Carolina rivalry—which is often larger than life—they did their part in the Big Four. N.C. State upset number-one North Carolina and Wake finished with a 16-14 record. But more important, each member of the Big Four was poised for the future. From now until who knows when, each of these four schools will face each other time and time again as the rivalry of the Big Four endures.

New memories will be forged as the whole world watches the state of North Carolina practice its time-honored tradition of playing quality ball. The 1997–98 season—with Duke and Carolina battling it out at the top—simply added to the drama that is basketball in the state of North Carolina.

"People can talk all they want about the Big Ten. About Michigan and Ohio State and Indiana and Kentucky or whatever, but there's no way that compares," Mike Krzyzewski said. "They're in different states. Here, we share the same dry cleaners."

Enough said.

Bibliography

Barrier, Smith. *On Tobacco Road*. New York: Leisure Press, 1983.

Brill, Bill, and Mike Krzyzewski. *A Season Is a Lifetime*. New York: Simon & Schuster, 1993.

Chansky, Art. *The Dean's List*. New York: Warner Books, 1996.

Golenbock, Peter. *Personal Fouls*. New York: Carroll & Graf, 1989.

Herakovich, Douglas. *Pack Pride*. Cary, N.C.: Yesterday's Future, 1994.

Jacobs, Barry. *Three Paths to Glory*. New York: Macmillan, 1993.

McKinney, Bones, with Garland Atkins. *Bones McKinney: Honk Your Horn If You Love Basketball*. Gastonia, N.C.: Garland Publications, 1988.

Morris, Ron. *ACC Basketball: An Illustrated History*. Chapel Hill, N.C.: Four Corners Press, 1988.

Mumau, Thad. *The Dean Smith Story*. Huntsville, Ala.: The Strode Publishers, 1980.

Valvano, Jim, and Curry Kirkpatrick. *Valvano*. New York: Pocket Books, 1991.

Index